D1370582

Vince Pesce is a sales trainer, consultant and professional speaker. As a senior sales engineer at Westinghouse Electric he received the President's Award for exceeding sales quota by at least 120 percent for four consecutive years, and as regional manager for Allis-Chalmers, he earned the "Outstanding Sales Manager" award. At the Siemens-Allis corporate headquarters in Atlanta, he developed their sales and sales management training program. He is a member of the Sales Executives Club of New York, and a member of the Board of Directors of Sales and Marketing Executives—Atlanta, and past president of the Georgia Speakers Association. He conducts seminars and speaks on professional selling and management development for associations, businesses, and at the university level throughout the country. He is the author of numerous articles and books.

Vince Pesce

the modular approach
to sales success

A Complete Manual
of Professional Selling

A SPECTRUM BOOK

Prentice-Hall, Inc., Englewood Cliffs, New Jersey 07632

Library of Congress Cataloging in Publication Data

Pesce, Vince.
   A complete manual of professional selling.

   "A Spectrum Book."
   Includes index.
   1. Selling.   I. Title
HF5438.25.P47   1983   658.8′5   82-21435
ISBN 0-13-162099-1
ISBN 0-13-162081-9 (pbk.)

This book is available at a special discount when ordered in
bulk quantities. Contact Prentice-Hall, Inc., General
Publishing Division, Special Sales, Englewood Cliffs, N.J. 07632

Fifth printing

ISBN 0-13-162099-1

ISBN 0-13-162081-9 {PBK.}

Editorial/production supervision by Norma G. Ledbetter
Cover design by Jeannette Jacobs
Manufacturing buyer: Cathie Lenard

Prentice-Hall International, Inc., *London*
Prentice-Hall of Australia Pty. Limited, *Sydney*
Prentice-Hall Canada Inc., *Toronto*
Prentice-Hall of India Private Limited, *New Delhi*
Prentice-Hall of Japan, Inc., *Tokyo*
Prentice-Hall of Southeast Asia Pte. Ltd., *Singapore*
Whitehall Books Limited, *Wellington, New Zealand*
Editora Prentice-Hall do Brasil Ltda., *Rio de Janeiro*

This manual is dedicated to all novice, veteran, and future sales-people. May their choice of the sales career provide them with the challenge, excitement, and success they want. May they make a living and a life for themselves.

A special dedication is made to the family and friends of all sales-people. Their support, understanding, and encouragement are prime motivators that keep the salesperson going.

Contents

Preface   ix

module one
THE SELLING PROFESSIONAL   1

module two
**ESSENTIALS OF VERBAL AND WRITTEN
SALES COMMUNICATION**   28

module three
THE TELEPHONE: A KEY SALES AID   52

module four
**REAL LISTENING:
IDENTIFY NEEDS AND WANTS**   71

module five
**GETTING MORE CUSTOMERS BY EFFECTIVE
PROSPECTING AND COLD-CALL SELLING**   80

module six
**SALES PLANNING FOR PROFESSIONAL GROWTH
AND PRODUCTIVE SALES CALLS**   98

module seven
**SUCCESSFUL TIME AND TERRITORIAL
MANAGEMENT**   112

module eight
**THE SALES INTERVIEW: IDENTIFY
YOUR BEST PRESENTATION APPROACH**   131

module nine
**YOUR TIME "ON STAGE":
THE SALES PRESENTATION**   139

module ten
**CREATIVE SALES STRATEGIES
AND TACTICS**   149

module eleven
**WIN/WIN SALES NEGOTIATIONS:
THE BEST KIND**   164

module twelve
**EFFECTIVELY HANDLING OBJECTIONS
AND CLOSING: THE MARK OF THE
PROFESSIONAL**   184

module thirteen
**KEEPING CUSTOMERS SATISFIED
AND STAYING COMPETITIVE**   203

The Final Wrap-Up   213

Glossary of Sales Terms   215

Appendix   221

Index   223

Preface

Now the student, novice, or veteran in sales has one source to look to for information on professional selling techniques. This manual clearly identifies what it takes to succeed in professional sales from pre-call preparation to closing. Featured are hundreds of suggestions, planning aids, self-appraisal checklists, and examples that illustrate what it takes to get *orders*. This book will benefit those who apply its techniques by increasing their sales. Its easy-to-read style details actual sales situations and then recommends the proper approach to choose—the approach and strategy that get orders.

The principles and techniques presented are effective, *they work*. The practitioner of this material should feel confident. The information is based on extensive research, observation, plus the author's over 20 years in professional sales, management, sales training, and consulting. Its practical approach to tough sales situations will be recognized as a very useful benefit to the salesperson. Salespeople must develop the skill of evaluating where they are in the sales situation and determine the best approach to take. Both basic and more involved techniques of the sales profession are covered. Those who are successful master the *effective application* of sales techniques. The consistent, effective use of successful techniques gives you confidence. Confidence encourages you to reach for higher levels of performance—confidence to set goals and get them, confidence to ask for orders and get them.

This manual has many *unique features* to help you. *Checklists* help you outline an action program for self-appraisal and *self-improvement*. Its modular approach makes it convenient to review each key area of professional selling. Modules can be grouped to be used as part of a complete sales course or training program. The manual is flexible enough to satisfy your individual desires and needs.

A key contribution this manual makes in improving sales performance occurs when the reader starts to use the exhibit forms included. These forms provide an ideal means of organizing sales efforts to help get more orders. They are an organizational aid to assist in preparing benefit statements and sales points in prospecting, sales planning, and sales call preparation. The forms included in our module on Time and Territorial Management will improve sales efficiency. The consistent, effective use of all the exhibits will provide a convenient method for measuring sales improvement.

The *review questions* following each module provide the opportunity to develop answers that apply to actual or anticipated selling situations. The answers help in developing *sales potential* to the fullest. Sales and training management will recognize the review questions as a convenient means of focusing attention on specific sales objectives and programs. The academic community will want to use the review questions as an ideal source to stimulate class discussions, role playing or other semester projects.

The unique *glossary of sales terms* is a handy reference to identify words and expressions often used in the manual. You save time by going to the glossary for terms, jargon, and word reference.

The first module highlights in clear terms what it takes to *sell like a professional*. It's the best place to start. In this module you will easily identify the key aspects of what and how the salesperson really sells. We sell benefits by asking questions and probing to determine buyers' needs and wants. You will learn to get the answers you want by reviewing the typical questions to ask. Each module covers important aspects of professional sales with suggestions for *improvement, action programs, strategies*, and *techniques*.

This manual is a sales aid. It will *help* you improve your performance. The more you know about what it takes to be a successful sales professional, the closer you get to being one.

This manual will help you if its contents are understood and applied regularly: effective techniques must be used habitually. The time-proven strategies and techniques mentioned in this manual should become habit forming. As you read this manual, use a pencil or high-lighter pen to *emphasize ideas*, suggestions, techniques, and sales points *you want to try* in your markets with your prospects and customers. Let the suggestions from each module help you get more orders.

As you read, make *marginal notes* listing one or more of your prospects or customers where the item or topic mentioned can be considered and used. Make this manual *your success book* to help you grow and develop as a sales professional. The successful application of its techniques has helped thousands. They will help you if you are committed to performance improvement and develop successful selling *habits*. As you read and reread this manual, think of ways in which you can apply its principles. One suggestion may be exactly what you need in your situation. Can you change a word(s) or phrase(s) to help with one of your prospects or customers? Customize the techniques to fit your situation. Use your creative abilities.

A *dialogue approach* is used to illustrate situations that often take place between a buyer and a seller. Analyze how you may fit into that same or similar set of circumstances.

The self-help checklists lay a solid foundation for your future sales growth. The professional knows that success comes to those who continually strive to improve their performance.

This manual contains *hundreds* of suggestions, ideas, and recommendations to help those interested in sales from the college student to the veteran. It is a *professionally prepared* sales aid. The material contained starts with the basics of what it takes to be a sales professional to detailed strategies on handling objections and closing, all in an easy to read format—all intended to help the salesperson get more orders.

This manual will help you to improve your sales performance, get more orders, and reach your goals—starting *now*!

ACKNOWLEDGMENTS

My sincerest appreciation goes out to my friends and business associates who have contributed to my interest and success in professional sales. Their support, experiences, inspiration, sharing, and suggestions will always be appreciated.

To my former prospects and customer contacts, thanks for the memories. Each experience, from my start in selling brushes and greeting cards door to door to getting orders for multimillion-dollar projects in high-rise office buildings, has sharpened my focus in recognizing what it takes to succeed in sales. To future contacts, I can't wait to meet you.

To the thousands of attendees of my sales training programs, I sincerely hope that your goals were exceeded. Set higher ones.

My family has been a continual source of support and encouragement. In my earliest years, my parents, Vincent and Irene, always encouraged me to be the best that I could be. They became my first customers. My wife, Camille, and children, Marie Angela and Vincent III, have always been my prime motivators. Their understanding, patience, and love are my driving force.

module one
The
Selling Professional

The principles presented in this module are the cornerstone of sales success. Knowledge of and by itself doesn't help an individual to succeed in sales. Knowledge must be applied successfully and continually. The effective application of knowledge, tied in with professional selling techniques and the proper attitude, is the foundation that builds sales professionals.

To gain professional status, the salesperson must be able to identify a prospect's needs and wants. This is done by asking questions, probing, and listening. Listening must be emphasized. We were given two ears and only one mouth for a reason. The best salespeople consider themselves problem solvers; they identify and solve problems. The professionals emphasize the benefits their products or services offer; they give their prospects a reason to buy. Prospects decide to buy when they envision the benefit they will receive when they will own the goods or services you are offering. Use the form at the end of this module to develop your benefit statements and sales points.

As you start this first module, make a personal commitment to strive for improvement through practice and dedication. The players on world championship teams must go back to basics each season if they are to maintain their positions as champions. Similarly, you must strive continually for improvement if you are to stay on top. This module outlines the basics of what it takes to succeed in professional sales. Read and study its contents.

THE SELLING PROFESSIONAL

The selling function is an important part of the *total* marketing function. The sales professionals are at the heart of new products or service introductions. They play a key role in moving their company's goods and services into the marketplace. The professional salesperson builds a rapport with accounts by pulling and leading, not pushing and shoving. Selling is helping a person make a decision that is for the betterment of all.

As a profession, selling is one of the most exciting, rewarding careers any person can consider when entering the business world. It is the epitome of the free enterprise system and spirit of competition. The individuals in sales must be committed to strive for improvement in performance, personal growth, and development. They are achievers who are always looking for more effective methods to serve their accounts.

The salesperson must be able to communicate effectively with prospects and customers, as well as within the company. The professional continually and successfully uses *sellatechnics*, studying and applying professional selling techniques effectively.

To handle effectively what is required, it is necessary for the sales professional to be versed in many areas. A simple checklist of critical areas includes:

1. Knowing customers
2. Knowing markets and competition
3. Knowing product application and features
4. Knowing customer benefits
5. Wanting to learn more selling skills and techniques
6. Setting goals, planning, and time management
7. Handling objections and closing
8. Understanding value of customer service
9. Understanding company policies and procedures
10. Having the positive attitude necessary to succeed
11. Knowing yourself

If you are not confident in any of these important areas, invest the time and effort to improve. This manual will be of significant help.

Desire, motivation, and persistence with the proper attitude are all essential. The professionals know the three significant areas of awareness and expertise they must continually develop. They strive to improve their *knowledge*, *sales skills* and *techniques*, and *attitude*. These are the three talents that require continual reinforcement through a conscientious effort. Each of these talents plays an integral part in the overall package that qualifies a salesperson for professional status. All are essential sellatechnic characteristics.

The primary difference between a salesperson and an order taker is knowledge of the product(s), service, and successful application of selling skills. The salesperson continually strives for improved awareness to help improve performance.

In addition to knowledge, sales skills and techniques, and attitude, we will cover other topics extremely important to the salesperson: preparing sales points by understanding product features and emphasizing their benefits, solving problems by asking questions and probing, preparing a presentation manual, and being prepared for a presentation.

If we take the first letters of the three key requirements for the sales professional, that is, attitude, skills, and knowledge, we get the word *ASK*. The success of sales professionals is based on their abilities to ASK questions of their prospects and customers. Of course after they ask questions, they must listen.

THE KNOWLEDGE NECESSARY TO SUCCEED

Knowledge in the selling profession includes many things—the features and customer benefits of your product or service; your markets and how you bring your products to these markets; your company; your competitors and how they bring their products to market; your prospect or customer's business, markets, and plans. Of course, knowledge of yourself is essential.

Knowledge is required to determine how many of the products you make or services you offer, and in what volume, would be of interest to your customer. Knowledge is needed to determine what type of approach you feel would best suit this prospect. In addition, you must know the terminology of your trade. You must be able to speak the language that is understood by the listener.

Professionals stay knowledgeable by keeping abreast of trends, innovations, and general market conditions. They join the necessary trade associations and professional societies.

Knowledge must be *specific*. It is meaningless to talk in generalities. Sales professionals know detailed information about their products or service. They discuss specifics about their operation, performance, aesthetic qualities, and other features. Their benefit statements and sales points must be specific. They know details on savings, costs, client benefits, materials, availability, terms of sale, and unusual requirements. They know exactly what are their company's policies and procedures, organization, intent in the marketplace, expansion plans, and programs.

They have a continual supply of factual information for minimizing the amount of friction that may arise when prospects or customers raise objections. They know how to answer objections by having specific knowledge about the company's products, benefits, markets, and competition. Sales professionals have this information now, and they keep abreast of what's going on to make sure they have it tomorrow.

The salesperson must be knowledgeable in many areas to achieve the status of a professional. Knowledge of products, company, competition, prospects, customers, and markets is necessary. We've prepared a convenient checklist to use in analyzing how much you know about your profession. Can you answer "always" to the following statements? We've divided them into Your Company, Prospects or Customers, Competitors, and Markets and Business. Rate yourself after each statement.

Your Company

1. I know how and where our products are manufactured.
2. I know the factory and headquarters organization and proper contacts.
3. I understand our warranty, guarantee, service, and other policies.
4. I understand all information contained in our company's advertisements and other literature relating to my industry.
5. I have the latest company publications and price books and know how to use them.
6. I use my boss, my peers, and others for their experience in solving similar problems.
7. I understand the prime benefits of our products or service.
8. I keep a file on each product's past performance; customer acceptability; competitive rating; and trends regarding size, lead times, and price levels.
9. I know the features and correct application of each of our products.
10. I am familiar with company and industry terms.
11. I submit reports on time.
12. I know how to handle negotiated projects.

Prospects or Customers

1. I know those who are key buying influences and how they purchase.
2. I know how prospects of customers use our equipment or service.
3. I know the buying cycle and necessary steps to get an order from my accounts.
4. I know technical evaluation criteria for all products or services.
5. I know equipment expansions planned for the future.
6. I update customers' organization charts regularly.
7. I know customers' preferred suppliers by product line.
8. I plan regular product briefings to keep customers apprised of our products or service.
9. I have a clear profile of what to look for in prospects I meet.

Competitors

1. I know who they are and where their facilities and offices are located.
2. I know their organization.
3. I know approximately what percent of business they receive and why.
4. I know their selling and warranty policies.
5. I know the features and benefits of their equipment.
6. I know who their "friends" are in customers' organization.
7. I know their strengths and weaknesses by product line.

Markets and Business

1. I read industry and trade journals.
2. I belong to industry or trade associations to get exposure for myself and my company.
3. I review industry trends and discuss these with prospects and customers.
4. I am aware of financial conditions that may affect purchase plans.

The professional knows that the pursuit of knowledge must be a continual process. One can never rest on what was learned at the last training session or sales meeting. Professional buyers list "product knowledge" very high on their list of desirable traits in salespeople calling on them.

Knowledge is the admission price that you must pay to enjoy the privilege of calling on a prospect. The successful application of knowledge, using effective selling skills and techniques, with the proper attitude helps you get orders.

SELLING SKILLS AND TECHNIQUES— THE SALESPERSON'S WORLD

Professional salespeople must continually search out, learn, and apply effective sales skills and techniques. They must strive for more and more useful information on effective salesmanship. Improvement must be sought in the ability to set goals and establish action plans, to call on prospects, to make cold call, to deal with and handle objections, to close, and to prepare and deliver an effective sales presentation. It's necessary to develop effective skills in writing sales letters and proposals, asking questions, listening to prospects, communicating to prospects in person and over the telephone, establishing sales strategies and tactics, negotiating orders, and managing your time and territory. All are essential.

Professionals learn from their experiences and observe how others have succeeded—how others handle selling situations and how they use effective skills and techniques. The goal must be to try not to make the same mistakes others have made. Professionals know how to use their sales aids effectively. They seek advice and support from other members of the sales team. They know the importance of good customer service in keeping out competition.

The effective application of sales skills and the continual effort for improved performance are what make a sales professional. The sales techniques must continually be tried and tested. What works with one prospect may not work with another. What is successful in one market may not apply in another. Professionals test the situation before they commit themselves to a set course of action. Close analysis helps determine what areas are touchy or sensitive to the prospect and must be avoided.

Practice of effective skills and techniques makes them habit forming, which gives you confidence when you are in front of a prospect or customer.

ANALYZING YOUR SALES SKILLS AND TECHNIQUES

To help you review your present level of selling abilities, we have prepared a convenient checklist for self-analysis. Review the following statements and decide if you can answer each one "all the time," "almost always," "occasionally," "almost never," or "never." The key to improving performance is to recognize where you are now, decide where you want to be, and then make a plan to get there.

1. I speak clearly and precisely at all times, particularly during the sales interview.
2. I use sales aids at my presentation.
3. I plan sales calls in advance regarding specific action I want the prospect to take. I have a contingency plan.
4. I handle objections effectively, trying to answer typical objections before they are raised.
5. I emphasize benefits of my products and service at every opportunity.
6. I get the customer involved in every presentation, eliciting positive feedback from my listeners.
7. I ask probing, open-ended questions effectively.
8. I plan and use my time efficiently.
9. I know the buying influences at my accounts.
10. I listen intently and objectively for the buyer's needs and wants.
11. I always ask for the order and look to close the sale.
12. I am honest in my discussions.
13. I am enthusiastic in my sales career.

14. I get agreement and identify the prospect's needs and wants before I start my sales presentation.
15. I act as a professional businessperson.
16. I always get the customer's attention before I continue to the next step in my discussion.
17. I handle the problem of price effectively.
18. I do not make assumptions without asking for the prospect's or customer's agreement.
19. I analyze sales lost and sales obtained to determine good and bad features of both.
20. I constantly try to obtain competitive data.
21. I use the telephone effectively.
22. My correspondence is accurate, precise, and as brief as possible.
23. I recognize written communications as important to my selling effort.
24. I know I must continually prospect to maintain a list of active buyers.
25. I fill in unforeseen changes in my schedule with cold calls.
26. I outline a strategic and tactical plan on major jobs.
27. I recognize competition and constantly analyze ways to beat it.

The more times you can say "always" to these statements, the more effective you are as a salesperson. In the following modules we will offer many suggestions to help you improve your sales skills and techniques. In six months go back to these statements and see if you answer "always" more often.

ATTITUDE—
PROBABLY YOUR MOST IMPORTANT ATTRIBUTE

The third essential ingredient of professional salesmanship is attitude. Attitude is how we face our job and each daily activity. It is the motivating force behind our wanting to continue to do, and be, the best we can. It is our desire to handle every situation in a professional manner in a positive way. It is facing every sales situation with positive anticipations.

Do You Have
a Positive Mental Attitude?

The individual who knows all the selling skills and techniques but does not have the motivation to use them is no better than the person who doesn't know any. Knowledge is only useful when it is put into action. The attitude salespeople have toward their careers must be one of commitment to serve their company and customers. You have a positive mental attitude coupled with positive sales anticipation. We've prepared a checklist to help you analyze your attitude. The more times you answer "always," the better is your attitude for the sales profession.

1. I am enthusiastic, self-motivated, and have a positive mental attitude.
2. I follow through on all promises so people learn to depend on me.
3. I am confident and not easily discouraged.
4. I use my cassette player to listen to my presentations as well as the sales and motivational tapes of others.
5. I accept constructive criticism graciously because I want to improve.
6. I am creative in problem solving to make effective decisions.
7. I am willing to use new approaches.
8. I have the persistence to follow difficult projects to completion.
9. I work well with other people.
10. I am aware of others' needs and wants.
11. I act like a professional at all times.
12. I communicate well with my superiors, peers, and subordinates.
13. I am well organized because planning is important.
14. I can think quickly in difficult circumstances.
15. I have common sense and use it.
16. I seek additional educational opportunities in and out of the company.
17. I believe in what I'm doing.
18. I keep a manual of useful ideas, suggestions, successful strategies, and tactics.
19. I read at least one motivational book a quarter.

Is your percentage of "always" answers as high as *you* want? If not, what positive steps can you take to improve?

SELLING IS PROBLEM SOLVING

The successful salesperson knows that to get results it's always essential to come up with answers to the prospect's or customer's problems. The real professional knows that accounts do not flash signs saying, "Help, I have a problem." The problem can be large or small; it may be obvious or not too obvious, but it exists and must be identified by effective probing, by asking questions.

With our prospects or customers competing in a free-enterprise system, they have the problem of continually searching for more effective methods of bringing their product or service to market. Your products or services can help them if you find out the exact nature of their problem and then offer a solution. Without a doubt, all progressive companies and individuals want to consider new ideas, methods, products, and services that can benefit them. If your product can help them save time, money, or effort over what they are presently doing or using, then what they are presently using is a problem to them, whether they realize it or not. More often than not, prospects will not admit they have a problem. If they did, they would be admitting their lack of action in not correcting it sooner. The problem may be hidden in their plant operations, purchasing policies, manufacturing techniques, technical specifications, stocking and inventory procedures, or any of numerous other areas. To identify their problem(s), the sales professional must learn as much as possible about what clients make, how they make it, the markets they serve, how they specify, and how they buy. Armed with this information the salesperson can become a problem solver.

A problem is nothing more than the difference or distance between what people or companies have and what they want. The solution you offer, by their using your product or service, can bring the difference closer or close the gap entirely. Salespeople, when calling, think of the prospect's or customer's business first: how can they help? True sales professionals must think of themselves as rendering a service. The most effective method of identifying the prospect's or customer's problem is by effectively asking open-ended questions, by probing. This technique, coupled with a strong desire to serve, is what makes a true professional. Probing usually takes place in an initial meeting, often called a sales interview.

ASKING QUESTIONS, PROBING

Sales professionals identify the prospects' needs and wants (problems) by learning as much as they can about them as individuals, their operation and methods of doing business. Salespersons get answers by asking questions in a manner that convinces the prospect that they are sincerely interested in helping. The true sign of a sales professional is the ability to ask open-ended questions, and of course to listen to the response to identify needs and wants. There are six effective words to start a question: who, what, where, how, when, and why. The journalist uses them in preparing a story. The sales professional uses them to get answers. The questions are not asked to solicit a yes or no answer only, but rather to encourage dialogue to learn as much detail as possible of how the prospects transact their business. Statements are made and questions asked to solicit a positive response; questions should never be asked to embarrass the prospect. This is important for many reasons. First, we want the prospect in a "yes" frame of mind and we want to make sure there is no misunderstanding; and of course embarrassment doesn't make for a pleasant buyer–supplier relationship.

If you are prepared properly, you will have many approaches from which to determine the best one. If you are interrupted or detoured in your presentation, you can get back if you have planned properly. Socrates, the Greek scholar, effectively taught his students over 2,000 years ago by asking questions and probing for solutions. Doctors and lawyers use the questioning technique in their professional practices, as must the sales professional. If you are asked by your prospect why you ask so many questions, simply say, "Mr. Prospect, I ask questions so I can better understand your requirements and how you prefer to do business. That way I will be equipped to serve you more professionally with less or no wasted time."

When asking questions to identify needs and wants, the salesperson starts out with broad or general questions; then as answers are given, the salesperson can be more specific in his or her questioning.

It is necessary to anticipate the answer you are looking for as you develop your line of questioning. The interviewing questions must be directed to emphasize a sales point or benefit that should interest the prospect. Customer probes are done in a fashion that encourages prospects to respond honestly because they know you are there to help. The sales professional can come up with ideas, suggestions, and recommendations that will help fill the needs and wants of individuals or their organization. Probing is an effective way to get answers. Questions are open-ended to allow the prospect to reply without restrictions. We often make a statement, first to emphasize a positive fact, and then ask a question. It adds depth and an awareness of business when a salesperson questions in this manner.

Some typical statement-first questions are these:

1. The cost of motor burnouts is high. How often do you have burnouts?
2. All companies are interesting in reducing their cost of employee benefits. What do you figure it costs you per employee?
3. With inventory costs a concern in all companies, what would you like to see happen to bring yours down? How often do you reorder?
4. We recognize that consultants have to satisfy their clients. We may be selling them services now in one of our sales offices. Who are your clients?
5. We recognize that distributors like manufacturers to be out front in promoting new products. How often would you want me to make joint calls with your salesperson?
6. With most of us concerned about inflation, how are you planning for your retirement?

7. I have a problem and I need your help. I've never met your new insurance officer. Where can I find him? I'd appreciate it if you would introduce me.

Be wary of questions that start with would, could, or should. They ask rhetorical questions that don't have to be answered. Or, if answered, they can very easily be answered with a curt yes or no. We'll give you a few examples.

1. With medical and dental costs rising all the time, wouldn't it be nice to be able to have fixed-rate coverage for an extended period?
2. With materials costs being a significant factor in your production, wouldn't it be great if you could cut your material requirements by 30 percent?
3. Spoilage and process control are real concerns in chemical reactions. Wouldn't it be remarkable if I could review how we've helped many companies reduce their rejection rate by 22 percent?
4. There are many new and exciting investment programs available. Is it important that you have one with high or low risk?

Examples of open-ended questions that can help you identify the prospect's needs or wants and give you the opportunity to suggest ways you can service them are as follows:

1. Whom are you buying from now?
2. Why did you decide to buy from them initially?
3. Are you satisfied with your present suppliers? Why?
4. What do I have to do to be able to quote on our services?
5. Who is involved in the buying decision?
6. Who else in your company would be interested in this cost-saving system?
7. What are your company's policy and procedure in reviewing proposals sent to you?

A questioning salesperson is generally recognized as a skillful salesperson, provided he or she listens to the answers. The salesperson must also be prepared to answer questions from the prospects. We suggest you consider answering some of their questions with a question of your own. They can be very effective closers. Examples follow:

Prospect: How much does it cost?
Salesperson: In what quantity?

Prospect: When could it be delivered?
Salesperson: When do you want delivery?

Prospect: How much do I have to order to get a good price?
Salesperson: How much do you want to order?

> *Prospect:* When does a new model come out?
>
> *Salesperson:* Do you want the newest model? This is it.

The number of questions you ask is only limited by the time you are allotted or how much time it takes to identify the problem. Once the problem is identified, you immediately get into your sales presentation, making sales points and stressing benefits to help prospects solve their problems.

Ask questions like, "Is that important to you, Mr. Prospect?" or "What do you think is the most important feature in a service of this kind?" or "In your application, Mr. Prospect, which would be more important—long service life or low initial cost?" The ability to ask questions effectively is the sign of the real sales professional.

ATTITUDE—SKILLS—KNOWLEDGE: ASK

The successful professionals get what they want out of their careers when they ASK. The ASK letters should trigger many action programs, which involve setting specific goals for measureable improvement in attitude, selling skills, and knowledge. First, ASK yourself at what level you are performing now. Then ASK where do you want to be. Next you must initiate action improvement programs to get from where you are to where you want to be.

Second, ASK your peers, manager, teacher, family, trainer, or others who have an interest in your development for suggestions on how you can improve.

Third, ASK your prospects or customers. ASK them for recommendations on how they would like you to serve them. Also don't forget to ASK them for orders.

If you want action, ASK for it, starting with yourself.

THE STATEMENT-QUESTION TECHNIQUE

The statement-question (SQ) technique in opening a sales interview and probing is one of the most important tools a salesperson should master. This technique requires a relevant statement, focusing attention on a subject or item of interest to the listener, which is followed by an open-ended question to stimulate probing when you are attempting to identify responsive chords.

Here's how and why the statement-question technique works:

1. You start with a statement that emphasizes positive action, results, or conditions that you are aware of from your customers, the market conditions, government regulations, or other sources.
2. Then, without waiting for a reply, you ask an open-ended question relevant to your statement.

It works because you don't start out "selling" your product or service before you identify problems and needs, and your initial statement is usually based on third-party testimony, not something you made up. Here are a few examples:

1. Mr. Jones, the U.S. government is giving a tax-saving benefit to people who are installing energy-saving devices. (*Statement*) What action is your company taking to save energy? (*Question*)
2. Mr. Smith, there are many areas of benefits that our customers enjoy when they take our service. What benefits are you interested in the most?

HITTING THE "HOT BUTTON"

The sales professional continually probes and asks questions to hit the buyer's most responsive chord, or "hot button." This expression is one that has been used by many sales trainers in identifying product, service, approach, or buying signal that is a positive indication of the prospect's interest. It's a visual, verbal, or written indication from the prospect that the salesperson is probing into an area of interest to the buyer. The sales professional hits and identifies hot buttons by probing, asking open-ended questions, and listening. Prospects then reveal their business tactics regarding how they buy, what they buy, when they buy, and who in their organization are the decision makers.

The salesperson probes for hot buttons on initial sales interviews and subsequently in building rapport, handling objections, and closing. Hot button salesmanship helps the salesperson take the most direct approach to an order.

THE POWER OF PERSUASION

Sales professionals use their persuasive abilities in a sincere attempt to convince prospects that they have a solution to their problems. Before attempting to persuade a prospect, the salesperson should probe for the problem and believe in the solution.

Salesmanship has often been defined as the art and science of persuading another to believe in the same thing you believe in. Hence, a strong conviction and personal belief by the salesperson is necessary. The successful salesperson is the individual who has the ability to constantly persuade prospects and customers.

Salespeople persuade their prospects and customers by knowing as much as they can about their products and services, markets, company policies, competition, and so on. They are confident in their application of this knowledge by continually improving their probing, listening, and other selling skills.

Let's take a closer look at how the sales professional goes about persuading prospects and customers.

1. A thorough knowledge with strong emphasis on the customer benefits of your products or services is necessary. Knowing and telling what the benefits mean in terms of dollars saved, improvement of the operation, or other *specific* benefit is memorable.

2. An awareness and appreciation of what your offerings have accomplished in similar situations is helpful. You can persuade when you are able to support your benefits with proof, past experiences, or other testimonies. You believe what you say because you know it is true.

3. Your eyes, voice, and mannerisms must all reflect the same truthful attitude.

4. Your sincere desire to serve and help the prospects and customers must be obvious. The commitment to service is upmost in the mind of professional salespeople. With a sincere belief in their product or service, their company, and themselves, sales professionals are on the road to persuading others to believe and buy.

PREPARING TO SELL

To help in a review of the many areas that are important for effective salesmanship, we've listed some key questions to consider. We suggest you feed the following questions into the world's most fantastic and original computer, your brain, before each contact with a prospect or customer to ensure maximum success:

- How will the prospect or customer benefit from my product or service?
- How will their company lose by not buying?

- Will the person I call on have the power to buy and the money to pay?
- Am I prepared to speak in terms of specific benefits?
- Do I have solid evidence—third party if possible—to prove my statements?
- Will I listen carefully when the client speaks?
- Will I be able to answer questions without hesitating?
- If presented with a logical, major objection, will I be able to handle it smoothly?
- Am I prepared to "draw the client out" with open-ended questions?
- Will I give up trying to convince prospects the first time they say no?
- **Am I prepared to ask for the order, identify what it takes to get an order, or for an appointment?**
- How many times will I ask for an appointment or an order?
- Do I have a really good opening and closing?

Preparing for a sales interview is every bit as important as the selling itself. The less successful salesperson will usually tell you that success is largely a matter of luck; however, isn't it interesting that the harder you work, the "luckier" you get? Luck is when preparedness and opportunity cross.

Other areas in which to prepare are these:

1. The sales professional may not know the prospect's needs or wants. Effective probing is required before they can offer recommendations and solutions.
2. The prospects may not recognize their needs or wants; the salesperson must help identify them.
3. The salesperson may first consider one product or service to recommend, then after probing, feel another one is better suited.

The salespeople must be prepared to appraise quickly the prospect's replies and decide what is the best approach to use to present their product or service. Sales professionals recognize that one of the primary means of discovering needs and wants is by asking questions. They must observe the individual's personal characteristics, facilities, methods of operation, and so on to be more aware. Sound advice to the salespeople who want to bring a prospect to their way of thinking or close a sale is *always ask another question.* The more professional a salesperson is, the more time is spent asking questions and listening for replies, replies that can help identify needs and wants.

THE PRESENTATION MANUAL

Salespeople must always be in a ready position to present, discuss, and review the products or services they offer. This is best accomplished if all the materials necessary to make an effective presentation are available in a presentation manual. The presentation manual is one of the most effective sales aids a professional salesperson can prepare and use.

This manual should contain descriptive materials, bulletins, brochures, copies of orders, installation photos, testimonial letters, lists and photos of satisfied customers, case studies, copies of your latest advertisements, photos of your plants and manufacturing facilities, technical articles and data, the latest pricing and shipping dates, competitive comparisons, government or industry reports, and so on. The presentation manual should contain any information that can show a feature, explain its function, show its benefits, or confirm its advantages.

The manual, to be effective, must be up-to-date and attractive. It's a working tool. It's important that salespeople check with local management and their factories and headquarters people to verify that the information in the manual is the latest.

Professionals know that while thumbing through the pages, looking for a particular piece of information to answer a prospect's question or illustrate a sales point, they can stop and say, "Take a look at this list of satisfied customers. Notice how many of the companies are in the same industry that you are in." Often while leafing through your manual, prospects may spot something that is of particular interest to them.

Important points to consider in preparing your presentation manual are these:

1. Use a heavy-duty, three-ring binder. The covers should be neat and clean; it should be sectioned off with tabs.
2. Sheets referred to frequently or those that may have to be taken out for closer inspection should be laminated or inserted in a plastic sheet protector. Replace all pages as they start to get frayed.
3. Review its contents with other company salespeople or sales management to see if they have additional information they can give you.
4. Continually look for new information that could be added that will help you illustrate a sales point.
5. Make sure you rehearse the sales point for each item in the manual.

FLEXIBILITY REQUIRED
FOR EFFECTIVE SALES INTERVIEWING

Professionals consider a sales interview or presentation as an opportunity to make the best impression possible. These salespeople are excited about their products, their services, their ideas, and the opportunity to share their enthusiasm with others. They are always using sales points to get the prospect's attention.

Sales interviews and presentations are given to accomplish key objectives. They are used to gather information, to inform, or to persuade. These key objectives can be accomplished better with previous knowledge of the needs, wants, ages, education, and experience of the clients. If you can get this information you will be able to relate to their frame of reference.

Salespeople must be prepared with options before they start. They should be flexible and determined to have their message understood. They are willing to try any approach necessary to meet those objectives. They know many sales points and techniques, and they use those that fit the best.

The sales professional's objectives must be determined before the interview and presentation and always remain absolutely clear in his or her mind. Every visual aid, every statement, every sales point, every physical action must strategically advance the interview or presentation toward those objectives. The salesperson must remain alert. Feedback from the prospect or customer must be monitored and analyzed. Positive reactions must be reinforced, negative actions counteracted, and neutral reactions intensified.

Through the interviewing and probing, needs or wants of the prospect or customer are uncovered. Salespeople point out how their product or service best satisfies those needs or wants. This is commonly called *need-satisfaction selling*. It is capable of satisfying many types of selling situations, including maintaining and building rapport with prospects and customers over a long period of time. To be prepared, the sales professional must have a series of sales points and sales aids available to handle any situation successfully. Flexibility is essential for the sales interview and for long-term survival in a sales career.

DEVELOPING SALES POINTS

The salesperson is prepared to make a favorable impression when he or she has sales points ready to be used to strike the most responsive cord of the client. (As we explained earlier, this responsive card is called the *Hot Button*.)

A sales point or selling statement is made when a benefit is given that should be of interest to the client. The more sales points a salesperson makes, the more effective is the interview or presentation. Prospects buy products or services when they envision the benefits they will receive when they own the product or service. The sales professional must be prepared to explain functions and give proof if asked. The amateur in sales can talk at great length about the features of a product when the prospect is really interested in benefits.

In developing sales points, the sales professional must know the product or service completely, then be aware of how it works, be able to explain its customer benefits, and be prepared to offer proof, if asked. This is commonly called feature-function-benefit-proof selling. It is the most effective kind of salesmanship.

> *Feature:* A fact about a product or service that is present in its design.
> *Function:* How the feature works.
> *Benefit:* Advantage to the prospect or customer because of this feature.
> *Proof:* Confirmation to back up your benefit statement.

The sales professional knows numerous sales points that can be made about the product or service. He or she begins with a customer benefit and mentions the feature in the product or service which enables the prospect to get that benefit. It is not necessary to go into how or why it works (function) or offer immediate verification (proof) unless it is necessary to reinforce your point.

It's important that as sales points are made, the salesperson receives an agreement or disagreement from prospective customers. This reaction is important to help them understand what is important to their customers so they can zero in on specific needs and wants—the customer's "hot button."

FEATURES—FUNCTIONS—BENEFITS—PROOF

Let's review in detail the important aspects of our sales points, starting with features:

1. *Features:* These are facts about the product, company, service, customers, or system. As long as they can relate to a customer benefit, there is almost no limit to the number of desirable features you can mention. They can be built into your product, the way you serve your customers, after-sale service, inspections, house calls, and so on. Research all aspects of your products, service, and company to discover all the features you can. They must be identified to help with your sales points for all your products and services. It is not necessary for the feature to be exclusive with your company for it to be effective.

2. *Functions:* An explanation of how your product works or what it will do doesn't have to be highly technical unless such information is requested. Don't hesitate to say that you may have additional technical support at a later meeting. We suggest you only explain the functions if you are requested to do so.

3. *Benefits:* This is really the heart of any sales point. The salesperson, in preparing a presentation with sales points, must realize that the prospect has two major questions: "What does that mean to me specifically?" and "What's in it for me?" Answering these questions before they are asked is at the very heart of customer benefit selling. Salespeople can go on and on, hearing themselves talk, but unless and until they are prepared to answer those major questions, they are not really selling.

A benefit is what that feature will do for the prospect and/or the company. Benefits, to be effective, must be specifically related to that prospect or customer. We've listed a few common features a company may have and their associated benefits so you can start to consider ways your product or service features can become effective customer-benefit statements.

Features	*Customer Benefits*
1. Large company	Well known, stable
2. Customer service department	On-time delivery, satisfaction
3. Worldwide company	Product and parts availability
4. Oldest company in field	Experience, leadership
5. Financially sound	Good investment
6. Quality controls	Trouble-free operation
7. Advanced products	Latest state of the art
8. Myself	Local office for service

More Features	*Specific Customer Benefits*
9. More efficient	Saves you $100 per unit
10. Smaller	Can save 40 percent of your stocking cost
11. Faster	Increases productivity 25 percent
12. Easier to install	Saves 30 minutes per unit

The more specific customer benefits you can identify about your product or service, the better you are prepared. All salespeople should prepare a list of every significant feature their product or service offers and relate to it a customer benefit. Specific customer-benefit statements should be the most heavily used tool you use. They are your sales points.

4. *Proof:* This is simply the evidence you can offer to substantiate the benefits you have described. It is not necessary to give the proof unless asked. You must be prepared, however. A good part of the time, your prospects or customers accept your word when you present the benefit, especially when you follow it up with the feature that produces the benefit.

The prospect, perhaps subconsciously, feels that you as a salesperson may be inclined to use a little "puffery." This prospect or customer may feel that your enthusiasm for your product or service causes you to overstate its benefits. At times like this, your unsupported word may not be enough and you may need to prove your benefits.

Types of proof you may consider are the following:

a. Technical data—Brochures, specification sheets, diagrams, or other technical data are essential to verify your statements.
b. Third party referral or testimony—Maybe a magazine article, technical paper, or letter from a satisfied customer will help.
c. On-site visit—Maybe a visit to an installation can verify your equipment's operation.
d. Case histories—Outline how other customers had a similar problem and arrived at the solution with your product or service.
e. Samples and demonstrations—Maybe a sample will offer the solid proof required. Do you have a model you can demonstrate?
f. Other sales aids—Maybe a flip chart with the required information or an audio-visual program will give some proof. How about a pad and pencil to sketch out or write out a proof?
g. Plant visit—Perhaps a visit to your manufacturing facilities will give the visual proof necessary to convince the prospect.

Your proof should be such that after it is given, shown, or demonstrated, the prospects or customers affirm the benefit(s) they will receive from your product or service. They are getting closer to being persuaded.

EMPHASIZING CUSTOMER BENEFITS

Sales points and hot buttons are more convincing if they touch one or more of the prospect's or customer's prime motivators. These prime motivators are pride, profit, fear, love, duty, and hate. Our prospects will take positive action if a benefit we can offer satisfies one or more of these motivators. Some typical motivators used as benefits are these:

1. Extra profits due to savings in dollars or time.
2. Security and emotional gratification.
3. Physical safety designed in product.
4. Proud to have the latest technology.

5. Being the best through newer products.
6. Ability to out-perform the competition.

Other points to consider . . .

1. Don't spend too much time throwing darts at competition—promote the benefits of your product.
2. Learn to sell with 51 percent—don't be afraid to concede good points of competitors' products.
3. Feature your exclusives, where your design is unique in some respect.
4. Make higher prices now a lower price later:
   - Feature savings on long-run basis.
   - Compare initial price versus ultimate cost by showing savings.
   - Don't be ashamed of the price.
   - Feature its value.

What a salesperson knows and sells as a distinguishing feature of a product or service may not be seen by a prospect as a reason to buy—as a benefit. Benefits are the end result of satisfactory use of a product or service, provided through distinguishing features. In the buyer-seller relationship, the buyer must be persuaded by the seller that use of the product or service will satisfy the needs or wants of the buyer.

Salespeople who base their selling strategy solely on a description or demonstration of features are gambling that the prospective buyer will accept the task of converting features into benefits in order to provide logical reasons to buy. We know from experience that most prospects do not have the time or inclination to do half the sales job for us; we also know that no sale is entered into without prospects anticipating some degree of benefit to them.

Providing the buyer with the reasons to buy (benefits) is important in all selling situations, and even more important when using the telephone, since the process is entirely verbal. The skill can be easily acquired through knowledge of the basics, and through practice.

Consciously, or unconsciously, the buyer has one primary question in mind when talking to a salesperson: "What's in it for me?" Salespeople make their presentations in a way that will answer that question; they answer it by selling benefits—selling features won't do the job.

"Double-plated, integrated circuit protector" is a feature. It is meaningless until the salesperson explains how it will benefit the customer. On the other hand some salespeople say that not all features are as obscure as the protector. Some are so well known as to be as self-explanatory. There's some truth in this, but can salespeople afford to take a chance that this particular prospect knows all about the benefits of this particular feature? Not really.

A benefit may seem obvious to you, but it may be less obvious to your prospects. Even if they are capable of translating the feature into the benefit, they may not make the mental effort. You do the translating. Don't just say, "It has a double-plated, integrated circuit protector." Subconsciously ask and answer the question, "So what?" It's better to say, "You get ease of installation, big saving in the cost of on-site testing, and no danger of hook-up errors; all these because of our circuit protector." Of course, if you have enough details about the customer's operation, it's more effective to give specific dollars or percentage savings. The prospect is primed to buy when convinced of and anticipating the benefits enjoyed from owning your product or service. Once the prospect envisions the benefits of ownership, the sales professional must close and complete the scenario.

In making a sales point, you may decide to present the feature first and follow up with the benefit, or present the benefit first and follow up with the feature. Although it's important to know the function and proof of each feature-benefit statement, it is not necessary to get into those details unless asked. If you hit a hot button after a benefit statement, the prospect may want you to give a more detailed proof or explanation. At this point, you consider the most effective proof you can offer from your sales aids and presentation manual.

Top-selling professionals agree that presenting the benefit first and following it up with the feature that produces the benefit makes a stronger presentation. For example, "This widget will increase your profit by 20 percent on each job because these simple, snap-in connectors save time for your installers on the site" is a statement giving the benefit first.

When the benefit is presented first and followed up with the feature, the feature tends to support the benefit statement. Most of the prospects who become customers are in a business of some type. They're interested in saving money, saving time (time is money), increasing production, making more sales, looking and feeling better, and so forth. They're interested in profit now or in the future.

Profit is the one ultimate benefit in which every businessperson is interested. Any benefit you can present that will help to increase profit in some way will be interesting to the business buyer. Even nonprofit organizations can be said to be interested in profit; they may have a different label for it, increased efficiency, higher productivity, but it boils down to the same thing. Individuals who are purchasing for themselves are looking for more value, dollar savings, an easier way of life, and so on. They are the same as profit is to a business—important.

Keep in mind, however, that business buyers don't buy only for business reasons. They also buy for personal reasons. Buyers may buy from you because your product or service can make their job easier, because it saves headaches. Your competition may have a similar line, selling at a similar price and offering similar service, but the buyer buys from you because of personal preference. Buyers may buy your product or service because it will enhance their reputation in their company. Make them look good. Your product or service may help them get a promotion or keep their job.

In a given case, the personal benefits may be more important than the business benefits. Naturally, since these benefits are personal, sometimes very personal, you may have to approach them indirectly and by implication. Don't overlook personal benefits: they can be the real key to making the sale.

SELLING IN ALL MARKETS

The opportunities and possibilities for career growth in the sales field are as many and varied as there are products and services available. Each product or service, whether sold retail or wholesale, through distributors, to manufacturers, to original equipment manufacturers, or to users, each requires the talents of a professional salesperson. This book, with its intention of emphasizing the essence of effective salesmanship, covers topics that are beneficial to all salespeople, regardless of the markets they serve. Although there are suggestions and techniques that would apply when making a sales presentation in a prospect's or customer's place of business, they may not be appropriate or relevant if you are in a retail sales position and someone visits your place of business. Nonetheless, the basics of knowing your products or service, effective use of selling skills, and the proper attitude apply in all professional selling.

Selling Retail

When selling retail, potential customers usually visit your place of business. They demand to be serviced. The professional salesperson does so by probing and asking questions to identify what is the best product or service that can be offered. Occasionally, people that are selling retail may have an opportunity to leave the store to address larger groups or meet buyers that might be interested in their products or services. All the skills in our modules on planning, communications, time and territorial management, strategies, handling objections, and closings apply.

Selling to Wholesalers or Distributors

Wholesalers or distributors can benefit greatly from this book's content because when selling to them, the sales professional has to work closely with their customers, management, and sales force to get his or her products sold to the distributor's prospects and customers. Building sales rapport with distributors involves prospecting, cold-call selling, and all the other items contained in this book for effective account coverage by the sales professional assigned. The professionals calling on distributor accounts know they are salespeople for the company they represent, and the distributor looks to them to behave like a sales manager and sales trainer. With that challenge, the skills that can be acquired through the effective utilization of the suggestions and techniques of this book would help in two ways: in their own selling capacity and in their larger responsibilities to the distributor's management of helping the distributor salespeople be more effective.

Selling to Manufacturers and Original Equipment Manufacturers (OEMs)

When selling to manufacturers and OEMs, it's important that the salesperson look not only at the way the customer can use and benefit from the products or services offered but also beyond the customer to the "customer's customer." What do the people who buy your product or service do with it after it is received? How does it help them in their businesses? The ultimate usage is an important consideration. Salespeople are more effective when they are always concerned with how the company who buys the products or services will benefit from it. Manufacturers are always looking for areas to increase their productivity and efficiency and to reduce their expenses, as well as for suggestions to help them in the marketplace.

Original equipment manufacturers are companies who buy a product or service and incorporate it in their equipment or service and then sell it as a completed system. Salespeople assigned to these accounts must be aware of the OEMs' customers, so they can be better prepared in selling their products and making more meaningful sales points.

The sales professionals, no matter what line of endeavor, recognize that all the ideas and suggestions in this book may not work all the time nor apply to their particular sales field right now. However, as you advance into sales and into sales management or higher level positions, it will become obvious that the contents and basic concepts in this book will help in most sales instances and can add to your knowledge of the sales profession.

CONCLUSION

There are many disciplines that a person wanting to become a sales professional must master. It is necessary to be continually committed to self-improvement in knowledge of products, customers, markets, and competitors. It is essential to learn and apply the many sales skills and techniques necessary to service your markets effectively. The ability to identify needs and wants through effective probing, questioning, and listening is basic. This skill helps salespeople identify problems that they can solve. Professionals sell customer benefits by making sales points. They know product features to support benefit statements, and they have the proof to back them up if necessary in a well-prepared presentation manual. Professionals are always looking for more effective ways to serve their prospects or customers. They are always searching for the best *sellatechnics* to use in a given sales situation.

Review Questions

1. What are three major areas the sales professional must strive continually to develop and improve? Why are they so important?
2. We know that talking in specifics is more meaningful to the listener. Write five examples of talking in generalities and five of talking in specifics. Assume you are talking to a potential buyer.
3. Pick out a product or service you are selling or would like to sell, and list ten areas where you should be knowledgeable.
4. List ten of the most important sales skills that must be mastered to sell this product or service.
5. How can you evaluate performance improvement in each of the areas mentioned in questions 3 and 4?
6. Why is it necessary to keep a positive mental attitude in sales? How do you do so?
7. Explain what a salesperson is selling in addition to a product or service when talking to a potential buyer.
8. What personal and professional characteristics do prospects and customers find most desirable in salespeople?
9. The statement-question technique is very effective. Write ten examples that could be effective in a buy and sell situation.
10. Why is probing necessary for an effective interview with a potential buyer?
11. How is asking questions and listening for the answers used in effective salesmanship?
12. Give ten examples of asking questions and probing that may be used in a typical buy and sell situation.
13. Persuasion is a strong tool that when used effectively can help others make a decision. Give five examples of how you have persuaded others to take the action you want.
14. Consider a product or service you are selling or would like to sell and prepare a typical presentation manual. It should list its contents and explain how each item could help the salesperson.

15. What are the four major aspects of a sales point? Define each.

16. Select five features of a product or service. Next, determine the functions and benefits, and proof for these features. Finally, write five sales points emphasizing the benefits.

17. Why is it more meaningful to talk specifics when you discuss customer benefits to a prospective buyer?

18. Why do your customers buy from you? What can you do to have them buy more?

19. Explain why it is essential for people in sales continually to strive to improve their performance.

20. Why should we consider sales a profession?

FEATURES	FUNCTIONS	BENEFITS	PROOF
The facts about your product, service, company, system, etc.	How it works. Why it works. How it is used.	What benefit does it provide? *Be specific*	How can you prove the benefit? (if necessary)
Salespoint: For each benefit make a statement or ask a question that is of specific interest to this prospect or customer.			

module two
Essentials of Verbal and Written Sales Communication

Communication is an interchange of information between two or more parties. To be effective, the information must be understood and accepted. From a salesperson's viewpoint, it must also be "acted on" in a positive manner. Certain words are action-packed; others are negative. The professional should always be positive in personal attitude and expression.

Salespeople must study and strive continually to improve their ability to get their message across in a clear, logical, effective manner.

A cassette tape recorder should be used to practice sales presentations, telephone prospecting techniques, probing skills, the ability to make effective sales points, answering objections, and closing.

Clear communications help get orders. This is an important module in your personal and professional development.

TOTAL COMMUNICATIONS— NECESSARY FOR SALES SUCCESS

The sales professional's position requires total communications— effectiveness in writing, speaking, and listening. The salesperson will not survive long if unable to communicate effectively. Unfortunately, effective communications does not come naturally to some people. It is a skill, to be practiced and learned. The investment in time and effort pays off in increased sales.

Salespeople must deal with and through people in order to achieve their objectives. This requires communication. Day by day they must plan and coordinate work activities and time scheduling with others; they must be able to make reports; write sales letters, sales proposals, and presentations; and ask effective questions and analyze the answers. All these activities require the exchange of ideas, facts, meanings, and feelings through written or spoken words. Let's look at basic communications.

WHY WE COMMUNICATE

Sales communication is the flow or interchange of information, thoughts, or opinions between a prospect or customer and a salesperson. When salespeople communicate, they are trying to accomplish four things:

1. *Being understood*—getting something across to somebody else so they know exactly what you mean. This "something" can be facts, or it can be your intentions, your feelings, your frame of mind.
2. *Being accepted*—getting prospects or customers to agree with you, or at least give you a sympathetic hearing.
3. *Getting something done*—getting prospects or clients to act because they understand what you want done and why they should do it, or helping them change their attitude toward something by showing it in a new light.
4. *Understanding others*—learning how they feel about you, a particular situation, or conditions in general. It's important to remember that all communications are two way—not just something that goes from you to others, but something that takes place between you and others. Unless you practice it this way, you'll be as handicapped as if you went about your job wearing blinders and ear plugs.

HOW WE COMMUNICATE

We can communicate with or without the use of words. Actions (what we do and how we do it) communicate our intentions and ideas sometimes more forcefully than what we say. Kinesics is the study of body language. How you say a word, your voice inflections, tone, attitude, facial expressions, and gestures—all add feeling and meaning to what you are saying. The salesperson studies body language.

Written words can be as profitable as spoken words, sometimes more so. They can be read over many times and a word not understood can be looked up in a dictionary. You can pick up and put down written communications at your convenience. Of course, there are disadvantages to written communications. You can't get the reaction of the reader if you are not present when the material is being read. Sometimes it is difficult to reflect the state of mind of the writer. With that in mind, a good rule of thumb is to use written communications as backup to your verbal communications with your prospects and customers.

This module will deal with a key to effective salesmanship—attaining good verbal and written communication skills. Since we know that words and ideas, seemingly clear in themselves, can be understood in different ways, this module will suggest ways we can reduce misunderstandings, thereby helping the salesperson get more orders.

VERBAL COMMUNICATIONS—
ARE YOU SPEAKING THE SAME LANGUAGE?

The language we use is a result of our total experiences. Our culture, country, province, section, neighborhood, profession, personality, attitude, and mood at the moment all bring us to where we are now. The chance of two people having the same background and meeting at the same time are remote. Since we have different backgrounds, it is absolutely essential to communicate in a language understood by both parties. This necessity requires a strong effort on the part of the salesperson in dealing with prospects and customers who have a different set of total experiences.

There are more than 3.5 billion different people in the world, and each talks, listens, and thinks in his or her own special language. Sometimes we use several languages, which contain slight variations of agreed-upon meanings that are uniquely individual and which may change each second. The 500 most common words in the English language have over 14,000 meanings. Sometimes it is a wonder that anyone understands anyone else. Sales communication is the thread that ties all our efforts together. How well we communicate with our prospects or customers will definitely affect how well we succeed.

Improving Your
Oral Communications

Two things to keep in mind when communicating orally are these: (1) your primary purpose is to establish or improve understanding between you and another person; (2) any communication will be accepted or rejected primarily based on your sincerity. Following are some specific suggestions to improve oral communications and sales effectiveness:

1. Be sure of what you say. Document your sales points and support them with proof prepared before you get into any discussion of a serious nature with a prospect or customer. Having proof handy gives you confidence.

2. Keep things in logical sequence. Your interview or presentation should be in a sequence that has a clear-cut beginning, body, and finish, properly communicated and not hidden among less important or trivial discussions. This requires sales planning.

3. Have your sales interview or presentation where there are a minimal number of distractions.

4. Consider your own experiences or the experiences of satisfied customers and how some of them may relate to or be of interest to your listener. Most prospects enjoy hearing stories of actual successful experiences and benefits that they may relate to and possibly draw from. Point out how similar benefits could be received by the prospect.

5. Establish mutual interests, a common ground between both parties that can be built upon. The salesperson is interested in serving the needs and wants of the prospect.

6. Talk in language that is understood. When we communicate with each other, it is useful to remember that our common words may not evoke the same image in someone else's mind as they do in ours. Knowing this, we can help improve our communications by being as specific as possible in the way we use words; also, if we are on the receiving end, it often helps to ask questions to increase clarification and understanding. Don't use unfamiliar words or ones that require a lot of additional technical definition, lest they distract from the smooth flow of your interview or presentation.

7. Get feedback. You have to watch for responses or positive feedback as an indication that what you are saying is getting through to the other person. You can see by their facial expressions or gestures if they are bored or confused. You are understood.

8. Check the emotional level of the prospects. See if they're getting a feeling for what you are proposing. Watch your timing. Try not to cover too much information that contains a lot of data, numbers, details, and so on in a short period of time without having a backup in writing for ready reference.

9. Answer who, what, when, where, how, and why questions to help you become more readily understood. This technique is commonly used by newspaper reporters, whose stories are composed to answer these questions so they can be readily understood by their readers.

10. Instead of asking, "What does that mean?" try thinking, "What does he (or she) mean?"

11. Your sentences should be clear and concise. Keep in mind that sentences with eight words or less are very easy to understand; sentences with fourteen to seventeen words (normal) are fairly easy to understand; and sentences with twenty-five words or more are very difficult to understand. Try recording your presentation and check the length of your sentences.

12. Use the word *you.* The more times the word *you* is used in a sales interview or presentation, the greater the degree of understanding. Using *you* or *your* will get the listener's attention and make your sales talk more personal.

Use Words that Motivate.   Eliminate words and phrases that irritate. Continually look for words that please and motivate. Some suggestions follow:

Irritate	*Motivate*
You know?	Will you help me?
Understand?	I'm so sorry.
Get the point?	It was my fault.
See what I mean?	Thank you.
You don't say?	Gee. I'm proud of you!
But honestly now!	Congratulations!
Not really. . . ?	Please.
Don't you know . . .?	You were very kind.
I'll tell you what!	I beg your pardon.
Old friend (Pal)	It's been a real pleasure.

Probing Words—Inviting Action.   Probing by asking questions is a key sales skill, and you should use words or phrases that invite action in your probing activity. They are important for getting a positive response. Some examples follow:

Probe
- What is your opinion?
- What do you think?
- Can you illustrate?
- What do you consider?
- What were the circumstances?
- How do you feel about . . . ?
- What happened then?
- Could you explain?
- Why?

- What would you suggest?
- Can you help me?
- How would you handle it?

Negative Words to Avoid.   Avoid using negative words that are not convincing and can leave a "hazy" impression. See the following list:

I think	Sometimes
Perhaps	I was wondering
Maybe	I might
If	I feel
I hope	I believe
Possibly	Only if

If you want to create and leave a hazy impression, use negative words. However, remember, *positives sell.*

Words that Trigger Emotions.   In your sales interviews, presentations, or writings, use words that trigger positive emotions. They will grab the attention and interest of your prospect or customer. Some words almost automatically have a strong emotional appeal. We'll call them *emotion-packed.* These action-packed words can be used very effectively in all sales activities. To make their use more meaningful, be specific when outlining customer benefits. Some of these emotion-packed words are the following:

1. Scientific	17. Quality
2. Durable	18. Bargain
3. Clean	19. Necessary
4. Efficient	20. Courtesy
5. Time-saving	21. Hospitality
6. Value	22. Status
7. Ambition	23. Enormous
8. Love	24. Low cost
9. Reputation	25. Genuine
10. Guaranteed	26. Progress
11. Safe	27. Thinking
12. Popular	28. Excel
13. Economical	29. Civic pride
14. Proven	30. Patriotism
15. Modern	31. Recommended
16. Health	32. Admired

33. Independent
34. Successful
35. Up-to-date
36. Tested

37. Expressive
38. Sympathy
39. Home
40. Growth

Is Your Sales Message Being Understood?

When you speak you want to be sure you are heard and understood. You want your audience to listen effectively. Following are some suggestions to increase the clarity of your message:

1. *Reduce the possibility of distractions.* When in a prospect's office, suggest that the secretary hold incoming telephone calls or interruptions. Don't discuss critical subjects in hallways, in reception areas, in parking lots, while waiting in crowded restaurants, at sporting events, or at other locations where distractions are likely. If you have a serious sales message to give, make sure the atmosphere is not distracting to the buyer.

2. *Get agreement as you proceed.* Look and listen for signs of agreement from your prospect. A shake of the head or a comment like, "Oh, okay, I understand, it's clear, it seems that it will work," are positive signs. Occasionally ask, "Am I making myself understood?" or "Do you agree?" or "What do you think about that?" or "What are your feelings in that regard?"

3. *Repeat key points.* Key sales points should be repeated at least three times during the course of your interview or presentation. Initially, highlight key points you want to review; next, review them in detail; then summarize. Emphasize the sales points of interest or the hot button that will benefit the prospect or customer the most.

4. *Watch your language.* Be wary of using jargon, slang, trade talk, or expressions that may not be clear or have two or more meanings. Listeners rely on their total life experiences to help them understand words and their meanings. Don't assume the meaning you place on a word is the same meaning your listener places on it. Clarify yourself at each key point to make sure there are no misunderstandings. Avoid this confusion by recording your presentation on a cassette player and playing it back. Technical terms and expressions may be an essential part of some presentations and cannot be removed to maintain integrity. Make sure these terms and expressions have the *one* meaning you want. Consider the different possible meanings of the following words: long life, high accuracy, small size, compact, reliable, minimum maintenance, relative performance, fast shipment, acceptable performance, high energy, low power consumption, miniature, durable, quick turn-around. Each of these words or expressions can lead to a question such as, "Compared to what?" or "How long?" or "What do you mean?" Unfortunately, many listeners don't ask a question to get clarification; they draw their own conclusions. This situation is deadly for the salesperson who must be confident that he or she is clearly helping and leading the listener to draw the desired conclusion. Words or expressions that have two or more meanings take the salesperson out of the driver's seat. *Remember, the responsibility for the listener being able to comprehend what is being said belongs to the speaker.*

Words to Avoid. Through the years, two words have crept into the sales professions that should be eliminated. These words give the profession a black eye because of the sly or sinister connotation often associated with them. The professional salesperson should eliminate the words *deal* and *pitch* from in-house discussions and those with their prospects or customers.

Eliminate	*Replace with*
deal	Transaction or offering
("I'm close to making a deal with that guy.")	(Dealers are in casinos.)
pitch	Make a presentation
("I'm going to the X Y Z Company and give them my pitch.")	("Pitch" men are in the carnival, not in professional sales.)

An expression that also should be eliminated is *sign here*. Most people have signed for too much already. Replace it with *please approve* or *O.K.*

The Importance of Remembering Names

In professional sales, a name is very important. To build the necessary rapport between buyers and sellers, understanding and acceptance is required. Using the prospect's name helps in this rapport-building process.

Prospects are interested in themselves first, in their business second, and last of all in you. When you mention their names and pronounce them correctly, you've got their attention focused on you. This is the simplest of all techniques for strengthening a sales presentation, yet it is too often ignored. A name is like a magnet. No matter how far your prospects' mind may wander, you can attract their attention back to you simply by calling them by name.

Prospects will be more inclined to listen to you and give you their full attention when you greet them by name and pronounce it correctly. Whenever you add a new name to your prospect list, make sure you write down the exact name and initial. Make sure the spelling is correct and you know how to pronounce it properly. Don't hesitate to ask, "What is the proper way to pronounce your name?" Also write down the title and responsibilities.

If you are blessed with an exceptional memory, be grateful. If you are like most of us and have trouble remembering names, we will offer you some suggestions:

1. The very moment you are introduced to a prospect, repeat the name. If during the introduction the name is mumbled or slurred and you don't hear it clearly, ask your prospect to please repeat it. He or she will not feel insulted. In fact, your show of interest in getting the correct name is flattering.

2. Try to use the name several times in your initial conversation with a new prospect. Start your questions with the name and use it to end your statements.

3. Every time you mention your prospect's name, take a good look at him or her. Try to pick up relationships in the name that you can identify with other places or things. Associate the name with something familiar. For example, Mr. Boston with the city of Boston. Perhaps you can associate just the first syllable with something familiar. Take the name *Stoneman.* Here you would remember just the first syllable, *stone.* Maybe you can recall that the person had a hard, stonelike stare. Association with other places or things is the best way to remember names.

4. Repeat the name over and over. Repeat it as often as you can during your conversation. The name will be fixed more deeply in your mind each time you repeat it.

5. Get into the habit of jotting down the names of prospects you meet during your working day. Seeing the name in writing helps you to remember because it uses another one of your senses, your sense of sight. At night run down your list and see how many names you remember as people, not as just words by which people are known.

Remembering names is key in effective sales communication. Always look for techniques and suggestions that can help you in this area.

Checking Your Communication

This module has many suggestions on how to communicate effectively. Read and apply them; they will help. You may ask, "How can I tell if I'm communicating any better?" "Are my presentations clear? Do they emphasize the action I want taken?" It may be hard for you to tell without outside assistance.

Let me make three more suggestions that will help you help yourself.

1. *Join Toastmasters International.* This organization is devoted to improving the members' ability to express themselves clearly and concisely. There are local clubs in every city. Look them up and be a guest at their meeting. You will quickly recognize that the members are interested in helping each other communicate better.

2. *Be a joiner.* Look for opportunities to join a civic, fraternal service, or political club. They are usually nonprofit and dedicated to many worthwhile, charitable activities. Don't just join a club or organization, but plan on taking an active part. Don't hesitate to get on your feet to express an opinion or volunteer for a committee. Look for occasions where your sales and marketing abilities can help the organization. Maybe you can make a presentation to the membership recommending a new building, borrowing money from a bank, asking for contributions, soliciting advertisers, and so on. The sales professional is a master at creating interest and desire so that action is taken. Don't hesitate to share these talents with organizations that are seeking more doers like yourself.

3. *Listen to yourself.* Take a cassette tape recorder and record yourself. Listen to how you communicate when you

- make a presentation to an individual or to a group, with and without sales aids.
- make a telephone call to a prospect, set an appointment, ask for an order, handle a complaint.
- answer a telephone call from a friendly customer, irate prospect, headquarters personnel.
- give directions to your secretary. Are they clear? Are there areas where misunderstandings can and do occur?

A cassette tape recorder with playback unit is one of the best investments sales professionals can make to improve their communications skills.

Why Your Sales Message May Not Be Understood or Accepted

There are many reasons why messages are not understood or accepted. Sales professionals continually analyze their interviewing presentations and closing skills and strive for improvement. Some reasons for miscommunication could be the following:

1. There may be suspicion or dislike on the part of the prospect that cannot be overcome at that particular time; hence, what is being said is not being accepted on a trusting basis. The salesperson must build trusting relationships by being sincere, believing in the product or service being offered, and acting in a professional manner.

2. There may be a failure to take into account the other point of view. Our minds are made up already and we don't want to be confused with any additional information. The salesperson earns a living by listening. Don't try to shove your point of view down a prospect's throat.

3. There may be poor timing. If you interrupt someone involved with other activities or at a time when they cannot give you the attention you require, you're better off rescheduling than trying to have a meaningful sales presentation. There is no way you can get acceptance of a sales idea or solution to a problem if you don't have complete attention. Avoid preoccupation that would occur at a social or athletic event. They are great for building rapport but usually not good for initial interviewing.

4. You may have a poor approach. The people you meet are usually preoccupied with other activities. Normally, they do not have a clean desk with nothing to do. Your approach should be cordial and direct with an initial benefit statement presented in a pleasant manner. This will usually get favorable attention and encourage you to proceed. Loud, boisterous approaches should be avoided.

5. People tend to receive or hear the message they want to hear, discarding the others. As a sender you have to be sure you are sending a clear, concise, and specific message which can be easily received and understood.

6. Insufficient proof is a main reason why an idea is not accepted. You may not have properly explained what the advantages and benefits of your products or services are.

7. Assuming that "everyone knows what you are talking about" and assuming "you know what others are talking about," without asking questions to make sure, are two common causes of communication failure.

Any of these miscommunications makes it difficult for prospects to understand and accept your offering. To communicate successfully, the sales professional must learn as much as possible about the customers or prospects. Try to identify what they are like, their ideas and thoughts, their experiences, their education, and what sort of approach will they respond to. All these suggestions will help develop customer rapport through clear communications.

Hiding the Real Meaning of What Is Said.   People occasionally hide from one another by putting on "verbal masks" and saying just the opposite of what they really mean. Gerard I. Nierenberg, a New York City attorney and founder of the General Semantics Foundation, gives some examples. The person who says

- "I'm not suggesting anything" is actually saying: "I'm telling you."
- "I would never do that." (I would do it if I had the opportunity.)
- "Do you think we are doing the right thing?" (We aren't doing the right thing.)
- "I'll never speak to you again." (Make me talk.)
- "You don't think I went too far, do you?" (I did, but tell me I didn't.)
- "I don't want to sound like I'm bragging, but. . . ." (I'm wonderful—admire me.)
- "What are you talking about?" (I know exactly what you mean but I don't like your attitude.)
- "Why did it have to happen to him?" (Just so it doesn't happen to me.)
- "Who could have dreamed it would end this way?" (I have—many times.)
- "I don't care what happens to me." (This is a launching pad for a defense of conduct elaborate enough to be used at a murder trial.)

If your prospect or customer hides behind a verbal mask, maybe some of the ideas in the module on handling objections can help.

How Do You Sound? Your voice over the telephone or in person must be an asset at all times and under all circumstances. The impressions you make are important. When meeting people face to face, poor diction may often be excused because of a winning smile or a warm personality. When using the telephone, your voice is all you have to reflect your personality. Before dialing an account, smile and keep smiling.

Let's outline some qualities of a good voice that can help either across the desk or on the telephone with a prospect.

1. *Alertness:* Give the impression you are wide awake and alert and interested in the person.

2. *Pleasantness:* Build a pleasant company image with a "voice with a smile." Pleasantness is contagious.

3. *Naturalness:* Use simple, straightforward language. Avoid repetition of unfamiliar words or phrases—particularly avoid slang, jargon, or technical terms which may not be understood.

4. *Distinctness:* Speak clearly and distinctly. Open your mouth so the sound can come out. Move the lips, tongue, and jaw freely.

5. *Expressiveness:* A well-modulated voice carries best. Use a normal tone of voice, neither too loud nor too soft. Talk at a moderate rate, neither too fast nor too slow. Vary your tone of voice. It will bring out the meaning of sentences and add color and vitality to what you say. Your voice reports whether or not you are thinking. If your mind is dull, your voice will be likewise. If you think and feel what you say, expression will find its way naturally into your voice

6. *Sincerity:* Convey the impression that you mean what you say and know what you are talking about. Your approach must be truthful by selling with facts and honesty. Whether talking to a prospect or to a customer, prepare for your discussion with pertinent information of interest. Nothing can be more damaging to customer relationships than "off the wall" statements not related to reality. Nothing can be more effective than well-planned sales points emphasizing customer benefits carefully personalized to the person with whom you are talking.

WRITTEN COMMUNICATIONS

Most of the daily communications of the sales professional involve speaking and listening to prospects and customers. Although skill development is important in these areas, no less effort should be made in improving writing skills. Your written word remains after you leave.

We will address our comments to any written information you mail or present to a company or individual. Although most of our comments will relate to correspondence between a salesperson and the prospect or customer, it can be applied within the company. Good written communications skills have no bounds.

For this module, we will consider any memo, letter, report, note, offering, or proposal that is written and intended to be read by a prospect or customer.

How Written Communications
Help Us Sell

Effective written communications should be an aid to any selling effort. It can have more of an impact than any sample, audio-visual program, or factory visit. As an aid, it is not expected to replace anything. It's expected to reinforce discussions or visual presentations. It helps build rapport.

The reasons why the sales professional should develop writing skills are many and varied. We list a few:

1. It is often necessary to confirm information given in person or over the telephone. The written document represents you, the salesperson, in your absence. It is a convenient, ready reference for the buyer to review your discussion. It can be read and reread time and time again as confirmation. It's a convenient way of forwarding information brochures, catalogs, or other sales literature.

2. By sending copies of correspondence to other interested parties, you can be sure that they all receive the same information at the same time.

3. Customers appreciate printed material and letters because this is an effective way for them to keep up to date on their many activities. Writing shows a concern for the customer because it's easy for them to keep their files and records in order.

4. A good letter or sales offering helps you sell. It is a base that must be touched by the sales professional. It is a very effective means of reinforcing sales points and hot buttons mentioned or observed during a sales interview or presentation.

5. Effective letters are an extension of you. They back up your promises; they can reach places you cannot go or cannot be. Marshall Field once observed, "One good business letter may be worth a million dollars."

6. Written materials not only carry information but also are an extension or your personality and attitude. They should indicate a respectful, trusting, and concerned nature. Good written communications must be an exact reflection of your attitude when you are visiting a prospect or customer face to face. The salesperson must present a consistent image. He or she can't be pleasant and desirous to serve in person and then appear cold, indifferent, or formal in writing. The prospect may wonder which is the real person.

7. A letter is an ideal way of focusing on situations by documenting past correspondence, activities, actions, and results. This is particularly important if for some reason a former customer is not presently buying from you because of a previous problem. If you have taken the necessary, corrective action, a letter outlining the problem, the steps you and your company have taken to correct it, and what you have done to prevent it from happening again will be very effective. By sending copies to all the buying influences who are aware of the problem, you can request to be considered for future business.

8. A brief memo, attaching an article or topic of interest to prospects or customers, will remind them of your thoughtfulness. When you read a newspaper, trade papers, or magazines, look for and cut out any article, promotion announcement, company activity, or advertisement that concerns or may be of interest to them and send a brief memo attaching the article. A simple comment, such as "I hope you will find the attached useful (or interesting)" or "Congratulations on your recent promotion" or "I'm pleased to see your completed plant expansion announced in the paper. I know you'll be satisfied with our equipment." These brief notes can be typed or written. They must be sincere and relevant to the readers and/or their companies.

9. Salespeople that have large territories have to rely on written and telephone contact with their prospects or customers between sales calls. Although recognizing that it's inopportune to telephone one prospect while visiting another, we heavily emphasize contact through the mails. Sales professionals should schedule mailings to their prospects or customers on a regular basis to continually keep their name in front of them. When on the road, they should be prepared with stamped envelopes and a mailing list.

10. A simple thank-you note after receipt of an order is a great way to show your customers how much you appreciate their confidence in you, your product, your service, and your company.

Deciding on What You Want to Write

Writing, like other aspects of professional selling, requires planning and organization to be meaningful. It's necessary to think about what you want to accomplish and identify the key points to make. Consider the following:

1. What's the objective I want to achieve?
2. What's the best way of approaching this subject?
3. What details should I state to support the message?
4. What action do I desire?
5. What's the background of the reader(s)?
6. What can I do to assume understandability?

Clear writing is based on clear thinking, and clear thinking begins with planning and organization.

When you learned to write school compositions, you were told to build up suspense gradually until you reached a peak, then conclude quickly. This technique, you learned, keeps readers interested and is the basis of good fiction. Unfortunately, many business letter writers learned this lesson too well and build their letters like a novel. The result is that long before the climax, they lose their reader's interest. Don't write with suspense, holding back the big ideas until last. You are not trying to entertain your reader. Your sales letter is intended to inform, create interest, and ask for action.

And since your reader's time is important, don't ramble on with too much detail. Decide what message you want to get across, and do it as clearly as possible. To do this you must *know your readers* and how much detail they are going to want. If you give them too much detail, they will either lose interest in what you say or miss the important parts of your message. If you give them too little, they may not understand. The two pitfalls are (1) assuming that the reader wants to know as much about your subject as you know and (2) assuming that they do know as much about your subject as you do. If you make the first assumption, you are liable to lose their interest, and if you make the second, you are liable to lose them.

Usually, you can spot the most obvious omissions or unnecessary details by simply rereading carefully. However, the closer you are to what you are writing, the more difficult it is to see errors. It would help if you could wait a day to read over an important letter or report after you have written it. This may help to be objective. Although not always possible to do under the pressure of business, it could be practiced more than it is. For major offerings, it is recommended that someone else read the offering before it is sent to a prospect or customer.

The ability to put yourself in your readers' shoes is basic to effective writing. Before writing, think about the readers' knowledge, experience, and interest in what you are preparing. When you do that you are in a better position to give them the information they need and want—enough, but not too much.

Just as a poorly organized sentence suggests incompetence, so does a poorly organized letter, memo, or report. A well-organized piece of writing keeps the needs of the reader in mind.

Is Your Writing Clear?

Effective writing consists of knowing what you are going to say and then writing it simply and clearly. The knowledge of which facts are certain and which are unsure is what the confident writer makes clear to the reader.

Who gives the best impression? The person who is always hedging or the person who speaks with confidence and who is not afraid to state the limits of his or her knowledge clearly and simply? Writing with confidence gives the same impression.

If your letter is going to be forceful, active, and effective, you cannot hedge. An over-cautious writer will be guilty of sentences such as, "It seems that perhaps it may be possible for us to complete your order by the 15th." Why not step right out? Never allow words to mislead. Be careful of the overuse of such words as *seems, may, perhaps, possibly, generally, usually,* and *occasionally.* Strive to be positive throughout your letter. If a qualification must be made, meet it squarely. The reader is more apt to trust you if you are confident in yourself. Trust builds rapport.

Word size and sentence length are two keys to clear writing. More important than sentence structure is making the intended meaning *clear.*

Often, two ideas not coordinated or closely related are hooked together with an *and* to distort them. When two ideas are parallel and of equal importance, you can use the connector *and* to continue your explanation. Don't use *and* for connecting unrelated ideas.

Thus, the person who writes, "I have only one pump order which appears to be on schedule and this is the unit for Midway Industrial Company," is writing a clumsy sentence and possibly a confusing one. It's better to write, "I have only one pump order which appears to be on schedule—the unit for Midway Industrial." The same can be said of the person who concludes his or her letter with, "We will make the shipment on the first of the month and your attention to the foregoing questions will be appreciated."

Similarly, the person who writes, "The price shows an increase of 11½ percent on bare surfaces and 18 percent if surfaces are painted," rather than "... an increase of 11½ percent on bare surfaces and 18 percent on painted surfaces," is causing the reader unnecessary difficulties. The structure of a sentence should reflect the intended meaning of the ideas in that sentence.

The words "prelubricated ball bearings" can elicit the same variety of responses. To the person who has had trouble, the phrase can mean more trouble. To the person who has not yet had an application, it means unanswered questions, perhaps doubt. When terms can be related to individual experiences, your story will stand a far better chance of reaching into your reader's thought processes.

Here's a more concrete example. If you speak of "corporation profits," it will mean many things to many people. When you narrow it to "money we earned after taxes," you are guiding your reader still further. But when you talk about "five cents on the dollar," you have painted a *specific picture* of a specific thing. Thinking is now in unison between reader and writer.

Again, being more specific in example, if you write, "The X–19 High Torque Pump has a stainless steel casing," you are taking a chance on the reader's experience with stainless steel. When you say "Stainless steel gives these pumps, pound for pound, nearly twice the life of older types," you have painted a picture. *People paint mental pictures of what they hear and read.*

Writing for the Reader

Confusion occurs when sales representatives attempt to convey what they believe to be a more businesslike form in their letters and write in a pompous, impersonal style. It may be confusing for the customer because this writing style is often completely different from the personal, natural personality the customer knows the salesperson to have.

The sales professional can't have two styles of personality, one for speaking and one for writing. To build rapport with a prospect or customer, there must be trust built through *predictable actions*. Different personality traits can hurt.

Compare the following statements. See how the personal statements are clearer and more natural than the impersonal, pompous statements:

Pompous	*Personal*
1. We solicit any recommendations that you might wish to make and you may be assured that any such recommendations will be given our careful consideration.	1. Please give us your suggestions. We shall consider them carefully.
2. This is in response to your letter of November 15th in which you request information in regard to the recent thrust increase in the subject apparatus.	2. I have enclosed the information you requested in your letter of November 15th on the recent changes in trust requirements.

Letters That Sell

There are many reasons why it pays to be "letter perfect" in sales work. A good sales letter covers a wide territory quickly. A good sales letter makes contact with prospects or customers at their convenience. And perhaps most important of all, a good sales letter helps the customers sell themselves on your product or service.

When you learn to write effective sales letters, you'll realize a rise in sales, and that rise in sales is only three steps away.

The first step, called the *grabber*, starts the prospect or customer on the way to a decision. When beginning the letter, the essential thing to do is *get the customer's attention*. The best way to do this is to appeal to their needs and wants for buying.

What are some effective grabbers? Many begin with a question or eye-opening statement. All grabbers must involve the customer personally. Here are a few examples:

- I'd like to take your computer out!
- If you found out that nearly 20 percent of all motors burn out in the first year, you'd want to do something to protect your good name.
- Tired of frostbite and cold hands? The first thing you must do is put half of your money back in your savings account.

Now you've got their attention. In the first example you're appealing to the customer's curiosity. In the second example you're a salesperson appealing to the customer's sense of business concern. In the third example you're a glove salesman with a special promotion. You're appealing to the customer's need to save money.

The second step is *proof* that you can come through with your promises. You've briefly explained why your products fulfill the customer's needs. Now what kind of evidence do you have?

It's time to give the facts. It's time to show the reputation of your product. It's time to make those comparisons with other products, time to be convincing about savings or protective benefits—whatever you promised in the beginning. It's time to itemize customer benefits.

Then comes the third and final step—the *action step*, what you want the reader to do. This is an effective close because it makes the customer's decision final, easy, and immediate. It helps nail down the sale. It helps the customer sell him- or herself. Take the time to consider how you can reinforce many of your sales calls with a brief letter confirming some of the key benefits you discussed. Letters keep you, your company, and the benefits you offer in the customer's eyes and mind.

A Good Start and Finish.   It's been said that in a salesperson's presentation, the greatest skill is required at the end, in closing. In writing, the beginning is as equally important as the ending. The beginning is the "attention getter." Make it *brief* and *powerful*. The first or second sentence should contain the subject. Slow starts put people to sleep.

Before you write, think. Think of the message you want to convey and how you would say it if you were face to face with the reader. Write as you talk—simply, using words your readers will understand. Know your audience. Will it or could it be circulated to others?

Consider Rudyard Kipling's six honest serving men; use them as a checklist to outline your message: who, what, when, why, where, how.

1. What is the subject of the material?
2. Who will read it?
3. Why would they be interested in it?
4. What is the story in a nutshell?
5. What action am I asking the readers to take?
6. Why should they do what I suggest?
7. When is a reply expected?

From an analysis of the message you want to get across, decide on an effective opening.

Courtesy and friendliness have a vital place in business letters as long as they are sincere. Furthermore, the reader must sense that they are sincere. You might say, "We are pleased to offer the following quotation," and sincerely mean it. But if you have used that phrase over and over, year after year, your customer is somehow going to sense it is a stereotype and react accordingly.

Why end a letter with, "We eagerly solicit any recommendations that you may wish to make and assure you that such valued recommendations will be given our careful and immediate consideration"? Why not simply write, "Please give us your suggestions. We will consider them carefully." If you have replied to a letter giving the customer the information asked for, there will be little need for a last paragraph such as, "We sincerely hope that this is the information you desire. . ."

A final point about concluding sales letters is: *Do not be afraid to ask for the order.* Done sincerely, it makes an excellent close.

Word and Sentence Size.   The size of the words you use and your sentence structure are important aspects of the impression your writing reflects. Never fear to use little words. Big, long words often name little things. All big things have little names, for example, life and death, war and peace, win and lose, day and night, hope, love, home, God, plan, sell. Learn to use little words in a big way. It may be hard to do, but they say what you mean and reflect your personality.

The average desk dictionary has over 500,000 words. The average high-school senior uses 10,000 to 15,000 words correctly. The average college graduate uses 40,000 to 50,000 words. Yet, of all our writing, ten words account for twenty-five percent of the total number of words we use. These ten, which tie ideas together to make meaningful sentences, are: *I, it, the, and, of, to, in, a, is,* and *that.* The length of your words and your sentence structure affect your clarity. Read your letters before you send them out to see if they are clear. Check to determine if you use any word phrases that make them hazy.

Sentence structure is also an important aspect of the writer's personality. Writing that is full of short sentences may suggest by their choppiness a curt or immature writer. Writing that is full of long and involved sentences may suggest by their complications a confused or devious writer. Further, unnecessarily short or unnecessarily long sentences may distort the intended meaning or attract so much attention to themselves that they distract the reader.

Understandability varies according to the average length of the sentences. The following list shows average sentence length and the level of understanding:

  8 words (or fewer) are *very easy to understand.*

11 words are *easy.*

14 words are *fairly easy.*

17 words are *standard.*

21 words are *fairly difficult.*

25 words are *difficult.*

29 words (or more) are *very difficult.*

Time and *Reader's Digest* average eighteen words per sentence. These figures will vary with such considerations as the subject, the degree of formality of the letter, and the personality of the writer. But those who find their sentences continually averaging under fifteen words or over twenty should analyze their writing carefully to be sure that they can justify the deviations. Thoughtful salespeople can often "feel" if their sentence length is proper by carefully reading what they have written.

Brevity is the essence of good communication. Julius Caesar wrote "I came, I saw, I conquered," to tell his friends about the outcome of a battle. He said it all in six words.

Watch Your "Person." Engineers and scientific writers tend to write entirely in the third person. Many of them avoid *I* and *we* entirely. There are times when the impersonality of the third person is desirable, but generally not in a business letter. Why write, "It will be noted that considerable savings have been accomplished through initiation of these methods"? You wouldn't speak that impersonally. If you were talking to someone, you would say, "We have saved many thousands of dollars by improving these methods." Let this conventional flavor carry over into your writing. Mark Twain wrote, "Nobody is entitled to refer to himself as 'we' except kings, editors and persons with tapeworms." When you are writing something to prospects or customers about what you, personally, have discovered or will do for them, use *I.*

Finally, don't neglect the second person, *you* and *your.* Get the other fellow's point of view always. Plenty of *you*'s and *we*'s add warmth to letters. Such warmth gives a better impression of you and your company and is more likely to hold your readers and, more important, to influence them.

Making Routine Letters
Not Routine

A real art in good written communications is the ability to write a routine letter without making it sound routine. Readers get the feeling that letters are routine when the reply is so impersonal, the language so common, and the phrases and expressions are so worn out that it appears that the only item which makes it individualistic is the name and address. Prospects or customers do not like a routine or "canned" reply any more than they like a canned presentation. Replies generated by using forms where items are filled-in blanks are convenient. Unfortunately, this isn't very original or personal. Writers who use "rubber stamp lingo" come up with a letter that is stereotyped and trite. Review your routine letters to see how they can be improved.

Letters You Don't
Have to Write—but Should

The information in this module refers to letters you initiate to transmit data or present a convincing sales story. These are letters you have to write to serve your prospects or customers effectively. The letters you don't have to write are sent to show your appreciation and interest in a prospect or customer. They help build rapport. Letters which can be included under this heading are many. The list of suggested situations which follows is merely typical and by no means complete. It is hoped that by including some of these letters at this time, your imagination will be triggered to think further about letters as a selling tool.

Headlining this group are the letters which say "thank you for your order." Then there are the many occasions to congratulate a customer on an award or promotion. Is a customer going on a vacation? How about a brief note wishing him or her a restful holiday?

If the customer is a golfer, maybe send a package of tees or a golf ball. The value isn't important; it is the thought that will pay you dividends in the long run.

The possibilities for vacation letters written in a light, friendly vein are unlimited. These little things are remembered—and so is the writer long after the vacation is over.

A thank you letter to a customer after he or she has placed a large order is an excellent time to work in a short, "plow-back" story. That is, after the order is placed, thank the customer and point out that a percentage of the purchase price will be socked back into research and development to make sure the next purchase from you will be of maximum value.

Never lose the opportunity to compliment a customer's organization or an individual. This could be an occasion of particular courtesy on someone's part in helping you identify an item or some information. Perhaps someone went out of his or her way to help you. Don't overdo this type of letter, but being sincere and warm can help build rapport.

If it's going to take you some time to gather data or otherwise hold up your reply to a request, why not drop a short letter to the customer, stating in one or two friendly sentences when a complete reply can be expected. Then don't let the promised date go by. If by that time you still haven't the full story, send another note with another date. This is certainly better than making the customer call you. All it takes is something like this: "Glad to have your letter. I'm getting the information together for you. You'll hear from me by August 27th or before, if possible."

One additional type of letter is the occasional letter that does not drive for an order. A letter which just tells a company how much you enjoy doing business with them is fairly well expected around Christmas time and will probably receive little notice for this reason. But when it arrives before Thanksgiving or on March 1st, it is sure to make an impression.

CONCLUSION

Good verbal and written communications are essential for the professional salesperson. A verbal presentation, letter, memo, or report not only carries content, that is, a body of information, but also reflects the salesperson's personality and expresses his or her attitude. Furthermore, word choice, sentence structure, and organization are important considerations in reflecting this personality or attitude.

The primary purpose of a sales presentation or a sales letter has always been to deliver a sales message clearly and unmistakably in such a way that the reader responds as desired.

For more sales punch in your letter writing, try once each month to write a letter you don't have to write.

Salespeople are constantly selling themselves, their products and services, and their company. Their oral and written correspondence must be an extension of them. If a salesperson's verbal skills or letters are hurried, impersonal, or dull, they will be received casually—or even resentfully; but if they communicate simply and naturally, if they reflect efficiency, cheerfulness, and courtesy, they will be certain of a welcome.

Review Questions

1. What is good sales communication? Why is it important to a sales professional?
2. What should you ask yourself when preparing to communicate verbally?
3. How can you determine if your communications are understood?
4. Prepare a brief product introduction using emotion-packed words, one verbally and the other written.
5. Explain the qualities of your voice or your personality that make you easy to understand.
6. Why is written communication important to a sales professional? When is it preferred over verbal communications?
7. What should all good written reports contain?
8. Why is the length of words and sentences important?
9. Write a sales letter on a product and another on a service you offer.

10. Write a letter to apologize for late delivery.
11. Write a letter to an old customer who stopped buying from you.
12. Why should salespeople send letters they don't have to write? Name three types of letters you don't have to write and write a sample of each.

module three
The Telephone: A Key Sales Aid

Salespeople receive and make many telephone calls daily. To a great extent, the telephone offers an opportunity to reach prospects and customers unattainable in any other way. Whether this activity is profitable or unprofitable depends largely on how it is conducted. Good telephone skills will help you increase your range of contacts and get orders.

When you pick up a telephone you are about to make an impression on someone important—the person on the other end of the line, a prospect or customer. Naturally, you want to make the best possible impression on this important person. You want him or her to feel that you are alert, efficient, courteous, and professional—nice to do business with. That's good sense and it's good business.

Telephone contacts warrant special consideration since the person on the line can't see you, your smile, or facial expression. He or she can only draw an impression from your voice, tone, and manner.

When talking on the telephone, the spotlight is on you; every time you make or receive a call, you are the company to the person at the other end of the line. Your company is judged by the voice that speaks for it over the telephone—by what is said and how it is said. If your voice is warm and friendly, if you are courteous and tactful, customers will enjoy dealing with you and your company. If you have a secretary answer your telephone, make sure he or she gives the proper impression to the callers. Check what is being done now and suggest improvements if necessary. Tape-record your telephone calls and play them back to see if you are as effective as you can be. Improvement in telephone techniques pays back dividends.

USING THE TELEPHONE TO INCREASE SALES

The telephone is a vital business tool, yet one that is often taken for granted. Effective use of the telephone, especially in sales, depends on careful planning. Here are six tips for getting better results from sales calls:

1. *Write a simple script,* a sample dialogue between you and your prospect. Cover all situations with a few standard paragraphs. Write down a variety of tested responses in fifteen words or less. Use phrases that have worked well for you or others.

2. *Speak 120 words per minute.* This rate takes practice, but it works better than either faster or slower rates. At this speed listeners won't get tired, and you can hold their attention longer.

3. *Smile.* Even if you don't feel like it, smile—a big one. It will make your voice friendly, keep you from getting tense, and keep your listener relaxed.

4. *Control the conversation.* Don't use questions that encourage only a yes or no response, but ask leading questions which imply benefits: "Haven't I heard that you're a leader in your field? That you always use the best equipment?" Then listen for "buy signals" that open the door to a sale.

5. *Don't hammer.* Recognize that the prospect who says he or she is too busy may really mean it. End the conversation politely and suggest calling back at another time.

6. *Build confidence.* Know your product or service, its features, benefits, availability, and prices. Keep data sheets nearby so you can answer technical questions confidently. It's important to know your competitor's products and services, too.

Success in selling on the telephone is very similar to success in all professional selling. Professional salespeople must know their products and services well, know their company and policies, and know and use proper telephone techniques. Here's a list of some ground rules to keep in mind:

1. The product or service must be of good quality, competitively priced, and have a good chance of being of interest to the prospect.
2. The prospect you call must be selected from your prospect list. Make sure your list is up to date.
3. The sales discussion on the phone must be carefully planned before the call is made, just as a salesperson carefully plans a sales presentation before meeting with the prospect or customer. A prepared script is very useful.

4. A company must be prepared to perform professionally based on the promises made by its salesperson over the telephone.

A sales professional can be successful in selling and/or prospecting by telephone. The key in telephoning is to keep trying and keep playing the numbers. The more calls you make the more successful you will become.

Effective Telephone Usage

With sales expenses continually climbing, particularly the cost of fuel for company cars and meals and hotels, increased use of the telephone can be the key for reducing overall operational expenses for sales offices.

Significant uses of the telephone that can help the sales effort are the following:

1. *To develop prospect lists*—This is an ideal way to contact prospective customers concerning their needs and wants and to obtain business appointments.
2. *To revive inactive accounts*—An ideal source of new business is to discover why former customers are no longer buying from you. With some research of sales reports data found in most sales offices, it is very easy to find information on customers you did business with years back.
3. *Advertising follow-up*—Many ads have business reply cards or other requested information where a convenient telephone follow-up can determine the sincerity of the inquiry and indicate business potential.
4. *Appointment confirmation*—This is an ideal way to reduce the amount of time wasted in reception areas. Try to schedule and confirm your appointments.

Appraising Your Telephone Habits

Consider the following questions and decide if you or your secretary's telephone habits are helping you or if improvement is needed:

1. How quickly do you answer your telephone?
2. How do you identify yourself—name? title? company?
3. Is the acknowledgment of the opening statement appropriate?
4. Do you interrupt the caller or fail to give way when the caller tries to interrupt?
5. If the call is suspended, do you leave the line and return properly in a polite manner?
6. Are you attentive to the caller's statements or do you ask questions which indicate you were not listening?

7. Do you express appreciation, concern, or regret where it is appropriate to do so? Do you apologize, if necessary?

8. Do you express in words or indicate by manner and tone of voice a willingness to be of help?

9. Is your attitude friendly, helpful, and interested, or does the caller receive routine treatment instead of individual consideration?

10. When the nature of the contact require that you provide information or explanation, is it given completely and concisely?

11. Do you use technical terms, slang, or arbitrary phrases which may be confusing?

12. Are the final arrangements clear?

13. Do you respond appropriately to a caller's "thank you" or other closing remarks?

14. Do you plan your calls ahead by outlining what areas you want to discuss?

15. Do you keep paper and pencil handy?

16. Do you treat your callers with the same attention and courtesy you want when you call?

SALES TECHNIQUES THAT WORK

1. *Be prepared* to talk when your prospect answers your call. Know about your product, its applications, availability, pricing, and benefits. Don't call unless you can devote your entire attention to the call. Review all past relevant information about the prospect before you pick up the receiver to dial.

2. *Speak distinctly* in ordinary conversational tone; you are talking with prospects and you want to make them friends and customers. Avoid technical phrases or jargon they may not understand. Talk your story; don't read it. Help your prospect to buy—use word pictures to describe specifically your product and what it will do. Be specific in size, color, application, and so on. Use sparkle in your presentation. Avoid generalities and vague comparisons. Give customers a choice when you ask for an order or set up an appointment.

3. *Be courteous—don't argue.* You may win an argument and lose the sale. Smile before you pick up the phone so the customer hears a smile in your voice.

4. *Follow through.* Do what you agreed to do, whether it was to put something in the mail, follow up at a later date, set up an appointment, or contact someone else. Whatever you discuss, make sure you follow through. Your voice is you. Don't be discouraged in the course of your selling effort. The cost of using the telephone is so low that you can afford many unsuccessful calls to develop one good prospect or sale. The more calls you make without a sale, the closer you are getting to one. You should understand how to improve after each call.

Dos and Don'ts of Telephone Selling

Don't	*Do*
1. Frown	1. Smile
2. Mutter	2. Speak clearly and concisely
3. Sound tired	3. Be enthusiastic
4. Speak in a monotonous tone	4. Lower the pitch of your voice for friendly conversation
5. Be negative	5. Talk in a positive mood
6. Be overconfident	6. Be prepared to answer objections
7. Talk down into transmitter	7. Talk directly into mouthpiece
8. Ramble	8. Come to the point—ask for the appointment or sale
9. Do something *to* the customer	9. Do something *for* the customer
10. Argue	10. Discuss
11. Hang up abruptly if service is refused	11. Politely thank the customer for listening to you
12. Assume you are understood	12. Ask to find out
13. Be overwhelming	13. Use a cassette recorder to hear how you sound

TELEPHONE HABITS TO UNLEARN

This module outlines many suggestions and techniques to learn effective telephone skills. To learn properly means to establish good habits and unlearn bad ones. Following are some myths about the telephone you should unlearn:

1. *The telephone is an annoyance.* It interrupts what you are doing; it's an intrusion. Instead, think of it as another sales aid that will help you get more orders.

2. *The telephone is inanimate.* It doesn't require personal attention. Instead, consider that when the phone rings, it is the same as a person walking up to your desk. Give it your fullest attention.

3. *The telephone is as easy as face-to-face communication.* It's really harder because we don't have our eyes, hands, or body movements to help us; we only have our voices. We have to work harder because of the loss of visual feedback.

4. *The telephone is a shield.* Don't consider it easy to hide behind the telephone by saying you are doing something other than what you really are, for example, too busy to talk now. Don't lie to the caller.

5. *The telephone requires no planning.* Instead, prepare yourself before you start to dial, just as you would before you go on a face-to-face sales call.

PROSPECTING BY TELEPHONE

To use your prospecting time effectively and minimize travel expenses, recognize the importance of the telephone. It is one of the most convenient, inexpensive methods of contacting potential customers.

Setting Your Objectives

Every phone call should have two objectives; everything you say should have two goals:

1. To qualify a suspect as a true potential prospect.
2. If qualified, to secure an appointment for an onsite sales call or get an order.

Making the Telephone Call

1. Get to the point quickly.
2. Be *totally prepared*. Have ready your prescreen information on your leads, your appointment calendar, and anything else that helps you get that appointment.
3. Don't let a "no" kill your appointment presentation. Tell enough to *arouse interest* and whet the appetite of the decision maker. Give the person any series of options, except the option of saying no.
4. Keep your telephone call short, clear, precise, and in good taste.
5. Use short, simple words that are friendly. Remember to smile while you are talking.
6. Use vivid and specific words that give the prospect a mental picture of what you're talking about.
7. Establish the reason for calling. Initial remarks should pertain to the logical opening on which you'll base your presentation.
8. Offer your prospect a benefit for giving you an appointment.
9. Don't try to close a sale over the telephone, unless it is customary in your business. It is your responsibility to end the conversation when an appointment is set if no order is received. Having met your objective, add a thank you and get off the line.

Advantages of Prospecting
and Cold-Call Selling

1. *Quick*—You can telephone three people in less than ten minutes, which would probably be the time it would take you to leave your office, get into your car, and begin to drive to the first visit.

2. *Convenient*—Your prospect or customer is as close as the telephone on your desk; there is no waiting or delay and thus no reason to make a long trip.

3. *Economical*—The low cost of telephoning a dozen prospects instead of visiting one personally is obvious.

4. *Flexible*—If one prospect isn't available, simply dial another. You can call people locally or out of town.

5. *Productive*—Telephoning can be used productively during spare time, which might otherwise be wasted.

6. *Profitable*—Probably the most important aspect of the telephone is to allow sales professionals to prospect for new accounts. New customers mean increased profitability. More presentations to prospects mean an increased chance of getting more customers. The telephone is the easiest way to set up appointments for customer presentations.

(*Note:* If you make many long distance calls you should consider a WATS line. It can save you money.)

GETTING THE PROSPECT TO SAY "YES"

It is important during the telephone call to have the prospect say "yes." This is done by preparing a list of the common objections and the best answers. (See module on handling objections and closing.) The primary objection you might encounter over the phone would be, "I'm too busy to talk, " to which you would suggest a better time to call back. This answer requires using more sparkle in your presentation to create more interest and desire.

Telephone calls can either be used to set up appointments or, in fact, to get the order, which very much depends on the product or service. If you have a product that can lend itself to being sold over the telephone, that is an ideal time to ask for the order. A sales interview or presentation is not complete unless the prospect is clearly asked to act in a favorable manner *now*. If you are expecting to close over the telephone, *now* is the time to ask the prospect to buy. If you are asking for an appointment, *now* is the time to do it.

Sales professionals should never be ashamed to ask for action. They will feel comfortable doing so only if they are prepared and have indicated to the listener the benefits received by taking the action suggested.

THE SEVEN ADVANTAGES
OF APPOINTMENT CALLS

Calling to make and confirm appointments has many benefits for the professional salesperson. Following are some benefits you can enjoy.

1. *Saves time*—The customer sees you more promptly, which means less waiting time. This permits you to schedule your time more efficiently, allowing you to cover more territory.
2. *Avoids disappointment*—Assures you that all contacts are in and have time to talk.
3. *Assures more receptive attitude*—Because you are considerate of your customer's time and schedule, his or her attitude toward you is more apt to be favorable.
4. *Improves your image*—Adds to your professionalism. A successful salesperson has a reason to take up the prospect's or customer's time. The professional can't afford to create the impression of being idle or completely disorganized by "dropping in."
5. *Flatters the customer*—Should an important businessperson see anybody at any time? Your recognition of the importance of his or her time is evident when you call for an appointment.
6. *Prepares the customer for the visit*—The appointment call will lay some groundwork for the visit, allowing the customer to bring in other people or gather material which will allow him or her to make a decision on your recommendation.
7. *Obtains background information for use in the presentation*—You may gain information on the customer's position, likes and dislikes, wants and needs, types of clients, and any special requirements.

Bear in mind that any excuse may suit a prospect's attempt to cut you off and avoid the personal meeting which is your goal. Do not lose sight of it— you want an appointment. A sample appointment call follows:

Mr. Jones, good morning. This is (your name) of (your company). Recently we've introduced new products and prices that executives such as yourself have been requesting us to do for the past four or five years. You've probably read about them. I'd like the opportunity to discuss personally these new products in more detail. That's why I'm calling. I'll be in your area next week. What day will be most convenient for us to get together?

Or

I would like a few minutes to discuss your company's needs and how we can benefit you. Would (day/hour) be convenient or would (day/hour) be more convenient?

You may encounter objections, be asked addditional questions, or be granted an appointment. If it is an appointment, set the time and day and politely close your phone conversation.

> Very good, Mr. Jones. I'll see you then at (day/hour).

When to Call

Remember, when we approach a prospect at the wrong time, nothing we say will bring a favorable response. Timing is of the utmost importance. The telephone company has prepared statistical information showing when is the best time for calling various people based on other priorities they may have on their time:

1. Chemists and engineers—between 4:00 and 5:00 P.M.
2. Contractors and builders—before 9:00 A.M. and after 5:00 P.M.
3. Executives and heads of business—after 10:30 A.M.
4. Lawyers—between 11:00 A.M. and 2:00 P.M. or after 5:00 P.M.
5. Public accountants—any time but avoid January 15th through April 15th
6. Housewives and families—between 6:00 and 8:00 P.M.

Sales professionals analyze the work and home habits of their prospects and call at the appropriate time. When they get to the appointment, they ask, "What time would you prefer I call you in the future?"

PREPARING FOR YOUR FIRST CALL

To prepare for your first call, first get the names and phone numbers on your prospect list. Some of the places where you can get names of possible customers are these:

1. Your present customers. Are you selling all your products or services (your complete line) to each of your present accounts? Present customers should also be considered prospects for more business.
2. Inactive accounts or old customers.
3. Mailing lists or information obtained from the Yellow Pages or other manufacturing or trade publications.
4. Names acquired from your present customers, trade associations, or service organizations.

Second, *plan* your telephone sales talk. A haphazard, rambling telephone call with a hit-or-miss approach wastes not only your time but also the prospect's time. Also, this is very rarely successful and can even lose customers. It is essential that you plan what to say and how to say it. Remember, when you sell face to face, you can vary your approach and your sales interview or presentation depending on who your prospects are and what you have to sell. A poor approach or possibly a poor presentation can often be overcome by a pleasant smile and good appearance or by a sample or other visual aid. But the phone will not allow this advantage, so you must plan to meet various conditions. When selling on the phone, you're selling by your voice alone. Plan your sales talk and organize your ideas so you will be successful. One method of organizing your ideas is by using this simple, three-step approach:

1. Get attention and arouse interest.
2. Create the desire for your product.
3. Get the prospect to say yes.

PROSPECTING, QUALIFYING, AND GETTING APPOINTMENTS

The telephone is a key instrument in all professional selling. In prospecting, qualifying, and getting appointments, it's essential for effective time and territorial management. Following is a seven-step approach that can help. Smile, dial, and when the prospect picks up the telephone

1. Bid your prospect a good morning or afternoon. *Set the stage* for a pleasant telephone conversation. If the call is in response to a prospect's request, thank the prospect for inquiring about your product or service. This simple courtesy creates enthusiasm and prepares for a productive conversation.

Example: "I'd like to thank you for your interest in our product—you sent us a coupon, requesting information on our . . . line" or "The card you filled in at the convention . . ." and so on.

2. *State the purpose of your call* and obtain permission to ask questions. Check the prospect's availability. If there's someone in the office, it's better to call back at a more convenient time. Stating the purpose of your call helps prospects focus attention on their needs, wants, and problems.

Example: "Mrs. Diamond, my purpose at this time is to ask you a few questions that will help me to understand your current needs. (Pause) Would you mind if I asked them now?"

3. *Ask qualifying questions.* Identify your prospect's needs (wants and problems) by asking specific questions such as, "What type of product (size, dimensions, grade, and so on) do you use?" "When would you need the product?" "Are you familiar with our product?" "What type of specific information would you need from us in order to make a buying decision?" "Have you considered alternative solutions to your current problem?" "Have you thought about financing?" or "How much would you plan to invest in this type of product?"

4. *Thank* the prospect for the information. Show your appreciation and understanding.

Example: "Thank you, Mrs. Diamond, for sharing this information with me; this gives me a better understanding of what you are looking for."

5. *Provide encouragement.* Explain to the prospect that you've been able to solve similar problems before and emphasize that you'll be able to help meet his or her needs.

Examples: "I think you'll be pleased to hear that we've been able to solve similar problems with companies in your particular industry. I'm confident that we'll be able to present you with a proposal that will meet your approval."

6. *Propose to "show" interesting information to the prospect.* Your final objective is to set up an appointment. You need to get a face-to-face interview. Propose to "show" some information (that can't be communicated on the telephone).

Example: "It will take me only a short time to prepare some interesting data for you, so I'll be able to show you in detail how much we would be able to satisfy your particular needs. When would you like to see this information?"

7. *Propose a choice of two meeting dates.* Should you propose only one date, you will give the prospect the choice between meeting that day or not at all. If you propose to meet either this day or that one, you will increase your chances for getting the appointment.

Example: "Would next week on Wednesday morning be suitable—or do you prefer to meet on Thursday afternoon?"

YOUR TELEPHONE PRESENTATION

Before we give some suggestions on preparing your telephone presentation, analyze what you are doing now. Answer the following questions and take positive steps to correct all your "No" answers.

	Yes	No
1. Do I use short, simple, uncomplicated words?	——	——
2. Do I mention a benefit to the prospect?	——	——

3. Do I express my prime message so it would be under-   —— ——
stood?

4. Do I maintain a positive mental attitude?   —— ——

5. Do I emphasize the benefits of doing business with me   —— ——
and my company?

6. Do I have a professional way of "qualifying"?   —— ——

7. Do I stick to a logical order in my presentation?   —— ——

8. Do I have all the facts about my offering so I can   —— ——
answer any questions?

9. Do I smile before I pick up the telephone?   —— ——

10. Do I ask for the order?   —— ——

Following are key areas that you should consider in planning your telephone presentation:

1. *Study* your product or service and write a list of all the important features and, more importantly, their functions and benefits. Consider their price, quality, availability, and how they have helped others.

2. *Analyze* your prospect list by determining which ones on the list are your present customers, what they have been buying, and whom they've been buying from lately. If former customers, why did they stop buying? What do you know about them? Have you done your homework to determine their possible needs and wants? Also, what might they know about you that would make it easier for them to understand your company? The more information you have, the easier it will be to select the proper opening remarks and the best sales approach to use.

3. *Write out* your ideas step by step—make sure all vital points are covered. This is convenient to do by developing a checklist of ideas that should be the sales talk. We are interested in developing a planned presentation, not a canned one.

4. *Get attention and interest*, which is the warm-up portion vital to success in any effort to sell by telephone. Always smile, then (a) greet the prospect by name. During your opening comments, refer to how you obtained his or her name and company; (b) introduce yourself by making a simple statement of your name and company; (c) make an attention-getting statement by appealing to the prospect's self-interest or curiosity. It should be brief and to the point. A statement such as this deserves a great deal of care and preparation.

5. *Create a desire* for the product or service; your voice alone has to do the selling. You have to tell your prospects what you are offering, why they need it; what it will do for them; and how, when, and where they can get it. The price and service may be discussed. Be creative and add a little sparkle to your sales talk. By knowing your product, you should be in a good position to create this appealing statement in such a way that the prospects can visualize from your words exactly what you mean.

6. You must *describe the product realistically*; talk in terms that your prospect will understand and relate to. Smile before you pick up the telephone.

7. *Give all necessary facts*; don't assume or leave anything to the interpretation of the listener—be specific.

GETTING BY THE SECRETARIAL SCREEN

Secretaries and receptionists are hired to screen for their employers. The salesperson knows the importance of developing a professional, pleasant relationship with secretaries and receptionists. They should want to talk to you on future calls. However, they must get as much information as possible from you so their employer may not have to talk to you. You certainly don't want a go-between representing you, so you have to penetrate the screen. It can be done with three little words: "Is he (or she) in?"

Reception Screen

Situation A: "Beta Company, good morning."
"Good morning. Please tell me the name of your president."
"Mr. Robert Jones."
"Thank you. Is he in?"
"Just a moment, I will connect you with his secretary."

Situation B: "Good morning, Jones, Smith and Brown."
"Good morning, Mr. Jones, please. Thank you."

In a company with names in the title, just ask for the first name and end your request with "thank you." This closes the conversation, and you will have penetrated the receptionist screen.

Secretarial Screen

Situation C: "Mr. Jones' office."
"Good morning. Is he in?"
"Good morning. May I tell him who's calling?"
"Yes. Tell him it's (your name). Thank you."

This should work most of the time. If the secretary persists: "Who are you with?" or "What is the purpose of the call?" then respond: "I'm with (your company). It's regarding an advertisement in this week's issue of *Business*

Week. Is he in?" or "It's in reference to a new (name of product) that he has probably read about. Is he in or should I call back?"

HANDLING TELEPHONE OBJECTIONS

Salespeople know that they must learn to deal with objections in a competent manner if they are to succeed. The most common objections to a telephone call requesting an appointment are these:

Objection: Too busy!

    Answer: I realize that a person in your position is very busy. That is why I phoned first so I would not disturb you at an inconvenient time. Our discussion will take just a few minutes. I am certain that you will consider your valuable time to have been well spent. Would (day) or (day) fit your schedule better, Mr. Jones?

Objection: Tell me what you have over the phone.

    Answer: Because the capabilities in this area will substantially benefit you and your entire organization (company), Mr. Jones, it does not lend itself to being discussed on the phone. It will only take about fifteen minutes of your time. Would (day) or (day) be a better time for you?

Objection: Drop it in the mail.

    Answer: Mr. Jones, I can certainly mail something to you. However, I sincerely believe that the benefits to you and your firm can best be explained if I were to discuss it with you in person. Would (day) or (day) suit you better?

Objection: I can't see you.

    Answer: Have I suggested an inconvenient week? How about the week after next? Would Tuesday or Wednesday be better? Would the afternoon suit you better than in the morning.

Objection: Are you trying to sell me something?

    Answer: Mr. Jones, I believe that it would be very premature to propose anything to you at this time. First, we need to discuss briefly what your company's needs are and how you can benefit from our products. At the conclusion of that short presentation, you will then be able to see how and where we can help you and (company name). Would (day) or (day) be more convenient for you?

Objection: You're wasting your time.

    Answer: Thank you, Mr. Jones, for considering the value of time. That's why I called instead of barging in on you. I am quite sure you will be able to see the benefits that (your company name) has to offer you. Therefore, I would like to meet with you at your convenience. Would (day) or (day) be better for you? Of course, there is no obligation at any time.

Or

Answer: Thank you, Mr. Jones, for considering my time. The reason I'm calling you for an appointment is because I also appreciate *your* time. That is why I will be totally prepared to show you all the benefits (your company name) can offer you when we meet. Would (day) or (day) be better for you?

Objection: Not interested.

Answer: I understand how you feel, Mr. Jones. I certainly wouldn't expect you to be interested until you allow me to explain fully what we offer and to discuss the many benefits to you and your company. It will only take fifteen minutes. This is exactly why I am calling for an appointment. Will tomorrow or (day) be better?

Or

Answer: What exactly is it that you are not interested in? (Allow for response and continue.) Would you be interested if I could provide your company with more value for the dollars you're spending? It will only take fifteen minutes to discuss the many benefits with you. This is why I am calling for an appointment. Will tomorrow or (day) be better?

Objection: I'm not the right person.

Answer: (In cases such as these, you have an ideal opportunity to find the real buying authority or the decision maker. The person you have on the phone is passing you on to the purchasing agent. In either case, get the person's name and title, and if possible have the call transferred. Then use Jones as the referral for the call.)

Hello, Mr. Smith. This is (name) of (your company name). Mr. Jones suggested I speak with you and set up an appointment to discuss some specific ways we can benefit you and (company name).

Or

Answer: Mr. Jones, does anyone help you decide what equipment your firm should purchase or rent? (Assume the answer is "Yes, Mr. Smith, our Purchasing Agent.") Well, then, I suggest that you and I meet with Mr. Smith and review how (your company name) can benefit your firm.

FORMS

The following forms are shown at the end of this module:

Telephone Call Preparation: The best way of getting a customer appointment is to be prepared before you call. Your research will identify details of the company that help you set your call's objectives, opening statements, and qualifying questions. You should also have your sales message and important customer benefits written down for easy reference.

Daily Teleprospecting Log: This handy form conveniently shows you the effectiveness of your efforts. It helps identify successful sources of leads, sales, and remarks that will help in the future.

CONCLUSION

In this module, we emphasized the important part the telephone plays in helping us handle our sales activities. It helps us get orders conveniently by keeping in touch with prospects and customers. It's an ideal aid in prospecting, qualifying, and getting appointments.

It's important to remember that the telephone requires precall preparation and commitment similar to an in-person sales call. As a tool for managing time, it's ideally suited for complete coverage of accounts and territory. We encourage you to continue to work on your skills of sounding good on the telephone. Record your calls and strive for improvement. Maybe a script would help you organize your thoughts and actions. Remember, when you use the telephone for prospecting, you are playing the numbers game. The more calls you make, the more successful you will be. *Keep trying; you will succeed.*

Review Questions

1. List ten areas where the *telephone* can help in sales.
2. Write out a typical telephone script for the following situations:
    a. An initial prospecting call to set up an appointment.
    b. An initial call to introduce your product or service and get an order.
    c. A call to solicit funds for a charity.
    d. Returning a call to a customer who is dissatisfied with your product or service.
    e. Follow-up on a mailed request from the prospect from your ad in a trade magazine.
    f. Call on an ex-customer who hasn't bought from you in three years.
    g. Follow-up on a written proposal you submitted earlier in the week.

Where possible, try to use these situations in a two-person role-playing activity for future emphasis.

3. List ten areas where the telephone cannot help the salesperson.

4. Why is it good practice to call for an appointment and reconfirm it where practical?

5. Record in a cassette two telephone calls you could make if you were a sales representative for the product or service of your choice: one, to introduce yourself, your product or service, and your company to get an appointment; two, to attempt to get an order on the first call.

6. What objections are often given by someone who can't talk to you or doesn't want to see you? How can you overcome these objections?

7. Why is it important to get as much useful information as you can about the company and the person you are calling before you pick up the telephone? Give some examples of useful information.

Telephone Call Preparation

Name of Company _____

Telephone Number _____

Decision Maker _____ Title _____

Address _____

_____

Call Objectives:

1. _____

2. _____

Opening Statement (Rapport & Interest-Creating Remark)

_____

_____

_____

Three Fact Finding Qualifying Questions (Who-What-Where-How-When)

_____

_____

_____

Sales Message

_____

_____

_____

Objections	Benefits
_____	_____
_____	_____

Forced Choice Question

_____

_____

Made Appointment? _____

When to Follow Up? _____

Daily Teleprospecting Log

Name _____

Date _____

Name/TelNo Called	Source	Prescreen			Appt.	Sale	Follow Up	Remarks
		Yes	No	Un-nec				

module four
Real Listening: Identify Needs and Wants

If we agree that salespeople identify prospects' and customers' needs and wants by asking questions and probing, then it follows that they must listen attentively for the answers.

Salespeople can't listen effectively if they are not giving 100 percent attention to the speaker. It's impossible to identify a responsive chord (hot button) if we don't listen for a response. Asking questions and listening are two essential sales skills.

IMPORTANCE OF LISTENING

One of the most important skills a salesperson should develop is the ability to listen effectively. The prime reason prospects consider placing any business with you is because you listen to and understand them and they believe you can fulfill their needs and wants. Your interest and concern in listening indicates your dedication to serving them.

Effective listening is more than mere hearing. It's striving to *understand* what you are hearing. Your attention not only is on what is said by prospects or customers but also includes all others you come in contact with. How often have we heard the expression, "I like them because they listen to me." Psychiatrists earn their livelihood by listening—so must the sales professional.

71

The inexperienced salesperson keeps telling prospective customers what he or she thinks they should have rather than listening for their needs and wants. The ratio of the number of orders to presentations rises when listening effectiveness goes up.

An important point about listening is that when salespeople are really listening, by definition they cannot be talking. Sometimes salespeople must keep their mouths shut. Listening helps them treat a disease that affects many—"hoof and mouth" disease. Experienced salespeople, as well as novices, have "sold back" a customer's order by talking too much. After an effective presentation, when a prospect is ready to order your products and services, is the time to keep your comments to a minimum. Gentle reassurance that the prospect is making the proper decision will help eliminate "buyer's remorse." These comments should be brief.

The salesperson who listens well is in the proper frame of mind to probe effectively by asking meaningful questions and listening for the reply. Everyone enjoys a good listener—entertainers, politicians, public speakers, husbands, wives, children, and very definitely, prospective customers and salespeople.

WHY WE LISTEN POORLY

There have been two primary reasons why people are poor listeners, both of which are misconceptions:

1. Listening depends largely on the intelligence of the individual, that bright ones listen well and dull ones listen poorly.
2. A good reader is a good listener.

Unfortunately, neither one of these statements is correct. Unless people acquire effective listening skills through training or experience, no matter what their intelligence, their ability to understand and retain what they hear will be low. In our grade schools, the ability to read is stressed but very little emphasis is placed on the student's ability to listen. As a fair reader and a bad listener, the typical student is graduating into a society where the chances of having to listen are three times as great as having to read. The schools are not preparing students for effective listening, although they spend 60 to 70 percent of their classroom time engaged in listening. Listening is the communication skill used most but taught least. *People in business spend their average day in the following activities: 45 percent listening, 32 percent speaking, 14 percent reading, and 9 percent writing.*

1. *Limit your own talking.* You can't talk and listen at the same time.

2. *Be interested and show it.* You must convey a genuine concern and a lively curiosity. This will encourage your prospects or customers to speak freely so you can better understand their needs, wants, and viewpoints.

3. *Tune in to the other person.* Are you giving your full attention or is your mind wandering? Concentrate by practicing to shut out outside distractions.

4. *Think like prospective customers.* They have problems, needs, and wants that are important. You'll understand and retain them better if you try to get their point of view.

5. *Ask questions.* If you don't understand something, or feel you may have missed a point, clear it up now before it embarrasses you later.

6. *Hold your fire.* Do you jump to conclusions without hearing your prospects or customers out? Plan your response only after you are certain you have a complete picture of their point of view. Prejudgments are dangerous. A pause, even a long pause, doesn't always mean they've finished saying everything they want to say.

7. *Look and listen for buying signals.* Remember to focus on key, hot-button comments. In our dealings with others, we must be cognizant of their prime motivating factors. Once we have identified these factors, we can gently "push" their "buttons" to get the response we desire.

8. *Listen for ideas, not just words.* You want to get the whole picture, not just isolated bits and pieces.

9. *Use interjections.* An occasional "yes," "I see," or "Is that so" shows the prospective customer you're still there, but don't overdo or use these words as a meaningless comment.

10. *Turn off your own worries.* This isn't always easy, but personal fears, worries, and problems not connected with the customer form a kind of "static" that can blank out the customer's message.

11. *Prepare in advance.* Remarks and questions prepared in advance, when possible, free your mind for listening. Prepare a checklist of items you want to discuss and clarify.

12. *React to ideas, not to the person.* Don't allow irritation at things people may say or let their manner distract you.

13. *Notice nonverbal language.* A shrug, smile, laugh, gesture, facial expressions, and other body movements often speak louder than words. Start to "read" them.

14. *Don't jump to conclusions.* Avoid making unwarranted assumptions about what the customer is going to say or mentally try to complete sentences for them.

15. *Take notes.* This practice will help you remember important points. But be selective. Trying to take down everything that is said can result in being left far behind or retaining irrelevant details. A short pencil can be more effective than a long memory.

16. *Get feedback.* Make certain you're really listening by asking questions to confirm with the speaker what you understood. In sales work, effective listening is extremely essential in the critical area of handling objections. These objections are not always clearly stated; hence, effective listening can help identify "sincere" and "insincere" objections. Listen to the prospect's or customer's objections and use them to help you close the sale. Psychiatrists and doctors make good money listening—so can a professional salesperson.

LISTENING CHECKLIST

Following is a convenient checklist to help you tell if you are a good listener. The range of your replies will probably go from *always* to *never*, including *usually, occasionally,* and *seldom.* Your answers may vary between questions and possibly even on the same question, depending on whom you are listening to, what else is on your mind at that time, and the subject matter. Continually strive to answer each question with an *always* reply.

1. Are you eager to learn about other persons, their problems, places, and things?
2. Can you put yourself in other people's shoes—can you emphasize with them?
3. Do you attempt to tune in on the speaker's feelings as well as the words being spoken?
4. Do you try to overcome your own emotional attitudes and prejudgments?
5. Do you work to identify the main ideas, attitudes, and feelings being communicated?
6. Do you avoid interrupting? Especially, do you curb the impulse to complete the other person's sentences?
7. Do you ever ask for feedback on how people rate you as a listener?
8. Do you consciously practice listening skills?
9. In short, do you listen to others as you would like to be listened to?

The constant striving for improvement is the mark of the real professional.

WHY PROSPECTS AND CUSTOMERS
DON'T LISTEN TO SALESPEOPLE

There are many reasons why prospects and customers don't listen to salespeople. Let's list the main reasons.

It's the same old story. Salespeople may never vary their presentations, tone, interest, or sales aids. This can be a particularly important point in getting or losing attentiveness because we never come up with anything new or refreshing to present to our customers. Prospects get bored by continually listening to the same old presentation delivered in the same manner with the same arguments. Remember, this scenario is played over and over to prospective customers countless times every day, and it is old hat to them. By using a refreshing, new approach, your chances in getting the attention needed are better.

This lack of creativity is one of the reasons why many salespeople continue to repeat the same mistakes over and over and make a sale only after more calls than are necessary. Usually what happens is that because of this repetition and lack of creativity, buyers, after a while, refuse to see a salesperson.

What is needed is the realization that buyers want to learn something new and different about the product or service each time a salesperson calls. This can be achieved by relating new information in the presentation on each and every call. Salespeople must appreciate the time and attention granted by the buyer and make it worthwhile for the buyer to listen.

Before you make a second or third call, try to think why you are getting this invitation to return and what you are doing to show your appreciation for taking up the buyer's time and effort. Two reasons why buyers permit salespeople to make *repeat calls* are

1. The buyer expects to learn something new about the product or service your company is offering.
2. The prospect or customer wants to know something new about your company, industry, or business conditions that could benefit him or her.

Let's look at these reasons in a little more detail. First, regarding something new about the product or service, each time you visit you should look at previous call reports—what was achieved, results expected, and what action has to be taken. Look at the time of the last call and decide if there were any new products, features, or benefits not emphasized to the prospect. Also look for new markets, industries, or other areas your product has served that your prospect may not be aware of. Are there samples, audio-visual programs, testimonials, or other sales aids you could use to possibly reinforce some of the points mentioned in previous presentations? If during your previous presentation you could not clearly identify what a customer's most responsive chord was, you may ask a question such as this: What appealed to you the most during our last meeting when we discussed our product or service? Maybe this response can trigger some positive comments from the prospective customer that you can then elaborate on.

Review something new about your industry or the prospect's business: if you are reading the trade journals, you will be aware of what's happening in the marketplace. This will give you a continual source of new information about the industry and the markets you serve as well as what markets your prospects or customers serve. You can review new applications of existing products that other customers have found useful and which could be of interest to your prospect. This requires homework on the salesperson's part. If you want to be considered a consultant in the eyes of the prospect, it must be done.

LISTENING TO PROSPECTS AND CUSTOMERS

Effective listening is an essential part of all selling. It is an essential skill that helps sales professionals strive to do better. Successful salespeople know that they must listen to prospective customers' wants and needs and be prepared to react to buying signals. Professionals continually work at better understanding and interpreting comments made by prospects to be in a better position of reacting favorably.

Studies show that if a message is read or heard only one time, within twenty-four hours 10 percent of it is forgotten, and within thirty days, it is almost out of our minds. With this in mind, the sales professional knows it is extremely important to repeat important points during the course of a presentation. In order to aid in the retention of the spoken word, sales letters, testimonies, brochures, and handout information, at presentation and as a follow-up, are important.

Poor listening is usually unintentional. Few individuals are born good listeners. The primary reason for poor listening is that there is not a sincere interest in what's being said, sometimes because of outside distractions, impatience, or disagreement with the speaker's approach. Lack of sincere interest allows us to hear but not listen, causing most of the important information that should be transferred successfully from one person to the next to be lost.

Effective salespeople know they cannot identify their customers' needs and wants, much less attempt to satisfy them, without fully understanding their customers, their organizations, and more specifically, their desires.

Effective Listening
Can Help You

1. It can help you get more out of your discussions with people in school and in your office, including secretaries, peers, and management as well as your associates in sales, plants, factories, headquarters, and home offices.
2. It helps you get more out of training programs and sales meetings. You have more time to listen to other people's experiences, to listen and understand and then determine how they can help you develop.
3. It helps in the negotiation of larger proposals and contracts by providing better understanding of what is actually said. Understanding voice inflections will give you a better understanding of what is meant.
4. It builds a better rapport with customers, distributors, associates, and fraternal and social contacts. Obviously, all these people are potential sources of leads and are important to your business.
5. It should reduce the amount of unnecessary paperwork by effectively communicating and being clearly understood. Confirmations may not always be required.
6. It is an aid to clear and more effective sales letters, telephone communications, and proposal offerings to prospects and customers.

Effective listening makes it easier for the prospective customer to understand and pay more attention to what you are presenting.

Active Listening

Listening is a significant part of learning. Surveys indicate that we hear about half of what is said because we are preoccupied with other thoughts. We often hear that actions speak louder than words, and effective listening demands active participation. Winston Churchill once said, "Speech is silver, while silence is golden."

Unfortunately, some people are so impressed by the sound of their own voices that they never stop talking long enough to listen to what is being said to them. In social conversation, you may miss something very important if you aren't listening attentively. Unfortunately in sales you can lose orders. The representative who listens for a prospect's needs and wants, and looks for ways to satisfy them, winds up on top.

LEARN MORE BY LISTENING BETTER

We would be remiss if we didn't highlight one of the most amazing ways to increase our salesmanship skills and ability to communicate: the use of a cassette tape recorder.

Improving your salesmanship skills by listening to yourself and the sales techniques of others on cassette tapes can be accomplished conveniently with a compact cassette recorder. Since the mid-1960s the compact cassette tape recorder has proved to be a simplified effective method of improving performance. It is used in every trade and profession and in education, government, and business. It is a boom to the sales professional. The success of cassette listening and learning is based on simple reasoning: it works.

Cassette tape listening and learning will work for you if you let it, because

1. You can turn your normally nonproductive time into learning time by listening to cassette tapes while you drive to appointments or to and from work, wait, eat, dress, or relax. Early in the morning or late in the evening are ideal times to set aside for your personal development.

2. Cassette audio learning is easier than reading and it carries a stronger impact. It takes effort to grasp information from a printed page. Contrastingly, a recorded message can be understood and enjoyed with no effort at all. Its message sinks into your subconscious.

3. Cassettes are convenient, portable, and relatively inexpensive. Good recorders can be bought for less than one hundred dollars, and pre-recorded sales, motivational, and inspirational tapes vary from five dollars to ten dollars; blank tapes are about one dollar each for sixty minutes—a nominal investment to make to improve skills and techniques.

You do have the time to listen and learn through the incredible retention power of "spaced repetition." You can listen as often as you like, and easily and effortlessly learn more and retain more every time you listen.

Whereas printed material is usually read only once and put aside, a good sounding cassette provides effortless, enjoyable repetition until its valuable knowledge becomes a part of the listener.

The cassette recorder is an ideal tool to record and play back your presentations, opening comments, telephone prospecting technique, handling objections skills, and so forth. By recording and playing back you can detect and eliminate unnecessary pauses, delays, repetition, and unclear statements, while refining what you want to say. By repeating this tape you can make canned presentations more planned, and hence, more effective.

CONCLUSION

The sales professional who effectively listens to prospects and customers will be a success. How well you listen will be in direct proportion to the number of orders you receive.

Good listening has nothing to do with intelligence or reading ability. These skills can be learned by anyone.

Good communication is a two-way street; not only should you listen to your prospects and customers but also they will be inclined to listen to you. One reason why a customer might not listen to you is because of lack of creativity in your presentation or your speaking habits. Try to present something new on every call, and show your enthusiasm in your voice and speech.

Listening to the comments of your customers will save you time, paperwork, and money.

Another aspect of effective listening is the use of cassette tapes. You can play back recordings of yourself giving presentations or listen to educational or motivational tapes of others during what was previously nonproductive time.

Review Questions

1. Why is effective listening a skill that must be developed by the sales professional?
2. Explain the real difference between merely hearing and listening.
3. Explain what can be done to improve listening comprehension.
4. How do sales professionals get prospective customers to listen to them?
5. How can a cassette recorder improve listening skills?

module five
Getting More Customers by Effective Prospecting and Cold-Call Selling

The search for new customers or increased business from present customers is never-ending. There are many sources of prospective customers. The effective salesperson must look continually for them.

With an average of 15 percent of our customers not in the market in any particular year, it's essential to get new customers.

Effective prospecting means identifying and separating those accounts that are not potential customers (suspects) from those that can be considered legitimate opportunities (prospects). Prospecting is a never-ending responsibility, not a part-time activity "when things are slow." If more prospects are uncovered than a salesperson can handle effectively, then management must decide if additional manpower is necessary.

Each market and industry has sources of prospective customers. You and sales management must know these sources and continually tap them. The Prospect List form in this module will help you organize and plan your prospecting efforts.

We acknowledge that cold-call selling is tough. The eternal fear of rejection is what deters most salespeople from trying. Cold-call selling keeps sales skills sharp and utilizes time efficiently. Regardless of what type of products or services sold, there will always be opportunities to present your product or service benefits to total strangers.

Develop an appreciation for the challenge you face in cold-call selling. Proper preparation in product knowledge, markets, competition, company policies, and selling skills will help to warm up the cold call.

Cold calling gives you the opportunity to use every day to the fullest. With accounts changing their schedules at the last minute, emergencies, and new businesses moving into your territories, there are always opportunities to cold call. The professional looks for opportunities. The amateur avoids them.

The salesperson should be prepared with excellent sales points, sales aids, and an up-to-date presentation manual when making cold calls.

PROSPECTING

For sales professionals to grow, it is essential that they maintain effective sales contact with their existing accounts and also develop new customers. The art and science of getting new customers is called prospecting. Cold-call selling is calling on someone for the first time. These two important areas of professional selling naturally belong together because very often in your prospecting you will cold call.

The Objectives of Prospecting

Prospecting is the *continuous* search and identification of individuals or firms who may be in the market for the products and services you offer for sale. Its objectives are the following:

1. To identify potential customers for your products and services.
2. To determine what products and services you offer can best satisfy the needs, wants, and requirements of these prospects.
3. To categorize these prospects as to their dollar potential based on your research.
4. To arrange telephone and personal contacts with these prospects on a scheduled priority basis.
5. To see the prospects with the highest potential first.
6. To qualify them as to their ability to pay for your products or services.

It's been said many times that "people buy from people." The product or service comes with the salesperson. Prospects have the same basic needs, wants, fears, and desires that we all do. The objective of all salesmanship is to determine what benefits in our products or service will help satisfy these needs and wants. We find most people nice to do business with. They are usually courteous and friendly, and if we illustrate a gain, advantage, or benefit to them, they'll buy. Individually, prospects have different personalities. However, as a group, they all have similar needs, wants, fears, and desires.

The professional who has the ability to relate to many different personalities is successful in sales. In fact, a difficult prospect presents a challenge to the experienced salesperson. This prospect could represent a great opportunity because in the past he or she has probably scared off many weaker salespeople.

There is one significant key in dealing successfully with prospects. You've got to be able to identify what their problems are and how you can help them. The sure way to do this is by asking questions about their business to determine their needs and wants. By asking questions you are giving them an opportunity to make decisions and you are not forcing anything on them.

When you properly ask a question you illustrate ways that they will benefit from your product or service. Their answers will be your guide.

Why Prospecting Is Important

New customers are the biggest opportunity for a salesperson to increase his or her sales. Present customers are essential. They deserve good service and contact on a regular basis. It is from new customers that the significant part of *additional* business must be obtained to offset the continual erosion of every salesperson's active accounts. New business will replace less active or lost customers and help better last year's performance.

The first effort executed in finding new customers will always be productive if proper planning and action are taken. With a list of pre-screened contacts, a certain number of customers will result.

Effective prospecting should be not only productive from a sales point of view but also enjoyable and very interesting. Prospects can be found everywhere. Experienced, successful salespeople seek them out as they cover the territory. Names of prospects come from many sources: published books, periodicals, trade journals, trade associations, existing customers, old customers, and others. By looking, asking questions, and listening, salespeople can establish and maintain a list of prospects.

Usually the salesperson who does not do well in prospecting is one who does not do it continually as an integral part of the job. He or she usually spends all his or her time calling on the same old customers month after month and year after year. A salesperson who is forced to prospect only when regular customers aren't buying in the necessary quantity usually has poor results. One week may bring good results, but many weeks may draw a blank. The successful prospector is the individual who continually looks for new customers and follows each lead.

Identifying, Qualifying, and Developing Good Prospects

To come up with a list of good leads, it is important to separate the prospects from the suspects. A good prospect is one who needs what you sell, can afford it, and has the authority to buy. Let's elaborate on these characteristics.

First, through your investigation and research you have determined prospects that have a need or want for your product and service, although they may or may not be aware of it. The sales professional must identify this need or want for the prospect, and establish a climate in which the prospect will want to buy. The need or want must exist.

Next, you know that the prospect has the funds available to afford your products and service. If the company has been in business a while it is reasonable to assume it can pay for its supplies. The professional in sales helps a prospect find a way of buying an offering. We'll mention briefly that many prospects say they can't afford it, as a means of discouraging a salesperson. The best approach is to illustrate to the prospects the benefits to them. Then, help them find a way to afford it. There are many sources of credit available. Time spent investigating the funding of prospects before you call them can save time and embarrassment.

Last, be sure the prospect has the authority to give you a purchase order. If additional parties are required for approval of funds, engineering, operations, application, or other persons, make sure you identify them. Your experience of the "typical" organization of a prospect should help identify the job titles or departments that would normally be involved in a purchasing decision.

Prospects Are Everywhere

1. *Look at your present customers.* Consider why they buy your products and services. What other companies manufacture or use the same products or services? What other companies serve the same market? Are there companies with similar wants and needs in related industries? While thinking about your present accounts, consider if you are getting as much business as you can from them. Are they buying all your products up to their potential?

2. *Ask your present customers.* Your existing customers are an ideal source of prospects. Don't hesitate to ask them for the names of other companies and individuals who could be interested in your products or services. Satisfied customers take pride in who they buy from and are often anxious to give a personal testimonial by supplying you with leads. If you are given a lead, ask your customer if you can use his or her name when contacting the prospect. It adds authenticity to your approach and prospects are impressed if you mention the name of the person who gave the recommendation.

3. *Check previous prospects or inactive customers.* Look over any lists or files of prospects or previous customers that you may have contacted but were unsuccessful with. Also, consider customers who bought from you before but with whom you might have lost contact because they were then inactive. Technological advances, markets, strategies, people, the national economy, and many other factors affect a company's needs and wants. Try contacting these accounts again; maybe now there is a need for your product or service.

4. *Ask noncompeting salespeople.* On your calls and at business functions, you continually meet other salespeople. They are an ideal source of leads. They know the territory. Ask them about new opportunities they have uncovered for their products or services. Perhaps these new opportunities may be interested in what you have to offer.

Sources: Published and Personal Contacts

There are many published and unpublished sources of leads. The sales professional takes every opportunity to look through trade journals, annual reports, periodicals, and business newspapers searching for leads. Usually these services reveal what companies are doing now and what they are planning. Plant expansions, managerial changes, contracts received, and new product introductions are opportunities for new or additional business. Following is a partial list of published information that could help:

> Annual reports of corporations
> Chamber of commerce reports
> Directory of associations
> Dodge reports
> Dun and Bradstreet reports
> Fortune 500 and 1000
> Fortune plant and product directories
> House organs
> Moody's manuals
> Standard and Poor's publications
> Telephone directories
> *Thomas Registry of Manufacturers*
> Trade magazines
> *Wall Street Journal*
> Yellow Pages
> SIC numbers

In addition to published reports, consider all the unpublished sources of leads through personal contact. Remember, the more contact points you have, the better the chances of coming up with a list of good prospects.

A list of personal contacts could include

Alumni associations
Business club members
Community clubs
Employees of prospects
Friends and acquaintances
Fraternal society members
Owners of businesses
Receptionists
Sales and Marketing Executives International
Salespeople for noncompeting companies
Service club members—Lions Club, Kiwanis, Rotary
Toastmasters

If you were asked, "Where do you look for prospects?" the answer would be, *everywhere*. The more opportunities you consider the more ideas you'll get. Prospecting should not be something you assign to only a specific number of hours per day or any fixed time period. To be effective, the sales professional prospects continually, always looking for sources of business.

Your Prospect List

The sources available to obtain the names of prospects are many and varied. The effective salesperson develops the ability to zero in on prospective clients and turn them into satisfied customers. They know that a continual source of potential customers is necessary to meet and exceed their sales goals.

To help in developing your list, consider the following:

- Why are my present customers buying from me?
- What other companies or individuals could use my product or service?
- What specific features and benefits of my offering appeal to this type of company or individual?
- Where are these prospects located in relation to my present customers?
- What new products have we developed recently that would now appeal to inactive customers? Check all previous prospect and customer lists.
- What new service could we now offer that would be of interest to lost customers? How could we get them back?
- What personnel policy or business change has occurred that would make my product or service more desirable?
- What people do I know that have left previous customers and formed their own companies or joined other companies? Do I have their names and telephone numbers? When should I contact them?

By analyzing the answers to these and other questions you may choose, you start to develop a list of possibilities. It is recommended that you get as many names as you can in your initial list. Don't eliminate possibilities from your initial list too hastily. You may drop off a potential customer.

Add new possibilities to your list as they are identified or discovered. Leads may also come in from management, promotional ads, trade shows, conventions, or other company activities. A sample form for listing your prospects is included at the end of this module for your use. In addition to the name and address, it covers the items of interest to the sales professional.

Once your preliminary list of names is complete, it is convenient to list formally the most promising prospects. In determining the prospects that offer you the best potential, consider the following:

- What is the firm's main industry? Do you serve similar industries?
- Is this location the main facility, branch operation, or other?
- How big is the operation? Can you get the sales figures?
- Does the company presently buy from your competitors what you have to offer? Can you determine how much it buys, from whom, and for how much?
- Is the firm already buying from your company in another location? Do you have a national account listing of it?
- If it was a firm that did business with you in the past, are files available? Are there people working there that you remember?
- The opportunities to reopen inactive accounts should not be overlooked. This can be one of your biggest sources of new business. Former buyers know you, your company, and your products or services. You know their personnel, their company, their industry, and their finances. They are well-qualified prospects.
- Examine your files to determine when they ordered last, what they bought, how much they paid, and why they stopped buying?
- If the firm is presently buying some products from you, what can you do to sell additional products and/or services?
- Do you know the purchasing agent or other contact in the company? Do you know any executives?

Salespeople know that most of their sales come from relatively few customers. Historically, 80 percent of your sales come from 20 percent of your customers. Similarly, when you look over a list of possibilities, experience helps you decide who will use the greatest volume of what you have to sell. These are accounts that should receive highest priority.

Your list should be active. Qualify it regularly to assure yourself of a sufficient number of active prospects. Your review will determine if more sales effort is required or if the prospect should be dropped.

Prospecting within Your Territory

The steps used to prospect in your territory are simple. Here's a suggested procedure:

1. Plot exact boundaries of your present territory on a map. Any map available from a service station or stationery store will suffice. Be sure it is large enough to pinpoint locations of prospects and customers and then plan travel routing to include them efficiently. In our module on time and territorial management, we cover in detail how to plot your territory efficiently.

The geography, business firms, organizations, and individuals within these boundaries are the raw material needed for your sales development. No matter what the demographics, it is from within territorial boundaries that you must develop sales. The act of plotting out and marking locations of prospects and customers on a map will help you become more aware of the real potential of your territory.

2. List the prospects you're either working on now or plan to contact in the near future. Then mark their locations on the map with a colored felt-tip pen or tack. Now you can easily check your weekly or daily call plans and travel requirements against the location of known prospects. This will save you time, and miles of driving. For example, by plotting a week's travel requirements for your regular sales and service calls, nearby prospects or those en route can be included more easily and regularly.

3. Add new possibilities to your prospect list as they are discovered or identified or as they are supplied by your manager, through call-ins or other sources. Be sure to add all new possibilities to your map also.

4. Your prospect list must be carefully policed periodically to make sure it contains an adequate number of active, qualified prospects for sales development. During this review, at least on a monthly basis, each prospect should be evaluated in terms of any strong sales effort required, reasons for suspending action until later, or reasons to drop completely.

Prospecting through the Mails

The mails can be an effective way to introduce your products or service to your prospects. You can conveniently enclose a brochure, flyer, announcement, or other eye-catching material. It's recommended that your mailings arrive on Tuesday, Wednesday, or Thursday. They then have a better chance of getting read.

An effective direct mail program boosts a salesperson's presentation by introducing the company's product or service to the buyer. The sales professional can reduce the average cost per call by securing an interview before he or she arrives.

A presentation will proceed much smoother if the salesperson is expected by the prospect. A good letter of introduction mailed beforehand can lead to a successful interview. If you are selling in a new territory, you can mail a letter to all customers and prospects in the area. Or if you're about to call on a new account, you might send a letter to the individual prospect. A telephone call before your visit will help you set a convenient meeting time.

Perhaps your prospects are overstocked at the time you pay your visit. Or they might feel they don't want to change suppliers at this time. Whatever the reason, the door is at least partially opened, and it's your job to make sure it remains so. How do you do this? Write a follow-up letter of thanks, reemphasizing the benefits you discussed and say you'll contact the company again.

Remember, most of us retain a small percent of what we hear. So whatever you do, don't expect a busy prospect to remember much more than 5 percent. With a good follow-up letter, you can reemphasize the remaining percent.

The letter will show the prospect that you're from a well-organized, considerate company that wants to establish good relations with its customers and prospects.

Prospecting by Telephone

With the cost of personal sales calls increasing yearly, the telephone is a convenient device to cover more people on your prospect list. Time and money can be saved by effective use of the telephone. When following up on requests derived from advertising, trade shows, convention booths, or hospitality visitors, the telephone may be your best approach. In our module on the telephone we cover prospecting, qualifying, and getting appointments through effective telephone use.

COLD-CALL SELLING

Warming Up to Cold Calling

Cold calling means making a sales call on a total stranger. It is a very effective way of getting new prospects. Although it is one of the toughest jobs a salesperson faces, it can be one of the most rewarding.

One thing that frustrates a salesperson more than any other is when a buyer calls up and cancels an appointment. The salesperson sees his or her very carefully planned day destroyed. How does he or she fill this void?

Does it make sense to sit around and wait for the phone to ring? Of course not. Use this valuable unexpected time to cold call on prospective customers.

The prime objective of cold-call selling is locating new customers. It's a fact that the more prospects you have, the more business you do. Based on this fact alone, calling on new prospects when you have a void in your schedule has to be more profitable than wasting your time in frivolous activities.

The real professionals in sales consider cancelled appointments not as problems but as *opportunities*—opportunities to use this available time to make a few cold calls. It's an effective way to get new prospects. The salespeople who regularly call on total strangers are always on their toes and are top performers. There are no mutual friendships or influence that can help with the new prospect. Cold calling is a sure way of improving and strengthening selling skills. Cold callers must know their products, their industry, their markets, their competition, and their selling skills. Effective cold-call sellers are sales professionals.

Benefits of Cold-Call Selling

The benefits of cold-call selling (above and beyond increased sales) are worthy of further comment. Four key benefits to a sales professional are the following:

1. Cold-call selling gives you the opportunity to meet new people, to face new situations, to keep your selling skills and techniques sharp. Somewhere in your territory new companies are starting up or existing ones are expanding. Competitors may be out of favor with some customers, offering an opportunity to you. Inactive accounts may benefit themselves if they listen to what you have to offer now. This business does not come to you; it's your responsibility to go after it.

2. It's an ideal source of new business. Approximately 80 percent of your business comes from 20 percent of your customers; the remaining 20 percent of your business comes from the other 80 percent of your accounts. This means you must continually have an active list of buying customers to replace those that moved or are inactive. A sales professional shouldn't always count on regular customers to buy in the same or increased quantities. Without new business, there is no growth.

3. It keeps the salespeople totally prepared. They must be competent in all key areas of selling. There is no friendship to rely on. They must believe in the product and service and be able to make strangers believe. Salespeople who call on only "old acquaintances" tend to become soft. They are leading a sheltered life. Cold callers stay competitive.

4. In a cold call, objections are usually mentioned right up front.

Whether sincere or insincere, the professional can handle them. Often your regular customers may hesitate to mention hidden objections.

Success through Belief

Effective cold-call selling requires all the sales skills of a real professional. The real key is the proper attitude. Your attitude must be one of total commitment; you must be committed to looking at a prospect as an individual who could benefit by using your products and services.

Sales professionals consider themselves problem solvers. Their prime objectives are to ask questions, listen for responses, and offer solutions to problems.

The right attitude means you must believe in what you are offering, believe in your product and service, your company, and most of all, yourself. If you don't believe, it is impossible to get a prospect to believe.

Change Fear to Love

Many salespeople avoid cold-call selling because of fear. The reasons are varied and understandable: the embarrassment of being considered a "peddler," the fear of rejection, the unfamiliar surroundings, and the recollection of past failures. None of these reasons should stop real professionals from recognizing that their time and talents could be used to the fullest in cold calls. With each attempt, they will gain experience and confidence, and ultimately new customers.

Professionals know that with each rejection they are getting closer to an acceptance. Professionals are driven to success; they get up one more time when they are knocked down.

Planning

Maybe if we used the words *warm call* rather than *cold call* this activity would be easier to swallow. In reality, if the salesperson is prepared, it is a warm call. The thought of getting a potential customer should give a warm feeling.

Preparation and planning should go into each call. Who you are going to call on and what you are going to say is basic salesmanship. In preparing for your calls, it is necessary to consider what motivates people to buy.

Major motives are *pride, profit, fear, duty, love*, and *security*. The active salesperson, through experience, can determine which of these motives hits the buyer's hot button. Pride in ownership, increased profits, fear of competition, duty to organization, love of power, and the security for family are a few positive motives for buying. You can think of many more.

In planning whom you should call on, pinpoint markets, companies, and individuals that have a need or want for your product or service. You know that in the course of their business, these companies and industries need what you have to offer. If they have a need or want, it's up to you to fill it.

The time of day that you make your call is an important planning consideration if you are to be successful in cold calling.

If it is possible, try to schedule your calls between 9:30 and 11:30 A.M. or 2:00 and 4:00 P.M., Tuesday through Thursday. Although this is not always possible, if you can arrange it you are less likely to wait. On Mondays and Fridays, and earlier or later in the day, the prospect is more likely to be busy and may resent being interrupted. Individuals can be called at home.

The AIDA and CIMA
Approaches to the Sales Call

The prime objectives of the call are to see the right person, get his or her attention and interest, and have him or her take the action desired. Two convenient approaches for achieving these objectives are the AIDA and/or CIMA formula.

Let's review the AIDA formula first.

A	Attention	Before you can proceed you must have the prospect's attention.
I	Interest	Your questions, probes, and benefit statements must create enough interest so that prospects want to learn more. They recognize that you want to help them solve their problem(s).
D	Desire	The listener must have the desire to own your product or service.
A	Action	The prospects take the action you want because you offered them a solution for their problem(s).

Another convenient reminder to help you make an effective call is the CIMA approach.

C	Communicate	Ask questions, probe, and listen to communicate your intention to identify problems.
I	Illustrate	Illustrate how your products or services can solve the problem.

| **M** | Motivate | Stir a feeling of positive anticipation in the buyer. Motivate their desire to own. |
| **A** | Activate | Emotionally move the buyers so they take the positive action you want. |

AIDA and CIMA are not two opposite approaches but convenient presentation reminders that can help you organize your objectives on cold calls as well as on existing accounts.

Your initial prospect contact is usually a receptionist or secretary. It is necessary to convince him or her that you have a product and/or service that the company would be interested in. Remember, you never get a second chance at a first impression; and if you don't get past the receptionist or secretary, you can't sell.

A courteous approach usually leads to the right person in the organization. Of course, proper dress, poise, and a pleasing personality are essential. Your initial contact should not be patronizing or arrogant, but sincere.

Getting the prospect's attention on what you have to offer is your first objective. This must be accomplished with your opening comments; you need an ice-breaker. Your initial comments have to be so impressive that the individual will give you the attention you require and listen to your presentation. They must be so stated that even the busiest prospect will feel compelled to listen further. They must emphasize a significant customer benefit.

Usually the best type of ice-breaker is to ask an interesting and provocative question. Here are a few examples:

- How much time per unit do you now spend on repairing defective motors?
- Do you want to see how to reduce your inventory by $1,000 per month?
- Wouldn't you like to raise your output by 10 percent per shift?
- How do you protect your family with life insurance?
- Do you presently sell through distributors?

Questions like these usually get the prospect's attention and give the salesperson an opportunity to explain further.

Approaches to Opening the Sales Call

Opening the call has one purpose, to get the meeting underway, to pave the way for the rest of your interview. Whether your objective is to sell something, perform a service, or pick up information, it cannot be achieved if you do not have the prospect's attention. What you say and do in those first few seconds pretty much determines how well (or how badly) things will go during the rest of the interview.

Thus, opening the sale is very important. Somewhere during the first thirty seconds you must

1. Clear the prospects' minds of what they were thinking about when you appeared at the door.
2. Plant the idea that you are a professional and you want to sell, that is, give an inkling of the benefits it is possible for them to achieve with your help.
3. Gain confidence and justify the time needed for you to conduct your interview presentation.

That's quite an order, but if you're going to make an immediate or future sale, the opening must be good enough to

1. Plant the germ of an idea or recommendation you'll develop later on in the presentation.
2. Pick up facts only the person you're talking to can provide.
3. Subtly suggest that perhaps you can serve the prospect better than the present supplier.
4. Change some ways of thinking the prospect has about you or the company.

There are dozens of ways to get calls underway. We will elaborate on the provocative question approach and four others.

1. *Provocative questions.* To use this approach effectively you must
   a. Know what type of information you need from the prospect, so you can frame your questions accordingly. A clear objective helps you prepare your questions.
   b. Develop logical reasons for the prospect to answer the questions you ask.
   c. Lead into your questions with emphasis on the importance of such key motives as saving money, product conveniences, reduction in time and effort, and so on.
   d. Ask questions conversationally—not like a detective probing an eye-witness. Don't ask questions that cause anger, create fears, or seem to challenge the prospect.
   e. Probe with open-ended questions. Don't ask questions that can be answered with a simple "yes" or "no." You want to find out the prospect's attitude toward you and your company, needs, wants, problems, opportunities, desires, and awareness of your product line and service. Let the prospect talk; you listen.
   f. Pick up on the prospect's response to decide what other questions should be asked during the balance of the presentation.
2. *Sincere compliments.* This approach is effective only when your compliment is sincere. It can relate to the office, furnishings, company awards or

recognition, trophies, and so on. "Mr. Jones, I notice you are an avid golfer. Do you get out often?" or "Mr. Smith, I read in the paper that your firm just received a large contract. You must be very happy with your business outlook."

For this approach to work it must be

a.   *Sincere*—Show your sincerity by the tone of your voice and expression.
b.   *Truthful*—There must be no phony or contrived statements.
c.   *Appropriate*—Negative or unflattering statements should never be used.
d.   *Timely*—Focus on current accomplishments.

3. *Benefit statements.* Selling customer benefits is a key ingredient to effective salesmanship, whether with prospects or customers. To make benefit statements work for you, consider the following:

a.   Learn as much as you can about the prospect's business, position in the company, personal status, buying habits, and so on.
b.   Arouse the prospects' interest by emphasizing how you can save money, increase sales, make them or their companies more secure, help their egos, improve their performance, and so forth.
c.   It's all right to discuss benefits in general terms while you are probing; however, remember to be very specific once you've identified how your goods and services can help solve their problems. Prospects become customers when they realize how they can get benefits by buying from you.

4. *Third-party referral.* This is an effective approach because it shifts the verification of proof to someone whom the prospect knows and/or respects. "Mr. Johnson, your friend at XYZ Company is using our products. He thought you may be interested. I promised him that I'd drop in to see you." The third-party referral can be used

a.   When you know the prospect faces a problem for which a solution has already been worked out by others.
b.   When the company you refer to is in the same or similar industry, markets, or activities as your prospect and has a good reputation.
c.   When you want to relate to a factual, timely experience which closely parallels the problem your prospect is facing. The experience must indicate the kind of benefits that are possible with your help.

After you evaluate the prospect's problem, point out how others solved similar problems. You may want to request another meeting when your presentation can then relate specific details and proof.

5. *Proof positive.* This can be a dramatic approach if the proof you offer is significant and/or unique. "Mr. Warren, this tabulation is dynamic proof of the positive results and benefits you can enjoy with our. . . ." This approach is effective if you

a.   Are certain the proof is accurate and fits into the problem the prospect is facing.
b.   Are brief and specific.
c.   Use it at the beginning when the prospect may be hesitant or suspicious.
d.   Try it on people that demand hard facts, figures, and documentation. Some individuals want proof of performance.
e.   Use impressive documents such as charts, graphs, computer printouts,

photographs, lists of satisfied customers, records, and letters. All these items should be in your presentation manual ready for use. Samples and models are also effective proof.

Whatever the approach you use, make sure it's sincere and gets attention.

Your product or service has numerous questions or interesting statements that can be made about it to get attention. Once you have the attention of the listener, cold-call selling is no different than any other type of selling. Start stressing customer benefits with sales points.

CONCLUSION

The need for continual prospecting for new customers is a never-ending one for the salesperson. The suggestions contained in this module, coupled with a positive mental attitude, will make prospecting a *rewarding* part of the sales profession.

Sales professionals who utilize cold-call selling techniques will find they are never at a loss for new customers and additional sales. It is also an excellent way for the salesperson to keep sharp and be prepared.

Although the term *cold-call selling* may have negative connotations, fear and false pride will not keep the true professional from trying and becoming successful at this type of selling.

Remember the AIDA formula—Attention, Interest, Desire, and Action—and the CIMA formula—Communicate, Illustrate, Motivate, and Activate.

Both of these convenient reminders can help you set your call objectives.

There are many approaches to use to begin your sales call, such as the provocative question or identifying a common problem. Always be sincere in whatever approach you take.

The telephone is a terrific sales aid. It provides convenience, flexibility, and productivity and saves time and money. Use it.

An important key is to get the prospect's attention. Once you have that, cold-call selling is just like any other type of selling. Preparation is essential.

Review Questions

1. Why is prospecting a necessary activity for the effective sales professional? What are the objectives of prospecting?
2. Pick a product you know and give ten areas where you will look for prospects to sell this product.

3. List the names of ten prospects that should have a need or want for this product.

4. Pick a service industry and give ten areas where you will look for prospects to sell this service.

5. List the names of ten prospects that should have need or want this service.

6. What methods and research can be used to determine if a prospect is a good one?

7. How does the telephone help in prospecting and cold-call selling? What about the mails?

8. What are the main benefits of cold-call selling?

9. Why do many salespeople object to cold-call selling?

10. How do salespeople identify what a prospect may need or want? Explain.

11. What does it take to succeed when prospecting and making cold calls?

12. Write a brief outline of a cold call, using the AIDA format, first with a product, then with a service.

13. Write a brief outline of a cold call, using the CIMA approach, first with a product, then with a service.

14. Prepare a list of ten industries or markets and record the best times to call on a prospect in each.

Prospect List

Names/Addresses of Prospects Located or Identified	Prospect's Potential in Dollars	Prospect's Present Suppliers	Products/Service Needed by Prospect	Dates of Calls Made on Prospects	Action Required to Get Business

module six
Sales Planning for Professional Growth and Productive Sales Calls

"If we don't know where we are going, any road will get us there," is a simple adage highlighting the importance of having a destination (sales plan).

Planning is necessary for sales achievement; it takes us down the road to meet our goals. A written plan that is measurable with time parameters gives us direction. Direction gives us confidence.

Specific plans and programs on how and where you are expecting your business indicate professional personal management. Identification in writing of the products or services you will sell by account, with a timetable for accomplishment, is basic to sales planning.

When making a sales call, it's especially important to identify clearly the call objectives. What do you want to achieve? Are you prepared to talk benefits? What sales tools will help you reach your objectives? The Sales Planning Ladder and Sales Call Planner forms in this module encourage you to plan and act in order to achieve a clearly defined objective. If you do not have a call objective, you react at the will of the prospect. You lose control.

PLANNING ESSENTIALS FOR BUSINESS GROWTH

Sales planning is essential for business growth. It gives us direction in our activities, it sets target objectives, and helps us devise action programs.

Effective sales planning includes the following:

1. Identifying prospects' or customers' needs and wants and then outlining a program to serve them.

2. Operating as effectively and efficiently as possible. It is necessary to define clearly all your objectives and plans. Set quotas in all the critical areas. You must first zero in on the right products, prospects, customers, and markets. Next, you should schedule activities to make sure you are doing the right thing at the right time.

3. Prioritizing your time and effort. Sales professionals know they must decide what is the best use of their time, how to handle their expense dollars, what products and services appeal to their markets, and so on. They know they can't be all things to all people. It's necessary to be selective by setting priorities.

4. Remembering that approximately 80 percent of your sales comes from 20 percent of your customers. You must spend your resources where they have the most *return*. Identify your key customers and develop them to the fullest. Next, spend part of your efforts in calling on prospects to develop them as customers.

Sales planning means deciding what you want to accomplish in the future and acting on those plans *now*. We use the words *sales planning* in the broadest sense. We mean all programs, plans, and actions that the sales professional takes to meet short- and long-term objectives. We include the sales interview and sales presentation as integral parts of sales planning.

Business management demands that objectives be established. Specific plans, priorities, and strategies are put in place to meet these objectives with a definite time set for their accomplishment.

Planning is the only effective way to run a business. Inspirational books are full of stories of individuals and the companies they formed who set out to attain a goal and didn't stop until it was achieved.

IMPORTANCE OF PLANNING

Proper organization is the foundation on which all successful sales careers are based. An organization plan is needed so that time, money, energy, and people can be assigned to the objective to be achieved. The secret of accomplishment in the sales profession is to know exactly what you want and how you are going to get it.

Top management must establish sales and marketing objectives for the organization before plans can be made by the sales force. These corporate objectives include marketing functions such as advertising, product introductions, sales aids and promotions, and trade shows. In addition, plans, classical objectives of sales dollars, number of units, new accounts, market penetration, personal growth, skill improvement, product mix, and other areas of interest are considered.

Historical data, business conditions, competition, facility expansion, product introductions, financial returns on investment, percentage of market share, and other factors make up what a corporation finally sets as its sales objectives for the coming year. It is often referred to as the *bogey*, the *goal*, the *plan*, the *quota*, the *nut*, or simply the *yearly objectives*.

Ultimately these corporate objectives must be divided and given to the sales and marketing departments responsible for making them happen. Annual objectives are further divided into quarterly, monthly, and possibly weekly or daily objectives.

The sales professional usually has his or her objectives set through discussions with a national, regional, district, or other product or territorial sales manager.

These individual objectives are usually reached by analyzing the salesperson's accounts, markets, potential, and past accomplishments, meshing them with other members of the product or territorial sales team. The totals of the objectives of each member of the sales force must equal or exceed the overall corporate objectives.

With individual objectives set, it is necessary to establish definite programs to meet them. The sales professional must have a plan, with an itemized list of what must be done, within a definite time period, to meet or exceed his or her individual objectives. This plan is the road map and guide to reach the ultimate destination, exceeding the yearly goal.

HOW ORGANIZATIONS PLAN

Management Planning

Sales management usually divides the served markets in a few classified methods:

1. *By territory:* A company may want its field sales representatives to sell all its products to all prospects and customers within a certain geographical area. In this arrangement, one person will have the responsibility to establish new accounts, increase business with present customers, and maintain commercial good will within his or her territorial boundaries. The boundaries can vary from certain floors in one skyscraper to many states or portions of the country.

2. *By product:* In this arrangement, a sales representative may sell only some of the company's products to all prospects and customers within a certain area.

3. *By markets:* A sales representative may handle some or all of the products the company sells to a particular market segment.

Most companies use combinations of these three methods in assigning objectives to their sales professionals.

Salesperson Planning

Key areas that must be considered by the salesperson and management to set effectively individual sales objectives and action plans are the following:

1. *Account listing and call frequency:* Each salesperson must have an up-to-date list of accounts, which should be divided into three categories: major, or A accounts; minor, or B accounts; and marginal, or C accounts.

A accounts are those called on most often. Most business comes from them. These accounts are frequently in the market for your products or services.

B accounts are those you call on less often because they are in the market for your products or services less frequently and/or they buy in smaller dollar volume.

C accounts are called on less often because they are in the market less frequently and/or buy in very low dollar volume.

Contact should be maintained with each account in proportion to its present and potential value. It is essential in planning for the year that each A and B account be given a dollar and a call-frequency objective.

This listing of dollar objectives by accounts and call frequency gives the salesperson and management the ability to analyze whether or not too much or too little time is allocated based on the potential, past activities, market conditions, and the salesperson.

2. *Product mix and market presentation:* When listing accounts and how often you plan to call them, also identify what you estimate they will buy. What products or service in what dollar volume must be considered. For established products normally sold to existing customers, potential sales are easier to identify. Market potential and penetration are based on information from surveys, research, annual reports, and other sources.

In this portion of your objective, you identify and set action plans by product and/or service into the particular market(s) in which you are interested.

3. *Skill improvement:* This is an essential area of consideration in setting short- and long-term objectives. Consider what you are planning to do today, this week, this quarter, and this year to help you reach your long-term sales objectives and skill-improvement objectives.

To plan effectively for skill improvement, the field sales manager and the salesperson must jointly analyze the following:

a. *Salesperson's ability to manage time and territory:* Is the salesperson using time wisely? Getting in as many calls as possible? Handling paperwork efficiently? Seeing enough "buying" people in the right markets? Submitting timely reports? Using the telephone efficiently?

b. *Product knowledge:* Does the salesperson continually strive to learn more about the company's products or service? The important features and associated benefits? Competitive products, present applications, and new applications?

c. *Prospecting:* Is the salesperson continually looking for new customers to replace those that are inactive or have moved? How is his or her prospecting technique—does he or she follow up on corporate programs?

d. *Product mix:* Is the salesperson selling all the products or services assigned in the volume expected? Should additional office, factory, or headquarters training programs be initiated to better equip the salesperson in the products he or she isn't selling?

e. *Selling tool usage:* Is the salesperson using all the sales tools at his or her disposal? Available audio-visuals? Samples? Brochures? Testimonials and sales letters? Does he or she ask for managerial support on difficult transactions? What about plant or job site visits with prospective customers? Headquarters or plant people visiting the prospect? Effective use of the presentation manual?

f. *Planning:* Does the salesperson have the ability to set objectives and effectively draw up a plan to meet these objectives. Does the salesperson do the things he or she set out to do?

g. *Organization:* Does the salesperson have a systematic approach to taking care of the company car, samples, catalogs? Does he or she keep paperwork moving efficiently? Submit reports when required?

h. *Selling skills:* How adept is the salesperson in the skills of the profession? Does he or she know how to get appointments by telephone? Close well? Handle negotiations effectively? Handle objections? Write effective sales letters? Have adequate oral communications skills? What should the salesperson do to improve skills to sell more?

i. *Development:* What is the salesperson doing outside of work to help his or her development? Following self-improvement programs? Belonging to any professional or trade associations for contact with prospects?

j. *Attitude:* How does the salesperson look at his or her sales career? As motivated? Enthusiastic? A team player? Committed to higher levels of performance. Cooperative? Does the salesperson take direction? Relate to the inside support people?

k. *Performance:* Is the salesperson meeting the objectives set out for him or her? Is he or she challenge-oriented? How are the sales volume and percentages? Is there positive improvement in the key areas assigned?

l. *Customer Relations:* How does the salesperson relate to prospects and customers? Accepted warmly? Sought out by customers for consultation before they go out and buy?

All these skills must be analyzed to determine present abilities and levels set for improved performance. Salespeople should remember that school is never out for the successful professional. They must continually strive to do the best they can. They need to improve their *sellatechnics.*

Your daily plans will probably include making sales calls. To help you maximize these calls, we've included in this module a *sales-call planner.*

The sales-call planner gives you one convenient place to identify the accounts you want to call on and set specific call objectives, sales tools required, results achieved, and so on.

In addition to sales-call planning, it is important to plan for overall sales effectiveness. We've included a convenient, twenty-six-question, yes and no checklist to help you identify your need for planning.

Another convenient planning tool is our *sales-planning ladder.* It encourages a step-by-step approach to meeting your objectives.

THE LADDER APPROACH TO SUCCESS

Sales-Planning Ladder

Planning is necessary if you are to schedule your actions to meet your objectives. As a sales professional, you must plan your personal and business growth objectives, including individual sales plans for each product in each account. Every objective must move you closer to the top of the ladder of reaching your final objective and keeping to your plan.

Preparing Your Ladder

1. You must identify and list all the objectives to be achieved. A separate ladder should be made for each major prospect or customer and each product or service line.
2. Establish a priority list based on your knowledge of the market, prospect or customer, competition, time available before purchase, effective time and territorial management practice, business goals, and so on.

3. Consider what items would naturally go together as an initial or secondary step up your ladder to get an order.
4. Set dates for the accomplishment of each item on your list.

PLANNING YOUR WORK— WORKING YOUR PLAN

We've often heard the adage: "Plan your work—work your plan," which means that to work effectively you must have a plan. You must identify what you want to accomplish. It is essential for effective time management and professional growth to establish a plan with measurable goals.

Following are some suggestions to help you in planning your work:

1. You must consider planning a top priority. It is necessary that you understand the importance of good planning and goal setting as ways of efficiently establishing the activities you set out to do.

2. Establish a regular time and place where you will do most of your planning. Whether at home or in the office, it should be a convenient location that will be conducive to reviewing your objectives. Some people plan better in the morning, whereas others are night people. It is important for you to determine when you do reach your most creative planning. By setting a regular time and place for it, you will eliminate any haphazard actions.

3. Set goals. You must set definite goals that are measurable, attainable, and realistic. You should consider such goals as the number of sales calls, number of sales dollars, dollars per product, dollars in minimum markets, new accounts, and other important areas that are essential for your particular activity. Write your goals down.

4. Keep your goals simple. You should not have goals that have a lot of ifs, whens, or whys attached to them because they get too difficult to follow; if too many things become dependent on others the goals are not clearly defined.

5. Be realistic. Consider the amount of time you have and what you want to achieve and decide on the amount of effort you must put forth to reach your objectives. Your goals should be obtainable.

6. Stick to your plan. Although your plan should have a certain amount of flexibility for some interference and slight deviations, you should not make changes just to suit your convenience. Significant changes to your plans should be given careful consideration and have managerial approval.

7. Evaluate your plan on a regular basis. As circumstances change, you may find that your work may require a slightly different course of action.

Take a look at your plan to make sure it's still practical. It is essential that you work with a plan; just make sure your plan is working for you.

8. Know exactly what you expect to accomplish by continually following your plan and keeping it in sight. Some people review their plans daily or have them in front of them so that they have a continual reminder of what they are expected to achieve. It is convenient to use checkmarks or a numbering system to keep track of what you accomplish while working on your plan. The "Things To Do Today" pads are very good for listing items that we expect to accomplish during a particular day. Get a calendar for yearly goals.

9. Keep records of your accomplishments so you can document the results and see how they compare with your overall objectives.

10. Strive to reach your goals. After you set realistic goals, make sure you put your plan into action so that you'll be able to work toward them.

11. Know your product. Be as prepared and knowledgeable about the features, customers, and markets of the product you are selling. Continually learn as much as you can about your competitor's products and your customer's organization.

12. Learn as much as you can about professional selling skills. Continually look for workshops and sales meetings where you'll be able to find additional sales material on skills and techniques that you may consider using with your customers.

13. Offer superior service. It's important to remember that when you sell a product or service, you are part of the offer. The customer buys a package consisting of your product, service, and company. Remember, when customers buy something from you they place confidence in this total package. Don't let them down.

14. Be enthusiastic. It's important that you maintain a positive and enthusiastic outlook toward your product, service, and job and that you reflect this in your daily activities.

The following is a checklist to indicate a salesperson's need for planning.

	Yes	*No*
1. Are you getting the sales volume you should based on the potential available?	——	——
2. Do you know how many calls per year it is economical for you to make on each of your accounts?	——	——
3. Do you always call on the right person in an account?	——	——
4. Do you get enough time to prospect and develop new business?	——	——

5. Do you spend a total of less than one day a week in the office? —— ——

6. Do you find that you very rarely have to wait to see people? —— ——

7. Do you always have a specific purpose for each call (not a social purpose)? —— ——

8. Do you know how many calls you have to make, on the average, to produce one order? —— ——

9. Is your desk free from unattended paperwork? —— ——

10. Do you set a dollar value on each hour of your time? —— ——

11. Do you set a dollar volume and/or number of units for each product or service that you handle? —— ——

12. Have you set a five-year income goal for yourself? —— ——

13. Do you set an annual income goal? —— ——

14. Do you allow time for planning? —— ——

15. Can you say that you never spend nights and weekends doing clerical work? —— ——

16. Do you always have enough prospects? —— ——

17. Is your sales curve rather constant and free from peaks of "hot flashes" and valleys of "deep slumps"? —— ——

18. Do you always have an adequate number of calls planned for a day? —— ——

19. When you first get up in the morning, do you always know where your first sales call will be? ——

20. After each call, do you always schedule the date of the next call on that account? —— ——

21. Do you have a program for improving all your selling skills? —— ——

22. Do you invest in your effectiveness by learning specific benefits about your product and service? —— ——

23. Are you striving to learn more about your customers, their markets, their motivation, and their methods of doing business? —— ——

24. Are you spending a portion of your time studying your competitors, analyzing their strong and weak points? —— ——

25. Do you analyze in depth the markets you serve to see if you are getting the penetration you want? —— ——

If you have...

0	"No" answers, you'd better take another look.
1–3	"No" answers, you are doing pretty good.
4–6	"No" answers, you could use planning.
7–9	"No" answers, you'd better use planning.
10 or more	"No" answers, you are in desperate need of planning.

Try this simple procedure for improving your planning. First, identify the areas in your sales career that need better planning. Where are *you* dissatisfied with your performance? List them in order of priority. Set a timetable for their improvement. Finally, define the positive action you will take to accomplish them.

SETTING SALES-CALL OBJECTIVES

The effectiveness of sales planning comes to a focal point when you are in front of a prospect or customer on a sales call. For a sales call to be effective you must have a specific objective. It is necessary to understand clearly what you want to accomplish and how you are going to accomplish it. A specific objective outlined *before* the call gives direction and definiteness of purpose. Being vague during the call usually leads to failure.

It is necessary to prepare an effective *opening statement* to get immediate interest so you can focus attention on your product or service. A poorly prepared or unprepared opening could easily dissuade a prospect or customer before you get going.

USING THE SALES-CALL PLANNER

To get maximum results from time and sales efforts on each call, you must have an objective. The sales-call planner in this module could be very useful in considering the products and benefits you want to present, what sales tools are required, the results achieved, and future action.

Key areas of interest in sales-call plannning are these:

1. Whom you want to contact and when—including the name of the contact, company name, and date. If more than one contact is to be made at an account, list them separately, each with a set of objectives.

2. The overall objective of the call—what are the major and minor objectives? What point(s) do you want to make? Think about the situation you want to discuss: what has preceded? What is next? How will you open the discussion? If you're sidetracked from your objective, how will you get back? If you are discussing commercial subjects, do you have the necessary supporting documentation? Do you know your competition? What about product and drawing availability? Terms of sale? Cost of enrollment? Length of policy, etc.?

3. Product discussion—If you are discussing a product or service, do you know the features, and more importantly, the customer benefits?

What about competitive products? What about availability of replacement parts? Service? Similar equipment in the customer's office or plant? Testimonies of other customers? Will a factory visit help? Will an engineering meeting at the customer's location help? Why should he or she buy this product from you at this time?

4. Sales tools—What tools or sales aids will help you meet your objective(s)? Audio-visual presentations, brochures, technical data, proposal information, publications, testimonial letters, lists of installations, service or quality control literature, samples, flip charts, sales management visits—who or what will help you prove your points? The more involved a client gets during a presentation, the longer he or she retains the message. Be creative.

5. Type of sales call and time required—Once you've identified your objectives and considered what you have to discuss and the sales tools you need, decide if the telephone or an in-person visit is best. Of course, sales tools are limited when you use the phone, although you can mention them and send a confirmation in the mail. With established accounts, telephone selling is very effective. It saves time and money.

6. Time required—How long are you planning for the call? How long did it actually take? This step will help you in your time and territorial management.

7. Results and actions—What results were achieved? What further action is required? When you leave a call, you should have a clear awareness of whether it was successful.

The sales-call planner is not just another form. It is an important concept of effective salesmanship. It covers significant ideas in setting objectives, planning presentations, managing time and territory, and achieving results. The real professional plans ahead.

CONCLUSION

Planning is an essential part of the salesperson's job. Without a plan of how you are going to reach your goals, you will never reach them; and without a goal you would never know what you had achieved.

Sales management will help you set your goals, but you must establish a definite plan of action. Each account should be given a dollar and a call-frequency objective. As a sales professional, you should also set goals for your personal enrichment and growth.

Good planning will definitely pay off when you are in front of a customer on a sales call.

Review Questions

1. Why are planning and setting goals so important in sales?
2. List the key areas for planning, giving specifics on measurable objectives.
3. Pick a product or service and a prospective customer. Complete a detailed sales-planning ladder showing specific measurable objectives, action programs, and dates for accomplishment.
4. Explain the advantages and disadvantages of assigning a salesperson's accounts based on (a) territory, (b) a specific product or service, or (c) a particular market segment.
5. Why should the sales professional establish a sales-call frequency on each account based on potential sales? Explain how it's done.
6. Why is pre-sales-call preparation so important?
7. List ten areas of interest the salesperson should direct attention to before stepping into a prospect's or customer's office. Explain why each is important and how the salesperson should prepare.
8. Select five different products or services that you sell or would like to sell and prepare a typical sales-call planner showing the call objectives, other details, and typical results expected.
9. Select three accounts from different markets and prepare a sales-call planner showing how you would sell them the same product or service.

Sales Planning Ladder

Planning is essential. You should identify what actions are required to meet your objectives. Number them in order of priority. Every action and objective must move you closer to getting an order. The top step is maintaining and/or increasing your level of business.

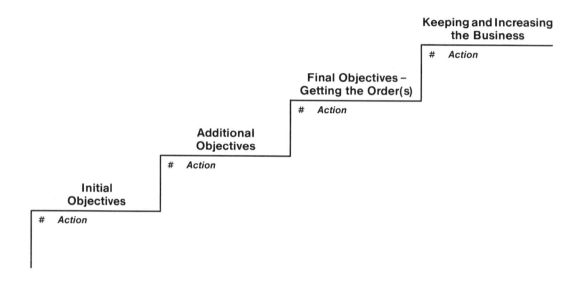

Sales Call Planner

Name _____ Office _____ Week of _____

Date	In Person	Phone	Account/Contact	Objective to be achieved	Hours plan/act.	Products features/benefits	Sales Tools	Results/Action

module seven
Successful Time and Territorial Management

To succeed in sales, it's absolutely essential to obtain enough business to justify your income and expenses while making a profit. To do this professionally, you must develop skills and techniques that enable you to make presentations and close on enough prospects and customers to reach your objectives. This is achieved by utilizing and controlling your time within your sales territory. This area of effective salesmanship is generally called time and territorial management.

The study of time and territorial management is important for effective sales coverage as well as for economic reasons. With fuel, meals, lodging, transportation, and other rising costs, the average cost per call is expected to exceed two hundred dollars before 1985. The sales professional must be cognizant of these expenses and make every effort to operate as efficiently and effectively as possible. The forms at the end of this module will prove very useful in helping you to control your time and to manage your territory.

SUCCESS IN SALES THROUGH EFFECTIVE TIME AND TERRITORIAL MANAGEMENT

The words *time management* are misnomers because we cannot manage time. Time cannot be stored; it can only be spent. What we are referring to is the control and management of ourselves. Time management involves the planning, organizing, and controlling of our sales activities to accomplish our objectives. It includes

- Separating the essential sales-producing activities from the less important activities and handling them by highest priority first.
- Writing a list of sales objectives which must be accomplished with a scheduled date for achievement.

Territorial management is preparing a call-frequency report on prospects and customers based on business potential and location. Territorial management is

- Analyzing and cataloging your prospects and customers to determine how often you should call on them based on their potential.
- Plotting on a map the location of your prospects and customers.
- Scheduling sales calls on a daily, weekly, and monthly basis, based on yearly objectives.

WHAT IS TIME AND TERRITORIAL MANAGEMENT—WHY IS IT IMPORTANT?

Time is a precious resource, and with it rests the success or failure of all your pursuits. The difference between sales achievers and the "I'm-still-thinking-about-it" people is effective utilization of time. Try thinking of time as the most valuable asset you can spend. Without well-organized time planning there will be fewer sales accomplishments and fewer resulting satisfactions.

You can't consider ways to use your time more effectively unless you identify what you do with your time now. After you have a detailed list of where and how you spend your time, you can effectively plan its use. A number of slippage points will reveal themselves in the analysis of your list, such as time spent with insignificant mail, unnecessary correspondence, personal office visits for matters which could have been handled by phone, unproductive socializing with office personnel, advancing opinions in matters routinely or best handled by another department, and so on. A time-analysis worksheet is included in this module to help you learn where you spend your time now.

Separating the absolutely necessary from the nonessential is a crucial part of reorganizing your time. Set about the task of eliminating those things which you need not be bothered with at all while directing your energies toward your sales objectives.

Next, you must assign priorities and learn to establish them correctly. Even after you have arrived at what you consider to be "must" duties, take a hard look at how these can be pared down, or at least scheduled for maximum efficiency.

Consider what is the best time of day for doing the following:

- Visiting customers.
- Handling phone calls.
- Conferring with subordinates.
- Conferring with the boss.
- Answering correspondence.
- Handling creative work or solving problems.

There is a "best" time for all your activities, and you must find it.

WHAT ARE THE BENEFITS OF EFFECTIVE TIME AND TERRITORIAL PLANNING?

Planning your territorial activities is good sales management for many reasons. It allows you to

- Get more selling hours into each working day by seeing more prospects and customers.
- Visit customers and prospects on a planned schedule.
- Improve customer service and build rapport.
- Reduce the overall cost of sales calls.
- Gain access to prospects and customers while the competition must wait.
- Eliminate costly waiting time and unnecessary traveling expenses.
- Increase the frequency of your coverage.
- Get more sales and more results at lower costs.

To plan your territory and account coverage effectively, you start by taking a close look at your prospects and customers. You must classify them by sales volume or potential.

WHERE DO YOU SPEND YOUR TIME?

The average salesperson spends between 2 and 2½ hours of his or her business day actually presenting the product in front of a prospect or customer. The majority of the time is spent in traveling, waiting in reception rooms, idle chitchat, meals, handling paperwork, and other time-wasting activities.

How many times have you charged out to talk to the boss, secretary, or co-worker when you could just as easily have handled the matter by telephone? A bigger time waster is jumping into your car to drive to a customer to ask a question that could have been handled just as effectively by telephone.

Through a concerted effort, a considerable amount of nonproductive time can be eliminated. It is reasonable to expect an increase in sales volume with a decrease in nonproductive time.

To reduce nonproductive time, you first have to identify it. This requires an honest inventory of what you are doing now, and a commitment to improve. We've included a time-analysis worksheet to help log your daily activities.

Select a few typical work weeks to identify and record your daily activities. At the end of the analysis, you can add up how and where you have spent your time and consider changes to give yourself more face-to-face selling time or more time on the telephone in an aggressive planned sales capacity.

Your first and best time investment is to log what you do each day. A short pencil is better than a long memory for this kind of elusive detail. This log should give you a clear picture of exactly what you do. It is not a reflection of your responsibilities alone; it's also a revealing portrait of how you spend your time, every minute of it. This time-analysis log, when completed, should be a real revelation if you have been completely honest in putting everything down.

PREPARING YOUR TIME-ANALYSIS WORKSHEET

We will consider five major areas in which salespeople spend their normal working hours—travel, office, service, personal, and face-to-face customer contact. You should log your activities in thirty-minute intervals between 7:00 A.M. and 6:00 P.M. The evening and Saturday activities can be recorded if business is transacted at that time.

Use activity codes (in parentheses) for convenience in filling in the worksheet. If less than thirty minutes are spent on one activity, draw a diagonal line in the time slot and list approximate minutes in each activity. Some estimations may be necessary from time to time; however, over the course of a week, the averages will give an excellent indication of where you've spent your time. The analysis should be conducted for several weeks or longer.

1. *Travel* (TR): Record the time you spend on travel to the office, on your first call, between calls, waiting in reception rooms, and on travel home.

2. *Office time and paperwork* (OF): Record the time you spend in the office reading, writing, listening or talking on the telephone, planning your calls, preparing proposals, meeting with inside support personnel and management, training programs, and all other inside activities required to move correspondence within the office.

3. *Service* (SR): Record the amount of time spent in servicing your customers rather than in actually selling to them. Include the time spent handling complaints, expediting orders, working on technical or design problems, instructing customer personnel, or any work *other* than selling.

4. *Personal* (PL): List the time you spend for meals, coffee breaks, fraternal or civic meetings, haircuts, servicing the car, or other personal activities.

5. *Customers* (C): Record the time you are in the presence of one or more buyers in an organization where you are face to face and building rapport to help you get an order. Idle association with a prospect or customer is not really face-to-face selling.

If in a typical week you spend a considerable amount of time in another function, devise your own code symbol and record it. Keep the worksheet on your desk, and each half hour log in what you did. At the end of the week, add how much time you spent in each activity. You will then see how much time you spend in your various activities. This is an excellent way to help plan a time-management program that will give you more time in category C, real selling time in face-to-face contact with a prospect or customer.

For the purpose of illustration, let's say you spend 2½ hours or 150 minutes per day face to face with a prospect or customer. If you can find a way to add 30 minutes of selling time, to visit or telephone additional prospects, this figure represents an *increase of 20 percent more sales calls.* If your orders per sales call remain the same (a reasonable assumption), your sales should increase 20 percent. Consider all the suggestions in this module and elsewhere to help you get more selling time and more sales.

WHAT HAS YOUR TIME ANALYSIS REVEALED?

Review your time analysis after you have logged in a few weeks' activities, attained the business, and realized your success in achieving your other objectives during this period. You can then analyze the following:

- Are you spending enough time in front of your customers or prospects?
- Are you spending too much time on lunches or personal activities?
- Are you spending too much time in service work?
- Is travel taking more time than expected?
- Are you spending too much time waiting to see prospects?
- Are you routing your territory effectively to reduce back-tracking?
- Are you concentrating on the high potential accounts?

Once you have completed your self-analysis and considered the answers to these questions, you can plan what is necessary to take better control of your sales territory.

PLANNING YOUR DAILY ACTIVITY

To accomplish effectively your daily objectives, it is essential to plan. Planning is best accomplished by writing down what you want to accomplish in order of priority. First things first.

We suggest getting "Things to Do Today" pads in a stationery store to help in listing your daily planned activities. Your list should be established early every morning when you plan the day or the night before. The highest priority item should be first on your list and handled first. Tackle each item until it is completed. Then go to the next item. If you can't accomplish everything you wish, at least you've handled the highest priority items. The following is the format of a typical "Things to Do Today" pad. Get some pads and use them—starting today.

Things to Do Today

1. _____
2. _____
3. _____
4. _____
5. _____
6. _____
7. _____
8. _____
9. _____
10. _____

Notes:

SUGGESTIONS ON GETTING MORE SELLING TIME

In addition to selling time, there are four major activities on which you spend your time—travel, office, service, and personal. Following are some suggestions to reduce your nonselling time to give you more selling time. With a little thought, you will think of many more.

Travel

Plan the route of your calls and appointments. *Plan and schedule* your calls as far in advance as practical. It saves unnecessary travel. Use the telephone for follow-ups and making appointments. Consider dictating in the car or listening to motivational and sales-training tapes while you are driving.

Allow for contingencies in mapping out your route. Schedule your calls so that they are in a line away from the office or your home. (Other territorial routing arrangements are previewed later.) If it is not necessary to go to the office or plan a return route on that day, try to avoid criss-crossing. The night before a call, review your presentation. Have alternative prospective customers near your scheduled sales call in case an emergency arises and your appointment must be cancelled. Extra time resulting from a cancelled appointment should be spent in prospecting and cold calling. Don't feel that all requests by a customer require immediate action on your part. Learn to "prioritize."

When confronted with a request, always ask, "When do you need this?" Don't assume that the customer needs an immediate reply or that an emergency exists when in reality there is available time. It is better to ask and schedule your response. It enables you to continue your planned calls. Customers respect salespeople who learn how to prioritize their time. Close coordination of your travel activities is probably the easiest way to save thirty minutes per day.

Office

This can be a key time to handle necessary paperwork or it can be time wasted. To utilize your office time to the fullest, consider the following:

1. Change the hours that you normally spend in the office. Try the early morning and/or late night. What about lunch time?
2. Avoid idle gossip sessions; don't hesitate to say you haven't the time.
3. Cut down meeting times by having an agenda and stick to it.
4. Establish a system of following up on outstanding propositions.
5. Create a system for preparing quotations.

6. Handle correspondence in the evening or on weekends.
7. Can the use of form letters help without slighting the recipient?
8. Make a list of the things you do in the office and estimate the amount of time involved.

A few concepts you might want to keep in mind are these:

1. Don't do jobs that are assigned to others. If inside support personnel have been assigned definite responsibilities, don't handle them. It may take a while to train these workers, but the time savings will continue once they are trained.
2. Communicate clearly, preferably in writing. Salespeople tend to give verbal instructions. Try jotting down the things you want to have accomplished so that inside personnel can proceed with clear objectives.
3. Businesslike handling of your office work saves time.

Service

The best action to take with service time is to convert it to selling time. Servicing the equipment or commercial aspects of your business takes away from your selling effort. We recognize that some servicing is required to maintain customer rapport; it's when a salesperson becomes a service-person that a change in priorities must take place.

Quite a bit of service time is wasted in "clearing up" matters that should have been settled when the order was placed. Bills of material, terms of sale, delivery dates, and other order requirements must be clear and agreed on *before* shipment. Consider a checklist and go over each item with the customer. It saves service time in the future and presents a businesslike appearance to the customer.

If the particular service is the responsibility of someone other than yourself, get that person involved when the service request comes in the first time. If you have a customer service department, use it. Customer service is an essential element in building customer confidence. It should not be neglected, but its time must be controlled.

Personal

The salesperson's job requires a great amount of flexibility. Don't let this flexibility make you fall into the habit of performing personal or family functions within the working day. Consider these positive steps to increase your face-to-face selling time:

- Get up earlier.
- Get your car serviced in the evenings or on Saturdays.
- Run personal errands at night or on the weekends.

Successful salespeople learn to discipline themselves and establish habits that enable them to devote the time necessary to reach their sales objectives.

With a little planning and a lot of determination, sales professionals can become more efficient in their utilization of time. Remember, for the sales professional, the real objective of all time management is to get more time for face-to-face contact with prospects or customers or more time on the telephone in a sales capacity.

CLASSIFYING YOUR ACCOUNTS

All accounts, including those of prospects and customers, should be classified to keep their call frequency as productive as possible. Sales professionals and their management must decide which accounts are most important to their companies. Classifying helps determine this. For every prospect or customer, there is a call frequency that will give you maximum return per call.

It is based on the belief that a greater portion of time should be spent on prospects or customers who offer larger volume potential. Less time should be spent on lower volume prospects or customers.

You will classify your prospects or customers as A, B, and C accounts. A are major accounts; statistically they number about 15 percent of your accounts and give you 65 percent of your volume. The following 20 percent of your accounts are B, or minor accounts. They give you 20 percent of your total sales. Of the remaining prospects or customers, 65 percent are C, or marginal accounts. They give you 15 percent of your total sales. These percentages apply in most industries and are an excellent rule of thumb for determining account classification and setting sales-call frequency.

To help in assessing account volume, we've included a prospect/customer assessment worksheet. This worksheet will help evaluate the potential of your present customers as well as the potential from prospects. You will use this information to help you decide which are your A, B, and C accounts.

In most sales territories, this simple analysis is rather startling. You will probably find that a small number of accounts produces the majority of your sales dollars, whereas a majority of your prospects or customers provide you with a small percentage of your sales. The classic statement that "80 percent of your business comes from 20 percent of your customers" is refined somewhat in the three account classifications.

Preparing the Prospect/Customer Assessment Worksheet

Let's create a hypothetical salesperson who calls on 100 prospects and customers. To help show how the classification works, assume your yearly volume is $1,500,000.

1. List each prospect's or customer's name on the worksheet.
2. Next to each name, write down your present yearly sales.

Let's assume that your largest account is Allright Industries, with present annual sales of $500,000. In column 2 record the total additional potential that Allright represents. In column 3, record what percentage of the total potential you can get. Remember, if you list potential percentage dollars, you must have a sales plan developed to indicate clearly how and what you have to do to get this potential.

Let's assume you show $200,000 as additional potential in column 2 and have a plan to get 50 percent of it. With 50 percent in column 3, the expected sales (column 4) from this potential is $100,000. The total estimated sales would then be $600,000. For effective territorial management and account classification, you should consider Allright Industries a $600,000 per year account. This figure would go in column 5.

Continue this procedure for all your prospects or customers. Account assessments may change from year to year and during the year; hence, professionals continually update their worksheets. Changes that can occur may include accounts moving out of your territory, mergers, new account assignments by management, new products, changes in the marketplace, increased or decreased competition, and so on.

Continually review your account classification to determine if you are going where the business is.

Classifying Your A, B, and C Accounts

When your prospect/customer-assessment worksheet is complete, use the information in column 5 to complete your customer-grading worksheet.

With 100 accounts: For customer Type A, you will show 15 customers in column 1 and 15 percent in column 2, 20 customers and 20 percent for customer Type B, and 65 and 65 percent for customer Type C. Of course, if we had picked more or fewer than 100 accounts for our example, the number of accounts in each type would change. But we would still use the 15 percent, 20 percent, and 65 percent as percentages.

Going back to the example:

1. A accounts (major)—15 percent or 15 accounts with the highest dollar amounts shown in column 5 of your assessment. They normally give 65 percent of your business.
2. B accounts (minor)—20 percent or 20 accounts with the next highest figures. They give 20 percent of your business.
3. C accounts (marginal)—65 percent or 65 accounts which offer the lowest sales or potential. They give 15 percent of your business.

This 15–20–65 split is a rule of thumb and may not fit every situation exactly. The salesperson has to look at his or her list and move borderline accounts up or down to get a more definite separation between groups.

Going back to the assumed annual volume of $1,500,000, note that A accounts give you approximately 65 percent of your business, or $975,000. B accounts give 20 percent of your volume, or $300,000; and C accounts give $225,000.

To emphasize the importance of account classification, let's prepare a chart showing the average sales per customer. (Column 5 in the grading worksheet.)

Account Classification	Number of Accounts	Total Sales in Classification	Average Sales per Customer
A	15	$ 975,000	$ 65,000
B	20	300,000	15,000
C	65	225,000	3,450
TOTALS	100	$1,500,000	

Note: This simple table shows dramatically what you felt all along. Few customers give you most of your business. In fact, one A account gives almost twenty times as much volume as one average C account.

This analysis emphasizes our concern about effective time and territorial management. Most selling time should be spent with type A prospects and customers. Conversely, you may have to allocate less time to the minor or marginal accounts. In many cases, your improvements in time management will enable you to make more calls.

Setting the Call Frequency per Account

Assuming you have 100 accounts that offer a potential yearly volume of $1,500,000, you must average 5 sales calls a day, or 25 a week. In 50 weeks, that's 1,250 calls a year.

The second rule of thumb to use after the 15–20–65 account split is the percentage of allocation of calls based on your account classification, which the following chart illustrates.

Account Classification	Percentage of Prospects or Customers	Percentage of Total Sales	Allocation of Calls
A	15%	65%	35%
B	20%	20%	25%
C	65%	15%	40%

This 35–25–40 percent allocation of calls helps you spend a significant amount of time with your major (A) accounts, while giving you an opportunity to develop your minor (B) and marginal (C) accounts. Try the 35-25-40 percent allocation split on your accounts as a first attempt to set call frequency. You may want to make adjustments to increase or decrease your call frequency on specific accounts later.

Based on this 35–25–40 allocation split, your estimated 1,250 calls per year, and information obtained previously, you can proceed to set the calls per customer as follows:

1. Determine the total number of calls to be made per year in each account classification by multiplying your total number of calls by your allocation percentage.

Account Classification	Total Calls per Year	Allocation of Calls	Total Calls per Classification
A	1,250	.35	438
B	1,250	.25	312
C	1,250	.40	500

2. Next divide the total calls per classification by the number of accounts in that classification to determine the number of sales calls you should make on each account.

Account Classification	Total Calls per Classification	Number of Accounts	Number of Calls per Account
A	438	15	29
B	312	20	16
C	500	65	8
	1,250	100	

You now have the number of sales calls you should make for each account. The A accounts deserve 29 calls per year, or about one every other week.

B accounts get 16 sales calls, or approximately one every 3½ weeks; and C accounts get 8 calls, or about one every 6½ weeks. Call frequencies may vary on some accounts. However, this method is an ideal starting place.

TERRITORIAL MANAGEMENT

Now that you've classified your accounts and come up with a recommended sales-call frequency, you are ready to group your prospects and customers by area and map out your territorial coverage. It's necessary to plot an itinerary consistent with sales potential.

Popular territorial patterns used by sales professionals to cut down traveling time and increase face-to-face selling are the following:

1. *Cloverleaf coverage*—One leaf or quadrant is covered at a time, and a new leaf is covered in each subsequent swing, until the entire territory is covered. Each leaf can take from one day to a week.
2. *Hopscotch coverage*—The salesperson starts at the farthest point from home base and makes account calls on the return home. In large territories, some may fly to reach the farthest points and drive back. Different directions are covered in subsequent trips.
3. *Circular coverage*—This route begins in the home office or the salesperson's home and follows a circle of sales calls which is completed upon return to the starting point.
4. *Straight-line coverage*—The salesperson starts from home base and makes sales calls in one direction to the very end of the territory, and on the return, either goes back along the same line or on a parallel line. Other lines are covered in subsequent trips throughout the territory.

Effective routing comes from trial and error through logging your calls, analyzing the time taken for calls and delays, and so on. A particular territorial routing may be used one month and be changed the next depending on account activity. The professionals keep evaluating what is the best way of getting the most from their travel time.

Plotting Your Coverage and Routing

As an example, we will consider cloverleaf or quadrant coverage. On a map of your territory, locate and mark all your accounts. Use colored felt pens or pins so that you can easily identify your A, B, and C accounts. You want to schedule your calls around solid A accounts every day. Then select B and C accounts that are clustered nearby in the quadrant. The map and your experience will help determine travel time, selling time, and the number of calls to be covered in each day of the week.

On your map you will see how many A, B, and C accounts you have in each quadrant. An inequality may suggest that one or more quadrants be made smaller or larger, or it may be better to divide your territory into fives for each day of the week. Plotting will be your biggest aid in this activity.

After you've plotted your accounts, you know the number of calls you want to make per week. Next, you want to define your weekly trip plan. Start with sales calls to your A accounts; then plan as many B and C calls as necessary to accommodate the call-frequency objectives. The time invested is well worth it by giving you more effective coverage of your territory.

GETTING A RETURN ON TIME INVESTED

After you've established and are following a territorial coverage program, you should continually monitor your results to determine if it's effective. It's important to know if you are getting an equitable return on your time. Let's review a few areas that could help you get a good return on your time. Consider the following:

1. Do you know exactly what you want to accomplish each and every sales call—and are you prepared?

2. Do you spend too much time in the office trying to determine where time can best be spent rather than being out in front of prospects or customers?

3. The best time to *plan* your calls is in the early morning, after hours, or on weekends. Prime selling time, between 9:00 A.M. and 5:00 P.M., should be on face-to-face calls or on the telephone with prospects or customers.

4. Statistically, most of your business comes from a small percentage of your customers. Maintain personal contact with the smaller accounts that have excellent potential and replace those that do not with good prospects. Use the telephone and mail to service the smaller accounts which are too costly for sustained personal sales calls.

5. Use a "Things to Do Today" pad for prioritizing each day's activities. Include sales calls and other "must" accomplishments. Should an event occur that prevents you from achieving this plan, use your checklist to get back on track.

6. Just as business uses the "Return on Capital Employed" (ROCE) to measure its overall efficiency, the professional salesperson should use "Return on Time Invested" (ROTI) to measure efficiency. ROTI is the actual or potential sales divided by the number of hours it takes to maintain or develop each account. This simple equation will establish a return on investment time on each of your accounts to make comparisons of one account versus another.

The improvement a salesperson gets from his or her effort in managing time can be based on the total sales volume or profit on what is sold. Sales management often uses the expression "cost of sales percentage" to evaluate sales effectiveness. Let's say it costs the company $75,000 per year to cover salary, travel and meal expenses, office support, rent, and so forth to support one salesperson. If he or she sells $1,500,000, the ratio of cost ($75,000) to sales ($1,500,000) is five percent. If, by improved time management, he or she increases sales to $1,800,000, with costs staying the same (it would probably go down with less travel), the percentage will go down to 4.17. The lower this percentage, the more the salesperson is doing to earn his or her salary. The same procedure would be followed in measuring cost of profit percentages, using profit instead of sales in the ratio.

The adage *time is money* was never applied to a more meaningful area than sales territorial management.

CONCLUSION

Time has often been referred to as a universal resource. Everyone has the same amount. It cannot be saved and used at a more opportune time. It can only be spent now. Before you can consider how to spend your time more efficiently, it's necessary to see how you are spending it now.

For a week or two, jot down what you are doing and when. Take a close look at your weekly activities and see where you can make improvements. These questions may help:

1. Are you spending time on something less important that could be spent on something more productive? Decide what is important on your list of objectives.
2. Are you spending most of each day moving toward one or another of your sales objectives?
3. Are you putting time and territorial management into your daily and weekly routine?

With a better awareness of where your time is being spent, you will be on the lookout for time wasters and will eliminate them as quickly as possible.

By classifying your accounts by potential volume, you will know where your most productive use of time is and increase the amount of your sales. The results will be immediate and significant, and your diligence will be awarded with success, in monetary gain and in the feeling of fulfillment that comes with knowing you have done your job well.

Review Questions

1. Can anyone really manage time? Explain.
2. Why does it make good business sense to use your time wisely?
3. How does effective planning help you get more time to handle the sales job better?
4. How could logging in how and where you spend your time now help you be more efficient in the future?
5. What sales benefits will you realize if you spend less time in travel?
6. Why is it important to map your territory and pinpoint each account?
7. Why is it important to establish a call frequency for each account?
8. Given a territory with 50 accounts, 8 A, 10 B, and 32 C: A accounts give you 65 percent of your business, B accounts 20 percent, and C accounts 15 percent. If your total sales volume is $875,000, what is your average sales per account?
9. Based on making 1,000 sales calls per year and an A–B–C call allocation split of 35–25–40, how many calls will be made on each account each year? What would be a suggested call frequency?
10. If you cover the previous accounts by being out four days per week, covering a quadrant of your territory each day, what could be a typical weekly routing?

Time-Analysis Worksheet

	MON	TUE	WED	THUR	FRI	SAT
7:00 - 7:30						
7:30 - 8:00						
8:00 - 8:30						
8:30 - 9:00						
9:00 - 9:30						
9:30 - 10:00						
10:00 - 10:30						
10:30 - 11:00						
11:00 - 11:30						
11:30 - 12:00						
12:00 - 12:30						
12:30 - 1:00						
1:00 - 1:30						
1:30 - 2:00						
2:00 - 2:30						
2:30 - 3:00						
3:00 - 3:30						
3:30 - 4:00						
4:00 - 4:30						
4:30 - 5:00						
5:00 - 5:30						
5:30 - 6:00						
EVENING						

Week Beginning_____

Code
TR=Travel
OF=Office, Paperwork
SR=Service
PL=Personal
C=Customer

Add Your Own Symbols as Needed

___ _____

TOTALS

Function	Total Hrs
TR	_____
OF	_____
SR	_____
PL	_____
C	_____

PROSPECT/CUSTOMER-ASSESSMENT WORKSHEET

	1	2	3	4	5
Prospect or Customer's Name	Present Sales ($)	Add'l. Potential	Potential Add'l. Business (%)	Expected Sales (2) x (3)	Total Est'd. Sales (1) + (4)

CUSTOMER-GRADING WORKSHEET

	1	2	3	4	5
Customer Type	Number of Customers	Percent of Total [Divide by Total Customers]	Total Sales	Percent of Total [Divide by Total Sales]	Average Sales per Customer
A					
B					
C					
TOTALS					

module eight
The Sales Interview: Identify Your Best Presentation Approach

This module will cover the two-way communication necessary to get an order. The word *interview* was selected because sales calls, particularly initial calls, must be two-way communication. A series of probing questions and their responses must be made and analyzed before a salesperson can identify the prospect's problem and recommend a solution.

For an effective interview certain actions should be taken before a call. Next these must be followed up with an impressive opening at the sales interview and then the close. Let's start with opening the sales interview.

OPENING THE INTERVIEW

A problem worse than the inability to close a sale successfully is the inability to open one. Professionals continually practice to improve their ability to open the sales interview, to "break the ice."

The opening comments have one purpose: to pave the way for the rest of the interview. It doesn't matter whether the objective of your call is to sell something, perform a service, or pick up information you need. What you say and do in the first few seconds pretty much determines how well (or how badly) things will go during the rest of the interview. Somewhere in the neighborhood of thirty seconds or so, you've got to

1. Clear the prospects' minds of what they were thinking about before you appeared.
2. Plant the idea you want to promote, that is, give them some inkling of the benefits it is possible for them to receive with your help.
3. Gain their confidence and justify the time needed for you to make the rest of your presentation.

That's quite an assignment, but if you're going to make an immediate or future sale, the opening's got to be good enough to

1. Change some ways of thinking the customer has about you or the company.
2. Plant the germ of an idea or recommendation (you'll develop later on in the presentation).
3. Pick up information that only the person you're talking to can provide.
4. Subtly suggest that perhaps you can serve the prospect better than the present supplier.

THE IMPORTANCE OF THE SALES INTERVIEW

When selling large-dollar projects, it's essential that the sales professional have a thorough knowledge of the buyer's organization. All buying influences and decision makers must be identified. The interview must help the salesperson get information on their markets, present suppliers, buying policies, organizational structure, buying influences, what it takes to get an order, and so on.

Some of this information may be attained before the interview through research of annual reports, trade publications, office files, managerial information, or other printed or unprinted sources. Unfortunately, the available information may not be up to date. Hence, the sales professional must obtain an up-to-date report of the prospect's state of affairs. This information is obtained by probing and asking questions in the interview.

The sales interview must establish a two-way communication, a dialogue, between buyer and seller. Usually a sales presentation is more one-way, with the salesperson doing most of the talking. In the sales interview, information is obtained that will help the sales professional decide on what products or services are best suited for this prospect.

The interview can range from one in which the salesperson is merely soliciting information for a future presentation or one in which he or she has the opportunity to review the entire line of products or services to see which creates the most interest. Once the hot button, or responsive chord, is identified, the salesperson can prepare an effective presentation.

Probing provides information about how prospects are presently doing business and what they consider important in their buying decisions. An effective sales interview enables the salesperson to make more meaningful sales points and benefit statements during subsequent sales presentations.

FIVE INTERVIEW OPENERS THAT WORK

To get your interview off to a favorable start, an effective ice-breaker, or "opener," is essential. Following are five opening techniques that you should consider.

1. *Third-party testimonials:* "Mr. Smith, Mr. Bruce of Acme Company, an old friend of yours, purchased equipment from us last year, and claims it does an exceptional job for his firm. I'd like to explore how it can do an exceptional job for your company."

2. *Sincere compliments:* "Mr. Barnaby, I see where your plant just received an award for a new multimillion dollar contract. You must be mighty proud of your efforts."

3. *Customer benefits:* "Today, John, let me show you how to save $3,500 a month on downtime and increase production by 15 percent. You are interested in reducing downtime, aren't you?"

4. *Probing questions:* "Mr. Kibler, what would turnover of 20 percent mean to your distributorship in profits—if it only requires a little extra effort?"

5. *Proof:* "These facts are dramatic proof of the results you can expect with our. . . ."

Each of the techniques for opening is designed to convey your sincerity, demonstrate your personal interest in handling each customer's needs and wants, and stimulate the prospect's desire to hear the rest of your presentation. Note, all the openings have one factor in common: they require careful *precall preparation* if they are to be used successfully. Let's take a closer look at these five openers.

PREPARING TO USE THE FIVE OPENERS

To use the third-party testimonial successfully, be sure to

1. Begin by outlining the prospect's current situation. Then, point out how others solved the problem he or she is now facing. Suggest a solution for which you will provide details later on in the presentation along with background facts and proofs.

2. Introduce a good customer (that you know personally) who is familiar to the prospect. He or she should represent an organization about the same size as that of your prospect. This customer should have a good reputation and be respected, you are sure, by the prospect.

3. Use this technique when you know the prospect faces a tough problem for which a quick solution is necessary.

4. Point out immediately to the prospect that others have faced problems similar to those they are now experiencing—and that a workable solution was found.

5. Make certain the prospect understands you are merely relating a factual, timely parallel of a situation successfully confronted and solved by the third party. The experience should indicate the type of benefits it is possible for this prospect to achieve—with your help and guidance.

Tips on using the sincere compliment follow:

1. Be honest. Demonstrate your honest sincerity by tone of voice, posture, and facial expression.

2. Be appropriate. Negative or unflattering situations are never good possibilities for compliments.

3. Be distinctive. Aim your compliment directly at the prospect. Stress any unusual circumstances surrounding the achievement.

4. Be factual. Nothing can spoil this opening quicker than a personnal compliment that is obviously phony or contrived.

5. Be timely. Focus on current events, not ancient history.

For the customer benefit opening:

1. Arouse the prospect's interest with a benefit you know he or she will be interested in.

2. Familiarize yourself with all important aspects of the prospect's status, business, buying habits, markets, competition, and so on.

3. Convey a definite impression that you can save the prospect money, reduce costs, generate sales, create excitement, increase efficiency, and stimulate productivity.

4. Discuss benefits in general terms, saving the specifics for the presentation which follows.

When using the probing question opening consider the following:

1. Develop logical reasons for the prospect to answer the questions you ask.

2. Know what kind of information you will need from the prospect so that you can frame your questions accordingly.

3. Lead into your questions with remarks covering the importance of such factors as saving money, product conveniences, energy savings, and savings in time and effort.

4. Ask questions conversationally, not like a lawyer firing away at a reluctant witness. Avoid questions that cause anger, create fears, or seem to challenge the prospect.

5. Probe with open-ended questions that can't be answered with a simple "yes" or "no" to determine the prospect's familiarity with your product line, attitude toward you and your company, needs, wants, problems, opportunities, and desires. Direct questions can be asked later when you have a better understanding of the prospect's problems and possible solutions.

6. Tie in the customer's responses to your questions to the balance of the presentation. Very often the manner in which prospects answer questions reveals their true inner feelings, their hot buttons.

Successful use of the proof opening requires that you

1. Make certain the proof offered is timely, accurate, and ties in with the situation faced by the prospect.

2. Introduce proof at the very beginning of the call when the prospect appears to be timid, doubtful, suspicious, or uncertain.

3. Be brief and to the point.

4. Make use of this opening when it is known that the customer is practical; feels more comfortable dealing with facts and figures; wants proof of performance at the very outset; and seeks specific values and benefits for himself or herself, family, business, or customers.

5. Utilize documents such as records, reports, letters, data, photographs, charts, and graphs.

A FEW MORE IDEAS
TO GET THE INTERVIEW UNDERWAY

It's been said that an impression is made within the first twenty or thirty seconds of a meeting. This is when the sales professional has to gain the prospect's attention. A convenient way to do so is to open with a benefit statement and a question that answers the prospect's or customer's question, namely, "What's in it for me?" Or, how will the product or service that this person wants to talk to me about help me and/or my company? The salesperson's initial statement, questions, or comments should always be related to a benefit that the prospect can enjoy, based on what other customers are now enjoying.

At the outset, salespeople should strive to get as many "yes" responses, or positive signals, as possible. They can get these positive responses by asking questions that obviously demand an affirmative indication. Some opening questions that may be used can be the following:

- "Mr. Jones, the purpose of my call is to ask you a few questions that would help me better understand your current needs and how I can serve them. Do you have a few minutes now?"
- "What type of product or services are you presently using?"
- "Are you familiar with our company and our products and services?"
- "What made you decide to buy from that company?"
- "What information do you need before you put a supplier on the bid list?"
- "Have you heard of some of the many customers that we have satisfied with our products and service?
- "Wouldn't it be nice if we were able to save 20 percent of your energy costs in the coming year?"

When meeting a prospect or customer, the sales professional always looks the person in the eye and extends the right hand for a firm handshake. When meeting a prospect for the first time, give him or her a calling card and make sure you get the prospect's name and title, the spelling, and the correct pronunciation. Don't hestitate to have a person pronounce his or her name slowly as you repeat it until you have it right.

The salesperson makes the interview call with the intention of learning more about the prospect. Usually, if prospects don't feel that the salesperson will ask for an order, they will be more open and responsive. It's necessary for prospects to be at ease and open during the interview. A successful interview will conclude when the salesperson and prospect open lines of communication that result in future meetings where an effective sales presentation can be made. This results in a win/win attitude that can be of benefit to both parties.

ICE-BREAKERS TO TRY

A salesperson uses an ice-breaker to warm up the prospect and break the ice that may exist between two strangers when meeting for the first time.

The ice-breaker can be a statement, comment, or question made at the outset of the interview. Let's consider a few more ice-breaking approaches you can try.

1. *Humorous approach.* You can try to get the prospect in a pleasant frame of mind with a humorous one-liner or a brief story. Of course, before you consider a humorous approach, you must feel natural and comfortable. It can't be forced. *Reader's Digest, Quote,* and other magazines and newspapers contain many quips, anecdotes, and humorous articles, and of course, there are many books in the library on humor. It's not necessary to be a comic or humorist to be effective in presenting a humorous story. However, you must feel comfortable. If you could refer to something humorous or unique about your business, product, or service, or the prospect's product or service, the humor may provide an ideal ice-breaker. When using humor, or any approach, avoid personal references, politics, sex, or religion if you are unfamiliar with the prospect's beliefs.

2. *Topical subject approach.* Initial discussion about the weather; popular hobbies; sporting events; or local, national, or international states of affairs can always be used to get the interview underway. Of course, the observant sales professional will notice photographs, memorabilia, awards, or other trophies in the prospect's office. They all provide material for initial comment to establish rapport.

3. *Industry-or business-related approach.* Of course any newspaper or magazine article or recent announcement relating to your business or industry can be a very effective way to break the ice. Openers may start out with a question:

- o "What do you think about . . . ?
- o "Did you like the way that . . . ?
- o "Did you see the recent article in the . . . ?
- o "Did you read how . . . ?

Industry- or business-related topics are normally well received because your prospect recognizes that the information may help him or her become more aware.

CONCLUSION

The salesperson that develops a systematic approach to the sales interview has a better chance to succeed. A good initial interview gives the salesperson the answers necessary to follow up with a sales presentation, a sales plan, and the basics for future strategy.

Review Questions

1. You are planning your first call on a prospect, what do you consider to be part of your precall planning?

2. How could information on what you've sold to similar prospects and the approaches you used help?

3. Write out how you will open the interview with your prospect, say Mr. Kramer. Explain why it will clear his mind of the previous activities he was working on.

4. What other approach will you try if this opener doesn't work?

5. Prepare a typical opening dialogue between you, the sales professional, and a prospective buyer.

6. Select a product you don't sell now but would like to, and write out five openers (ice-breakers), using third-party testimonial, sincere compliment, customer benefit, probing questions, and proof.

7. Write a list of ten sources for important market, industry, or other business trends or activity could be researched about the product.

8. How can you tell if the sales interview was successful? What information should you leave with? What should be the buyer's disposition?

9. List at least ten important pieces of information the salesperson should have at the conclusion of the interview.

10. How does the salesperson use the interview information to help in future sales calls and product presentations?

11. Why does an effective interview set the stage for future relationships between buyers and sellers?

Note: Many of the buyer-salesperson situations just outlined can be used in role-playing activity for added emphasis.

module nine
Your Time "On Stage": The Sales Presentation

When salespeople are in front of a prospect or customer, rehearsals are over. They are now "on stage"; it's show time, the time to give their best performance.

A sales presentation might well be defined as a vehicle for conveying to a prospect or customer an understanding of something the salesperson is attempting to interest them in. The presentation can be in words alone, or as a way to obtain more understanding; an appeal to additional senses by more dramatic means: photographs, audio-visual aids, models, samples, flip charts, sales bulletins, or similar items which are generally classified under the names of sales tools or sales aids. They are used in a well-done presentation. A sales aid is simply any person, place, or thing that helps the salesperson get an order, or get close to one.

A good presentation is an essential part of professional salesmanship. Explaining the benefits of the product or service is at the very core of the selling process.

If a presentation is to be effective, it must:

- Get the customer's attention.
- Ask questions to determine clearly needs and wants.
- Establish interest in the offering.
- Answer relevant questions and handle possible clarifications.
- Touch all essential bases.
- Create desire to buy.
- Achieve objectives.

For each presentation to achieve results, it must offer a benefit to prospective customers and get them to want to take the positive action you suggest.

The feature, function, and benefit of your product or service must be important considerations in the development of your presentation. The development of a presentation based on this technique helps strengthen the acceptance of an offering because it emphasizes the benefits to the prospect or customer.

PLANNING— THE KEY TO A SUCCESSFUL PRESENTATION

Sales professionals know that the level of their success is a direct yardstick of their ability to plan: planning to meet their objectives, planning the daily use of time, and planning an effective sales presentation.

The conclusion of an effective sales presentation is when the prospect or customer believes in your product or service and is prepared to act in a manner you suggest.

The key planning consideration for a presentation is the information on that account that you've recorded from your prospect list, previous telephone contact, or interviewing meeting.

REVIEW OF THE FEATURE-FUNCTION-BENEFIT PRESENTATION

Sales professionals know and show features of their products or service, and are able to describe how each feature works. They explain its function in language the listener understands. But most important they emphasize every possible benefit relating to the feature and function. A benefit should be in terms of dollar savings, profit, cost reduction, sales increase, health and safety improvements, or another measureable or emotional value that interests the prospect or customer.

To have the feature-function-benefit presentation give the desired results, you must have a thorough knowledge of your product or service, your customer's business, and personal communication skills. Product knowledge is basic.

EMPHASIZE CUSTOMER BENEFITS

Obviously, each feature of a product or service makes an important part of a well-prepared presentation. The benefits of each feature (telling what the feature will do) are essential and must be included in any presentation. Ultimately, each feature must be turned into a benefit, which is an explanation of the feature and the advantages for the customer.

The individual making the presentation should watch for the listener's response to determine whether some key issue hits a responsive chord. The customer's wants and desires, as determined by reactions to the benefits mentioned, should be used as guides to stress some areas and play down others. The past experiences of the customer, if known, are effective guides to those things which will probably be of most interest.

A presentation using a hit-and-miss method, even though it includes all the features and benefits, leaves much to be desired. A presentation which has benefits presented only in the order of their magnitude and importance will lack logic. Therefore, in a presentation the benefits should be stressed in logical sequence with primary emphasis placed on their order of magnitude and importance to this prospect or customer at this time. Time permitting, minor points can be included in their proper position in the presentation.

MOTIVATING BUYING

The purpose of your presentation is to motivate buying. The point to remember is that you must take the initiative and ask for an order. The prospect will not close the sale for you. If your presentation has aroused enough interest, you will get buying signals; be alert for them.

To motivate buying you must relate and appeal to *this* prospect at *this* time. You must consider the prospect's experience, education, position, and business or personal objectives or tailor your presentation accordingly. Your products or services may appeal to a broad classification of people, all for different reasons. The professional determines what motivates this prospect and stresses personalized benefits in planned presentations, not canned presentations.

You can make your presentation more effective by making it appear as if it were tailor-made for your prospect. Personalize some of your sales material by writing your prospect's name on it. For example, if you have a catalog price list or other material you want to leave with a prospective buyer, write or print his or her name on it. Some professionals insert a front page in their presentation on which they note that it was specifically prepared for Mr. Prospect. When you personalize your sales material, you make sure your prospects understand that you've been thinking specifically about them and their business problem and that you have something worth their time and attention.

A SUREFIRE FORMULA TO GET ATTENTION

There are two points that will pave the way to favorable attention. They will achieve results—use them.

1. When you talk to prospective customers, appeal to their innate curiosity.
2. Plan your talk so it highlights customer benefits.

1. *The grabber*—Arouse initial interest with an opening statement or question that will demand attention. It emphasizes a customer benefit and asks a question.
2. *Why bring that up?*—Answer the question you brought up.
   a. Bridge the gap between the benefit you mention and the client's business.
   b. Use the *you* formula: "When *you* enjoy these benefits it will mean. . . ."
   c. Tie in a and c with your second sentence, which highlights your product or service.
   d. Explain how your proposition will help the customer and how it ties in with the objective of your call.
3. *For instance*—This should be the body of your presentation. These are the most important words you can use here.
   a. Use these words once a minute and it wouldn't be too often.
   b. Commit yourself to telling a story or presenting a concrete example.
   c. Completely handle one "for instance" at a time in an orderly fashion.
   d. Present examples in logical sequence.
   e. Never return to a point covered before except for a brief summary.
   f. Don't repeat yourself in the body of your presentation; however, cover everything thoroughly.
4. *So what*—This is the reason for your presentation and why you want the listener to act.
   a. Get the order now or determine what it takes to get the order.
   b. Don't hope or hint for your desired results—*ask*.

Visualizing yourself as a lecturer and your prospective customer as an audience will squeeze out unnecessary words and actions from your presentation and bring results.

The exact amount of time it takes for an effective presentation will vary with your product or service, customer involvement, and questions. You should determine ahead of time the length of time needed for a complete presentation. We know that occasionally a presentation developed to take one hour may have to be presented in abridged version in ten to thirty minutes. Situations may arise in which the listener asks for a presentation in the reception room with some statement like, "Show me what you have." Obviously, these circumstances require salesmanship of a high order to get the necessary time and suitable spot for the presentation. Say, "Mr. Jones, what I'd like to discuss can save your company thousands of dollars. Let's pick a better time for our meeting! Will 2:00 P.M. tomorrow afternoon or 9:00 A.M. the next day be better?"

In order for you to put on an effective presentation, *you must have favorable attention.* This is achieved within the first thirty seconds you spend with the prospect.

This critical introductory time will decide if you get the necessary attention when presenting what you have to offer.

Once you get the prospective customer's attention, he or she is in a positive, receptive mood. You can start to point out benefits you can offer, benefits that satisfy basic motivational drives—pride, profit, fear, love, duty, and hate. Don't start discussing your products or service. Start highlighting what your offering will do to give more profit, protect their investments, reduce expenses, stimulate pride or increase efficiency. Buying decisions are made when prospective customers envision themselves enjoying the benefits you describe. The product or service you offer is the means to the end. It is not the end.

Once you've recognized the benefits the prospect is interested in, you can proceed to outline how your product or service can help realize these benefits. Asking probing questions that appeal to basic motivators is a skill that all salespeople must master if they want to be successful in the sales profession.

With the proper attention, the next step is to present the product or service effectively.

TECHNIQUES THAT WILL HELP CREATE THE BEST PRESENTATION

Interest-arousing and challenging openings will frequently help get proper attention. The use of questions is an effective technique both to get the customers' viewpoint and to make certain the products and service fit their needs and solve their problems. The use of vivid words of description will increase the understanding of examples you use. Creating images with words, wherever possible, will also make the listening experience more pleasant. Describing products or services and their features, advantages, and benefits in terms of a listener's experience will make them understood.

GETTING THE CUSTOMER INVOLVED

One of the most effective means of making a periodic appraisal of the degree of interest and understanding is to get client participation in some fashion. One effective means is the use of questions, properly phrased, to bring customers directly into the discussion to determine their viewpoint. Statements which are deliberately made to challenge and to get them to state their feelings can frequently be used to determine buying interest. Customer participation could well be solicited at all stages—start, middle, and end—of a presentation. Proper planning should include customer participation.

USING SHOWMANSHIP
TO MAKE YOUR PRESENTATION COME ALIVE

A bit of drama in sales presentation can be a very effective sales technique. In this age of electronics—of television, instant replay, and electronic games and productions—customers are very aware of and constantly being bombarded with many types of electronic gadgets. Although we normally do not spend the same amount of time and money as a television production, we can add a bit of showmanship to make our presentation more effective. Don't hestitate to be dramatic as long as it's in good taste.

A bit of showmanship pays off because it helps imprint important points on the prospect's or customer's mind. A sales presentation can include product demonstrations; visuals of many types; and printed materials such as brochures, charts, graphs, and letters. All these items emphasize desirable benefits. The intent of all the sales aids you may use is to hold the prospect's attention and make a favorable impression about your product, your service, and you.

The more senses the prospect or customer uses during your presentation, the more likely he or she is to remember what you talked about. Statistically, we retain 2 percent of what we hear, 10 percent of what we read, 30 percent of what we see, and 40 percent of what we see and hear together.

The use of any of the tools mentioned is only effective when the following requirements are met:

1. The sales aid should be a natural part of the sales presentation, not something that is the main attraction. All the visuals, demonstrations, samples, or printed material are for reinforcing what is being said and demonstrated.

2. The aids should qualify the points discussed and not confuse them. Visuals and demonstrations should illustrate a particular product feature and its associated benefit so that the customer can logically draw a favorable conclusion.

3. Where possible, the presentation should involve the customers so they can relate to it and come up with the conclusion themselves.

4. If the demonstration is intended for a customer's desk or table top, make sure you bring a piece of felt or heavy material to place on the desk to avoid any scratches. A scratch caused by a sharp object on a customer's desk not only loses attention but also may antagonize.

5. Make sure the demonstration is a part of the presentation, but not the only part. The demonstration should not replace the salesperson. Demonstrations are used to illustrate the particular points that require more emphasis. All demonstrations should show the feature involved and how it functions, and more importantly, it should clearly emphasize the benefit in terms that are meaningful to the customer, such as profitability, convenience, and safety.

6. Where possible, a customer should become part of the demonstration by either starting and stopping the equipment, seeing and touching a sample, and so on.

7. Demonstrations should be simple and to the point.

8. Make sure your point is one that customers recognize as being an objective they want to see and will accept.

When using printed materials consider the following:

1. Make sure that what you are planning to use ties in with the overall objectives of your sales call.

2. Make sure you are familiar with the literature you are about to show so that if any questions are raised regarding its content, you are able to answer.

USING VISUAL AIDS TO HELP YOUR PRESENTATION

Many visual aids could be used in a presentation. The following suggestions will help you be more effective when using an audio-visual program:

1. Set up equipment beforehand whenever possible. If it requires a screen be sure it is in place and make sure the film is available. Note the location and type of electrical outlet. Is it the proper voltage? It's very convenient to keep an extension cord with you in case the electrical outlet is far from the table where the projector will be mounted. If the projector is rented from a hotel or convention center, be sure it is in place and you, personally, inspect it and try it before your presentation.

2. Check the audio system to make sure that everyone will be able to hear your presentation. Once the equipment is in place, be sure it is in focus, it is running smoothly, and the audio is set at the proper level.

3. Run through your slides or overheads to be certain they are in the right sequence and placed in the slide tray properly.

4. Check the location of the light switch so that you will be able to use it conveniently.

5. Carry a spare lamp in case you have a bulb failure.

6. If during your visual presentation you want to stop for a discussion, use a curtain or black slide so there is nothing distracting on the screen. This keeps the attention on you, the presenter.

Flip charts and a blackboard can be very conveniently used by a professional salesperson because they can, in logical sequence, highlight all the areas that should be covered in a sales presentation. Remember these pointers:

1. Have enough chalk and an eraser handy.
2. Print big enough for everyone to see.
3. Talk as you print so that there is no loss in communication.
4. Stand to the side as you are printing so as not to have your back to the group. Where possible, underline, circle, or use stars to highlight particular points.
5. When using a large chart, start each new idea with a new page. If it's necessary to refer back to a page already used, it's wise to carry a large role of masking tape to tape the papers to the wall, or use push pins and affix them to a cork wall if that is what is in the room.
6. When using a blackboard erase the previous words, then start a new idea.

You should always have a clean pad, felt pen, and pencils so ideas can be written, emphasized, and discussed across the desk from a prospect. This gives you the opportunity to amplify some specific details of the presentation; draw layouts and dimensions; and sketch products, ideas, or points of interest. In addition, if items have to be discussed later on or additional people are involved, you can jot down their names and why they are interested in your sales presentation.

The sales professional knows what sales tools to use and what are available that could be of benefit in a sales presentation. When you sell visually, you get the customer involved and it makes an impression that's lasting. Outstanding salespeople continually use showmanship to make their sales presentation more successful. When prospects are using their eyes, ears, and hands, they are obviously more involved, making the sales presentation more meaningful.

CONCLUSION

The creation of an effective sales presentation is a real challenge. The presentation must be flexible because it will be made to people with different backgrounds. It will be used for various purposes, from arousing interest for getting orders to showing company versatility for future business or to establishing a favorable corporate image. The benefits inherent to the product or service must be brought out and tied in to the customer's experiences to appeal to specific needs, wants, desires, and problems. The key points made must be presented with full consideration of logical sequence and order of magnitude and importance.

The presentation must be built around the various sales tools available to make it more understandable to the customer and to increase desire for the product.

Sufficient flexibility must be incorporated in the sales presentation to permit its being told to a variety of people, in a variety of settings, varying from a long to a short time. The customer's available time must guide the time a presentation takes or the types of devices which may be included.

The task of creating an effective presentation is a continuing one; it is never final and complete. Modifications and polishing are always in order to suit it to the different uses to which it will be put and to keep it up to date with product modifications that are taking place. In this lies the challenge of the creation of a useful and effective presentation.

You must remember that the sales presentation is really your time on stage. Be prepared.

Review Questions

1. Explain why some consider the sales presentation the most important part of the selling function.
2. What plans and actions should be taken before making a sales presentation?
3. How does product feature-function-benefit-proof details give the salesperson confidence when making a presentation?
4. Explain the significance of emphasizing customer benefits in a sales presentation.

5. Why is it necessary to get favorable immediate attention when starting a sales presentation?

6. Name five techniques that can be used to make a presentation come alive and be more memorable.

7. Pick a product or service and prepare a separate sales presentation to each of the following: (a) president of a multinational manufacturing company, (b) accounting manager of a hospital, (c) purchasing agent of an electrical utility, (d) buyer for a government agency, (e) maintenance manager of a large office complex, (g) personnel manager of a major airline.

module ten
Creative
Sales Strategies
and Tactics

There are many steps required to service large accounts successfully. The ultimate purpose of good customer service is to build business rapport that encourages the prospect to buy from you. In this module, emphasis is placed on analyzing the importance of the purchasing function and other departments within a prospect's organization to identify the buying influences (where and how the prospect buys its products and services). Once these influences are identified, the sales professional must then determine the best course of action to take to get this business. You must consider the most effective overall strategy and then identify the specific action plans and tactics necessary to achieve your objectives.

It's important to recognize the significant part team selling plays when calling on larger accounts where there are many buying influences.

In this module, significant emphasis is placed on the hazardous areas or low wires that a salesperson may face on significant projects. The salesperson should identify possible ways to lose an order and then make sure to cover that base so the order is not lost, but won. Remember, there may be individuals in the buyer's organization who can't give you an order but who can prevent you from getting one.

The importance of knowing your product or service, knowing the markets, knowing your customers, and knowing professional selling skills tied in with the proper attitude cannot be overemphasized. It is the key in coming up with effective sales strategies and tactics. The outline form at the end of this module will help you organize your strategies and tactics.

149

SALES STRATEGIES AND TACTICS

When selling capital goods, large projects, detailed systems, personal development, insurance or health programs, or other services that require extensive discussions between the buyers and suppliers, more than one sales call is usually required. A sale may finally be made after many calls and much probing. Large offerings may take weeks, months, or years between the time of initial contact to the receipt of an order.

To sell effectively in this environment, it's necessary to recognize the importance of teamwork within the organization, to analyze how the prospect looks at the salesperson, and to understand the buying sequence within the prospect's organization. When the professional recognizes these and other factors, a program of positive action can be initiated. This program establishes what strategies and tactics are required to get the order. Let's define these terms as they relate to the sales profession. A strategy is identifying a course of action to achieve a desired sales objective with a prospect or customer. Its ultimate objective must be to get an order. *Tactics* are the actions or methods taken to carry out the strategy. What must be done to get the order?

A LOOK AT REASONING, LOGIC, AND EMOTIONS

The sales professional probes for problem areas, then makes a presentation and offering leading to an order. The objective is to convince and persuade prospects or customers that the offering can solve their problems. A very effective method of having an offering believed is by appealing to the prospect's senses and by using reasoning and logic while recognizing that emotions may be the ultimate deciding factor.

Although many buyers respond favorably to logical presentations, they may ultimately buy because of their emotions. They are emotionally satisfied that the sales professionals and their companies can supply their needs and wants. The buyer is content. The buyer believes. Salesmanship has often been described as the art and science of getting someone else to believe in the same thing you believe in.

To make the buyer a believer, attitude, sales presentation, and strategies and tactics must start with a truthful benefit statement or question of what is to be proven or shown. Then,

1. The buyer must accept it as true without an argument.
2. The salesperson must then follow with a series of benefit statements and

questions derived from answers to questions or previous comments to prove the initial point.

3. In the message, the salesperson emphasizes the specific benefits that the prospects and their companies can enjoy when they own the equipment or start the service.

4. The buyer trusts and believes the salesperson and has a desire to possess the product or service. This leads to emotional satisfaction and an order. Salespeople must adjust their probing, interviewing, and sales presentation techniques to establish the best strategy and tactics to fit the buyer's logical and emotional reactions. Whether the salesperson puts these strategies and tactics in writing or not, the thought process must still follow from general probing to specific strategies and tactics.

SELLING NEW CONCEPTS

Concept selling is one of the toughest challenges a salesperson can face. It is the selling of an idea, product, or service which is new or a different approach to an old problem. It is difficult selling new concepts because it requires a prospect or customer to change a habit. Habits are repetitive reactions to a similar set of circumstances and are hard to break. Typical reactions are these: "It has been this way for years, why change now?" or "My boss put in that system ten years ago and I don't want to be the one to suggest a change."

In concept selling, the salesperson must be prepared with extensive product and market knowledge to make specific salespoints. Before contacting any prospects or customers, the salesperson should prepare the answers to the following questions:

1. What areas needed improvement in previously available products or services?

2. Why are these improvements important now?

3. Upon what basis (surveys, reports, requests, government regulations, new inventions, research discovery), did your company decide to venture into these new areas?

4. How much research, development, and testing were involved prior to going on the market with the new product or service?

5. What assurances can you give that the new product or service will work as described?

The salesperson that introduces a new (concept) product or service must be equipped with these answers to be able to convince a prospect or customer. New concepts show advances in the state of the art by progressive companies. Prospects like to deal with forward-thinking suppliers as long as the salesperson can demonstrate product and market knowledge, to show how and where it can be used, to help solve the prospect's or customer's problems.

SYSTEMATIC APPROACH
TO SALES STRATEGIES AND TACTICS

Establishing sales strategies and tactics can follow from the consideration of many sources—gut feelings, other people's experiences, a flash of inspiration, or an organized system of analyzing the buying and selling process.

Let's start by considering the four key areas of involvement that the salesperson may face in the buying and selling process.

1. *The buying cycle*—We analyze the role of the prospect and identify all the steps that may take place when a product or service is bought.
2. *Key buying influences*—As sales professionals, we must identify key buying influences in the buying cycle.
3. *Selling Tools*—We identify the selling tools and aids available to us and decide which we should use at each step.
4. *Hazardous areas*—We identify areas that may prevent us from getting an order and take corrective action.

By considering these key areas in the buying and selling process, a salesperson has a guide to selling tactics. Most salespeople enter the situation after the prospect has already taken certain buying steps. The salesperson has to identify this step to be able to respond. Then, an analysis of previous actions is made and strategies and tactics are established to influence future action.

A CLOSE LOOK AT A COMPLETE BUYING CYCLE

To better understand where the sales professional may enter and start to sell, let's identify some of the major steps that take place in the buying cycle.

1. *Identification of needs.* Companies or individuals identify their needs or wants. They may consider new plant construction, building expansion, more or different products or services, new markets, supplier improvements, value-analysis program, and so on and decide to do "something" about it. That is, they recognize that they have a problem (whether they admit it or not).

2. *Consideration of alternative solutions.* Companies or individuals review their problem and consider possible solutions. They may analyze what is required, such as new tooling, additional personnel, increased facilities, finances, higher return on investment, market potential, new departments, new equipment, or new services.

In this phase of the buying cycle, a decision is made by management to proceed, and a timetable is established, or the project is rejected. We'll assume the former. The individuals and departments that are involved all become part of the buying chain. Operations, personnel, finance, installation, purchasing, engineering, and other support activities are brought together, and objectives and procedures are established.

3. *Review of available products, services, and consultants.* Once the objectives are set and the buying team established, a review is made as to what companies or individuals can supply the products and services required. Consideration may be given to whether the technical, commercial, or other operational advice and support can be accomplished in-house or if an outside consultant is required. An analysis of the suppliers and consultants used in the past for similar purchases are considered to determine if their performance was acceptable or if new sources should be evaluated.

4. *Analysis of sources.* To determine acceptable suppliers, buyers may contact any member of the buying team. For listings of suppliers they can look up national trade organizations, books and registers of manufacturers, or the yellow pages. They will rely heavily on their own purchasing records and input from company members for recommendations and references. A list of acceptable suppliers is then prepared.

5. *Preparation of specifications.* Technical, commercial, and other specifications must be prepared either in-house or by an outside consultant. A clear description of the product, systems, or materials required must be generated. Manpower requirements may be discussed at this time. Specifications are prepared so the purchaser can get the required quality, quantity, and uniformity in the products or services received. Technical specifications, essential for competitive bidding may contain details on appropriate codes and standards for materials, installation, and so on. Commercial specifications may include pricing details, warranties, terms of payment, type of delivery, and shipment requirements. Occasionally, a buyer, in order to get the best proposals, may indicate what items must be supplied as specified and what items can be altered or substituted. A procedure for evaluating competitive proposals and reviewing alternatives is usually established at this time.

6. *Request for quotation.* The purchasing or other involved department takes the list of acceptable suppliers and sends out a request for quotation transmittal. This usually includes the name and/or reference of the project, specifications of the equipment or services required, and other commercial terms and details necessary.

7. *Prebid meetings.* Before suppliers send in an offering or quotation, they may be called in, either individually or as a group, to review the specifications and discuss the request for quotation. This is sometimes called a prebid conference. Questions can usually be asked by potential bidders. The buying company also takes that opportunity to go over any technical or commercial areas which require clarification or elaboration. The buyer may ask for details about the bidders' ability to supply the equipment or services required. Request for samples, testimonial letters, factory or installation visits, and other graphic or verbal facts may be demanded to prove that the bidders are able to supply what is required.

8. *Notices of bidding change.* Occasionally during a buying cycle, possibly following a prebid meeting, changes to the specifications are made. In order to advise all the bidders of these changes, a change notice is normally sent. When this happens, the bid due date is normally extended so that the suppliers can prepare their offerings in line with the revised specifications.

9. *Submission and evaluation of offerings.* Upon receipt of all the proposals or quotations, the buying committee starts to review the submittals. Some firms have a policy requiring that technical or operational evaluations be made separate from the pricing and commercial evaluation. The operations or technical group will look for favorable responses to their specifications. The purchasing personnel, legal, and commercial group will be concerned about their requirements. Evaluations are usually made on the technical and commercial merits of the offering. A well-prepared offering will appeal to all evaluators.

10. *Selection of preferred supplier.* After evaluation and review by the members of the buying committee, a bid evaluation sheet is usually prepared. This sheet will highlight significant details of each supplier's offering. Included are price, delivery, exceptions to specifications, alternates proposed, and all other technical and commercial terms necessary for proper evaluation. A decision may be made to call in the supplier who has the most favorable evaluation to negotiate an order, or several suppliers may be called in.

11. *Negotiations.* Vendors that have submitted acceptable offerings may be called in to negotiate. Any or all of the technical and commercial terms are possible topics of discussion. Areas for negotiation can include increases or decreases in quantity, raised or lowered standards, previews of software or accessories, installation or maintenance service, variances to specifications, shipment dates, terms of payment, warranties, and price. There is virtually an unlimited number of areas that can be negotiated for the astute buyer and seller.

12. *Decision to buy.* Once negoations are completed, a selection is made by the buying committee or project team, and purchase orders are issued.

We've identified twelve steps that can be part of what we call the buying cycle in project buying. When you call on a prospect for the first time, you have to probe to find out where you are in the buying cycle. Then you can plan your strategies and tactics.

BUYERS OF ALL SIZES

The owner of a small business may decide one morning to increase productivity by adding a new piece of equipment. He or she may telephone a preferred supplier or two, tell them what is wanted, get a verbal quotation, and place an order before noon. That's a buying cycle. The only positive action sales representatives could have taken in that situation was to make sure they have established themselves as a preferred supplier before the owner decided that new equipment was needed.

On the other end of the scale, a large industrial company, a utility, or a bank that has many people and departments involved in the buying cycle, could include in their considerations for capital purchases appropriations committees, board of directors, real-estate transactions, labor unions, building permits, contractors, and consultants. Also involved could be buying influences from many departments. The timetable from identification of needs to a decision to buy can extend over many months or years. Sales representatives must identify where they enter the buying cycle so they can start to plan strategies and tactics. The salesperson, after getting a prospect to become a customer, by building rapport, will know about future purchases before they go out for bid. The professional salesperson will be a strong influence in the specifications prepared by customers.

THE IMPORTANCE OF KNOWING
ALL KEY BUYING INFLUENCES

All prospects or customers have individuals who are the decision makers. The salesperson who identifies them finds the key buying influences at the same time. Key buying influences are the members of a prospect's or customer's organization who decide what product or service to buy and from whom. Knowing these buying influences and building rapport with them is essential for effective sales coverage. In order to determine strategies and tactics, it's necessary for the sales professional to identify each department and individual in those departments that make key buying decisions. Some suggestions for identifying these key buying influences are the following:

1. Look at a prospect's organization charts. If none can be obtained, make your own chart showing departments that may be influential in one or more of the buying steps.
2. Next to the department name, write down the names and exact titles of the department manager, assistant managers, or other key individuals.
3. Set up a schedule of appointments to visit these people to determine their contribution to the buying decision, their needs and wants, supplier preferences, past experiences in similar projects, and so on.

REACHING THE KEY BUYING INFLUENCES

The prospect's decision to make a project purchase invariably touches a great many people, particularly when a large investment in time and money is required and the purchase has a significant impact on the prospect's business.

Key buying influences are at different position levels and have varying job responsibilities within the prospect's business. The final decision may be based on a group's or committee's recommendation. With this in mind, the sales professional must make certain that any offering appeals to individuals from several different backgrounds, education, experience, goals, objectives, needs, wants, and methods of decision making.

The involved departments and the buying influences vary from account to account; hence, the salesperson must develop the talent to locate them quickly. Influence by different departments may change within an account, depending on the type of equipment or service considered, the dollar value of the project, or other factors. Salespeople must continually probe and research the account to be sure they are up to date on who are the buying influences. Sometimes they may have to go over the head or around an obstructive buying influence. They should decide on this course of action only after they recognize that there is nothing to lose. That is, if they don't try, the sale is lost anyway. Offending *any* buying influence should be avoided if at all possible. If they go around someone and are successful, the offended person may make it impossible for them to get any future business. They shouldn't win a battle and lose the war.

Educational background, position, and individual style can help a salesperson determine factors concerning how and what prospects consider important before they decide. An executive with an engineering degree will probably follow a different road than one with an accounting or legal background. Marketing and sales executives will have still another viewpoint. Some will want many details; others, a summary of facts. Some are partial to a verbal presentation; others prefer concise offerings in writing; still others may respond to an audio-visual presentation.

A certain group will be interested in the latest technology and state of the art. Style and image, or esthetics, may appeal rather than details on function. Understanding these personality differences in the buying influence and responding properly will make the difference in closing a sale.

The *perceived value* of the product or service offered will depend on the buying influences involved. Each person will assess the product or service for the impact it will have on his or her area of responsibility.

Since the buying decision hits at the heart of a business, it is the responsibility of the sales professional to relate carefully the product's sales points to each person's responsibilities and concerns. Remember, buyers do not leave their human instincts at a consumer marketplace— they are extended to their business purchasing decisions as well. By identifying human factors early in the buying cycle, a salesperson will be able to develop a selling approach to win over each individual involved in the purchasing decision.

CONSIDERING WHAT SALES AIDS WILL HELP

Consideration must be given to all the selling tools and aids you have available to help convince the key influences. Review your literature for information that makes specific reference to the equipment or service you are offering. If you are going to hand or send it out, circle this information with a felt pen or highlighter for emphasis. Consider using satisfied customers' testimonials, installation and application photos, advertising reprints, samples, cutaways, technical articles, charts, or graphs, dimensions, return on investment figures, and so on to emphasize the key benefits of your products or services. Review your presentation manual and literature for any information that could help. Think about using an audio-visual program that shows and tells about operational procedures, detailed close-ups, plant and manufacturing locations, or other important details.

You may consider making a sales call with support from other individuals in your company (that is, technical, commercial, or other managerial people who can help your presentation). Their presence can reinforce some of the sales points you have made or suggest additional benefits. To emphasize equipment quality, you may consider a visit with this prospect to one of your manufacturing facilities or to a typical installation. To emphasize satisfied service, you may consider a visit to one of your customers.

Anything that can reinforce your presentations should be considered. Remember, each buying influence will respond to different stimulus. Technicians may want data, specifications, bills of material, lists of engineering comments and exceptions, performance curves, charts and graphs, references to appropriate standards, weights, dimensions. The operations or maintenance people may want details on installation, testing, servicing and repairs, performance characteristics, parts. Purchasing departments want to know all the details of the commercial offering, names of other satisfied customers, and reliability of your commitments. Management is primarily interested in return on investment and how the equipment and/or service fits into the overall corporate objectives. Personnel may be interested in how it effects health, welfare, training, and insurance plans. Each department may react to different stimuli, sales presentations, and sales aids. The sales professional considers the selling tools and aids available and plans strategies and tactics to make the most effective approach with each buying influence.

HAZARDOUS AREAS—AVOIDING LOW WIRES

The sales professional knows that it takes a lot of planning and effort to get an order of a capital purchase. You want to be sure that no problem or situation arises that will prevent you from getting the order. You want to prevent any unfavorable "surprise" from appearing before an order is placed, so you look for hazardous areas, or "low wires." Important points to consider and check in an attempt to identify possible hazardous areas are these:

1. "If we submit a responsive offering, is there anything that would prevent us from getting an order?" Answers to this simple question, asked of all the buying influences, often bring out the names or departments of buying influences that you may not have considered.

2. Have your sales and marketing management, service headquarters, and other sales offices calling on different locations of the same company had any problems? Consult with the engineering, personnel, accounting, or legal departments to determine if they have any pending actions with your prospect. Make sure past problems are resolved.

3. Are the prospect's requirements compatible with the equipment or service you can offer? How will you minimize the effect of any deficiencies, exceptions, or variances?

4. Are the delivery schedules, performance warranties, start date, data required, or other terms of sale acceptable to your company, or will you have to quote exceptions?

5. Did you identify your competition to determine if there are any areas where they can perform better than you? What have they offered in the past? Consider the price, delivery, terms of sale, product quality, service, parts availability, operating experience, unique features, or other desirable features or benefits. What can you do to neutralize or minimize competitive strong points?

6. In addition to the key buying influences, are there individuals in the prospect's organization who, although they can't give you an order, can prevent you from getting it?

Researching hazardous areas is looking for low wires. It's brainstorming to identify what can prevent the order and taking positive steps to correct that situation. It answers the question, "Is there any way I can lose this order?" followed by a set of strategies and tactics that will counter any hazardous areas.

The obvious hazardous areas are usually recognized early in the negotiation. It's the not too obvious pitfalls that you really have to dig out.

THE IMPORTANCE OF TEAMWORK IN SALES

Outstanding salespeople continually search for ways to improve their performance by building a stronger relationship with members of their sales team. They are aware that without effective support and teamwork, many orders could not be obtained. The team, including office staff, management, headquarters, service, manufacturing, and others all must have the same objective: "What can I do to help our sales department get the order?"

When getting an order a sales professional must have the same feeling of satisfaction that a baseball pitcher has after a winning performance. The pitcher knows that the support of his teammates made the victory possible. The sales professional must feel the same way about the sales team.

Teamwork requires uniformity of purpose concerning a particular prospect or customer. The prime account objectives must be understood and committed to by each team member. With this commitment, effective strategies and tactics can be discussed openly and positive steps outlined. The salesperson assigned to the account must be the team captain. All presentations, communications, or other actions contemplated with an account must be taken after discussions and approval of the salesperson.

The salesperson knows the importance of praising other team members to customers. It is necessary to recognize that the team's contributions are all parts of the benefits the prospect or customer will receive. Prospects get the salesperson, the product or service, and the company when they become customers.

NATIONAL ACCOUNT SELLING— TOUCHING ALL THE BASES

Major prospects and national accounts are commonly sold by team effort. The best team approach is to appoint the salesperson who will get the purchase order to be captain. All other salespeople must coordinate and support the captain. Coverage may include users, consultants, other plants, headquarters, contractors, OEMs, or any buying influence. Frequently an overall strategy and series of tactics are established with support from people in different locations. To succeed in project and national account sales, effective communications is essential between all involved salespeople. The team captain must decide on the strategies and tactics to use.

In establishing strategies and tactics, all salespeople and other team members must know what they must do to put the firm in a preferred position. A prime objective of the team is to have all buying influences prefer their products or service. Most major project sales are lost because all the bases weren't touched (that is, a hazardous area was discovered too late to take positive action). Possibly buying influences in one or more locations weren't receptive to the offering. Maybe they weren't called on by a salesperson because of oversight, or maybe they weren't considered influences. The key in major project and national account sales is understanding the buying cycle, identifying *all* buying influences in all locations, and making sure all members of the selling team have the same set of objectives.

It's recommended that on all major projects a *written* outline of strategy and tactics be prepared so all members of the team know their responsibilities. This will help identify where each buying influence is located, who will call on each, what the strategies are, and what the tactics are for timetable and results.

PREPARING A WRITTEN OUTLINE OF
STRATEGIES AND TACTICS

Once you determine where you enter the buying cycle, you should prepare an outline of strategies and tactics. This outline helps establish the "game plan" for getting the order. Possible sources of information include the purchasing, technical, headquarters, operating personnel, or other involved departments. All sources should be considered in identifying where you are in the buying cycle and who are the key buying influences.

Your outline starts after you identify where you are in the buying cycle. Calling on a prospect for the first time, you can come in at any step in the cycle. Calling on a present customer, you are in on the ground floor. You should be involved in preparing specifications and identifying solutions to problems.

Once you determine where you are in the cycle, it is important to review what has preceded so you can establish tactics for where you want to go. Your purchasing, marketing, headquarters, service, or other departments in company contacts are all sources of information to consider when setting strategies and tactics.

For each step in the cycle, identify the key buying influences and any hazardous areas you may be faced with. Next, based on input from your team members, formulate a strategy on how you can get the order. Then establish a set of tactics specifying how, what, and when the actions must be taken to carry out your strategy. Clearly determine what tactics you plan to use. Then determine what sales aids could best help and write down the date you want to complete the tactics.

After you have identified your strategies and tactics for a buying cycle, draw a horizontal line and list the next step in the cycle; then start again with the analysis just reviewed. You should show the results and any follow-up required after determining tactics.

It's important to list all the remaining steps in the buying cycle so a total strategy can be considered. Help from management, service groups, headquarters, and all team members should be considered in your outline.

Tactics may include product presentations, executive contacts, factory or field trips, sample reviews, offerings, service department corrections, or any of the many activities you must do to have your products or services preferred by a prospect or customer. Each should have a date set for its accomplishment, leading up to the purchase order.

CONCLUSION

The pivotal point upon which all sales strategies and tactics are based is discovering where you are in the buying cycle and planning accordingly. If

161

prospects are in step 1 of the cycle—identifying their needs—and you come in and try to close without getting sufficient details, you may have wasted an important sales call. More importantly, you may have discouraged future business.

Recognizing and contacting the key buying influences in your sales situation is essential if you are setting an outline to get an order. Watch for low wires. Learn all you can about these people—their responsibilities, interests, and styles of decision making. There is no such thing as knowing too much about them. The outline of strategies and tactics can be a very effective sales-planning tool.

Make effective use of all the selling tools available. Brainstorm with your sales team to determine the best approach in project buying. Thorough planning alleviates fear; lack of fear means you are confident and ready for anything. You are a professional.

Review Questions

1. Why is the establishment of sales strategies and tactics an important area of interest to the sales professional?
2. Why is selling a concept a challenge for the salesperson? How does it differ from selling a product?
3. Select two examples of a concept you would like to sell and prepare a five-minute verbal presentation on each.
4. Why is it important to identify where you enter the prospect's buying cycle before you proceed?
5. You are assigned to sell all the construction materials on a new municipal airport. Prepare a report on each of the key areas of sales interest. For each department in the municipality that may be involved in making a buying decision, outline the sales strategies and tactics you will take.
6. What are some of the different personal and business characteristics that may be displayed by the individuals in each department?
7. How does planning and research help in setting strategies and tactics?
8. You are calling on the owner of a small office building to sell your extermination service. What would be your tactics?
9. Pick five sales situations and describe sales aids that may be helpful. What hazardous areas should be avoided?
10. You sell industrial lighting. You've found out that a very large new plant is being built in your territory. The architect-consultant is located in another state and is called on by another salesperson in your company. Outline what is involved in the team selling effort between you, the other salesperson, and your respective accounts.

Strategies and Tactics Outline

Buying Cycle	Key Influences	Hazardous Areas	Strategy	Tactic	Selling Aids	Date	Results Follow-Up

module eleven
Win/Win
Sales Negotiations:
the Best Kind

In this module the emphasis is placed on identifying the negotiation points that a sales professional may be confronted with on a particular proposal or offering. It offers suggestions on sales approaches that may give you a competitive edge.

Although all orders are not negotiated, the thought processes emphasized in this module help prepare you to understand your total offering better.

Prior to negotiating, you must identify what parts of the offering are firm, what parts can be negotiated, and what the limits are of your negotiation authority. It is important to stress the positive win/win approach toward a negotiation. The salesperson and the buyer should feel that they have attained the best arrangement possible for both companies when the negotiations are concluded. Salespeople must recognize that buyers are paid to buy services and products at the most competitive offering, just as salespeople are paid to get the most for their products or service. If a win/win approach is taken by the buyer and seller, then they will strive to come up with the best arrangement. It is necessary to consider price, delivery, and all other negotiable terms of sales in your preparation. It is important to evaluate your relationships with purchasing and all other departments involved to identify sources of information. You can then determine how that input can be utilized.

Pre-negotiation is important to help identify as many options, alternatives, and contingencies as possible. A game plan or approach should be

164

established for each identifiable negotiation point. Although negotiations and sales tactics may vary from job to job, preparation is always required.

The sales professional must consider all possible strategies and tactics to get the order, including the handling of negotiations between companies. The salesperson must be capable of planning and carrying out the tactics necessary to find a satisfactory level of doing business and to be able to convince the prospect or customer. The salesperson is striving for a long-term buyer and seller relationship, which is only achieved through an association that lets both the buyer and seller feel that they've won after a negotiation is complete. The buyer would have liked a little extra but is satisfied; the seller would have liked a little extra but is satisfied—it's a win/win situation.

A sales negotiation is defined as mutual discussion and arrangement of the terms of a buying and selling transaction or agreement. In sales, it's usually considered searching for an acceptable level of price, product, or service for transacting business.

The situation salespeople often find themselves in is where the buyer no longer inquires about how good the product or service is but starts with the premise, "Let's talk about the terms—the compromise we're going to strike between one another."

In recent years, the art of negotiation and compromise has entered the sales picture as a vital element. The reason for its growing importance stems from three factors:

1. Companies are getting larger and fewer in number.

2. Buyers are becoming much more skilled. They have to look closer at the bottom line; they have to understand marketing and recognize sales techniques. Companies send their buyers to sales-training courses so they will know what they are going to be exposed to.

3. There is now a tacit and growing recognition between buyers and sellers that they need each other to succeed. Salespeople are paid to sell and buyers are paid to buy. There is very little tolerance for gamesmanship but plenty of room for professionalism.

THE SALESPERSON AS A NEGOTIATOR

Most salespeople have received very little training in negotiations. Usually, a few reminders given them by sales management or other veterans are their only real guidelines. Below is a list of often used reminders:

- Aim high—if necessary, adjust down.

- Keep the whole offering in mind. Avoid splitting it up.
- Keep searching for variables and alternatives.
- If you are turned down, give yourself time to think before you go back.
- When you desperately need a delay, excuse yourself to go to the restroom or make a telephone call.
- Allow the buyers to feel they are in control, although actually you stay in control, of the situation.
- Never make a concession without getting a purchase order or something significant in return.
- If you start backing down, it's a tough job climbing up.
- Absorb as much as you can of the discussions by taking notes. They come in handy if you want to review the past actions and reactions.
- Never make an offer the company is not willing to stand behind.

These reminders only start to scratch the surface when preparing a salesperson for negotiation. The professional must know about balance sheets, profit and loss, the bottom line.

For salespeople who can relate their product or service features into customer benefits and dollars saved, lower inventories, faster manufacturing, less employee turnover, and so on, negotiation is natural. They are prepared.

HOW SALES PROFESSIONALS NEGOTIATE EFFECTIVELY

The important personal and business characteristics that are found in successful salespeople are found in the successful negotiator:

1. A high degree of self-control; being patient when necessary.
2. The ability to express oneself—communicative skills, in particular, probing by asking questions.
3. Mental toughness, tenacity: ability to look for solutions to problems.
4. A positive outlook; the ability to approach a negotiation with positive anticipation.
5. Listening effectively; attentive to what is being said and meant.
6. Continually striving to learn more about products or services, features and benefits, customer's organization, marketing.
7. Ability to identify key issues in the negotiation that must be resolved.
8. Persuasive talents to convince others of the value of the proposal.
9. A sense of timing; knowing when to make offers and counteroffers.
10. Tactfulness; a clear understanding of buying influences and how to use them.

11. Open-mindedness: ability to listen to all suggestions and considerations and be flexible enough to accept alternatives when necessary.
12. Ability to take charge; acting as quarterback between customer or prospect, headquarters, and manufacturing operations.
13. Constant search for alternative offerings to present and discuss when price levels are changed.
14. Recognition that people need time to get used to new products and services.
15. Ability to plan a timetable for actions to take place that help close the order.

All these talents are needed to negotiate effectively. Additional support and suggestions from other members of the company are important for background information. The experiences of veteran salespeople or managers may shed additional light on the negotiation. Continually strive to learn as much as you can about the negotiation and the negotiators. It will help you to increase your sales.

WHAT CAN YOU NEGOTIATE?—ANYTHING

Following is a list of major items that can be negotiated. There may be others that apply to your product or service. Any area which can be discussed or offered can be negotiated, or "is open for discussion." Always consider what can be negotiated to determine what will help you get the order.

Basic price	Consigned stock
Special terms and conditions of sale	On-site installation service
Drawings schedule	Patent protection
FOB point	Special tests
Delivery or storage	Return materials policy
Shipping cost	Software review and training manuals
Special warranties	Special packaging or handling
Length of guarantee	Industry standards and testing
Quality or quantity pricing	Cost of changes or cancellation
Early payment discount	Sole source supplier
Replacement parts	Territorial protection
Progress payments	Service after delivery

Simply stated, anything that can be discussed can be negotiated.

TACTICS THAT HELP NEGOTIATIONS

The sales professional is continually looking for new tactics to consider and use, such as the following:

- Looking at the present way of doing things and considering how they can be improved.
- Studying the competition to better understand their marketing strategies and tactics.
- Seeking to penetrate prospects and customers more thoroughly by building a better rapport and remembering that negotiation is an effective sales tactic.

Every successful sales negotiation terminates with the transfer of a service or product for a price. To the customers, the offering bears a fair and equitable relationship to the price they are paying. The customers have decided that they want your product or service, are willing to pay the price agreed upon, and want to buy it now.

TIE-BREAKERS THAT HELP GET ORDERS

In contemplating negotiation tactics, consider all possible areas of "leverage" that can help get the order. If the sales situation is close or tied between you and a competitor, you need a tie-breaker to swing it your way.

To help you decide what negotiation tactics to use in beating the competition, we've prepared a list of items that could help you get an order. This list contains items that are dependent on the product, the factory or field performance, sales creativity, or the prospect or customer. You should prepare a similar list for your products or services. Each key buying influence must be approached and be convinced of the tie-breaker that applies to his or her involvement in the buying cycle.

Tie-Breakers Dependent on Products

1. Higher efficiency—With energy concerns a national interest, all customers are interested in what it costs to run electrical equipment.
2. Less weight—It can mean lighter, less expensive support materials.
3. More weight—To be used if appearance of ruggedness is more important than the weight.
4. Unique design—Features with customer benefits are stressed.
5. Ease of cost of installation—Time is money.
6. More effective shipping or packaging—This reduces receiving or inventory costs.

Tie-Breakers Dependent on Factory or Field Performance

1. Competitors' products or services cause trouble.
2. Competitors had poor shipment performance in the past.

3. Your manufacturing facility or office is more convenient for customer inspection prior to shipment.
4. Your parts inventory is larger for ready shipment.
5. You have more local support for application and service.

Tie-Breakers Dependent on Sales Creativity

1. You offer unsolicited alternatives.
2. You out-engineer the competition.
3. You offer coordinated package or project management services.
4. You are a more creative salesperson.

Tie-Breakers Dependent on Customer

1. There is duplication of earlier equipment.
2. You can match up earlier equipment.
3. There is a division of business.
4. There is unified responsibility—all equipment comes from one supplier.
5. The customer is convinced of your superior product or service capability.
6. The customer wanted to give the order to you.

The most valuable tie-breaker is: The customer wanted to give the order to you. If this is true, the customer will suggest or help you identify and evaluate the right tie-breaker. He or she will help you negotiate the best order for both sides, a win/win order.

Review this list and add as many other positive tie-breakers you can think of to answer the simple question, "Why should the prospect give me this order?" Do some brainstorming with your peers, managers, factory, or headquarters. Consider what you need in the way of sales aids, timing, customer contacts, company support, sales skills, and so on to make sure your positive tie-breakers are understood by the key influences.

Consider your products or service and your competitors. Answer the question, "Why shouldn't the prospect give the order to my competitors?" What can they do or not do that will help or hinder them on this project? How can I counter it? How can I convince the prospect that my product or service should be preferred?

GETTING READY TO NEGOTIATE

Major sales negotiations, like all other aspects of professional salesmanship, are more successful when you have as much data as possible, you have planned, and you have prepared a review of the following:

- The prospect's or customer's annual reports.
- Actual buying and proposal history.
- Top personnel.
- The customer's markets and competition.
- The importance of this negotiation to the customer.
- What party will negotiate for the customer.
- The strengths and weaknesses of each negotiator.
- The strong and weak points of your proposal.
- The customer's probable position.
- The complete history of discussion of activities relating to written proposals and verbal agreements.
- Identification of the roles of all negotiators on your team.

To get a better feel for what you want to accomplish, "role play" the entire negotiation. Have someone in your company play the role of the devil's advocate. Look for inconsistencies that poke holes in your sales presentation. Let this person present possible objections to your approach so you can rehearse and plan strategies and tactics. Consider who should actually be in the negotiation and who should remain outside the room, available for consultation. Agree that there should be no disagreement around the bargaining table.

These are part of what sales professionals must consider and review with the negotiation team. This preparation can mean a great deal in giving your team background and confidence.

THE IMPORTANCE OF ASKING QUESTIONS

The salesperson must prepare a suitable reply to the prospective customer who interrupts early in a negotiation to ask, "What is your price?" or "How much is it?" It is important to stay in control by quoting price only after properly preparing the way for it to avoid unnecessary sales resistance. By asking questions, the salesperson can make certain the customer's requirements are understood. With discussion of these requirements, and working to fit the features and benefits of the product to best fill the needs of the customer, a professional presentation is made before discussing the price.

By leading the prospect through various probing questions designed to identify needs and requirements, the professional salesperson gets agreement that the offered benefits are the best ways to fill these needs. The salesperson is then in the best position to have the price accepted when it is quoted.

Only after the salesperson is certain that the prospect fully understands the value and suitability of the products or services should the salesperson quote the price. Skill in this phase of selling is one of the marks of a real professional.

The salesperson should be prepared if after telling the product story, making the presentation, and submitting and discussing the offering and then the price, the prospect says, "Your price is out of line" or similar comments.

Let's take a look at the price objection.

CONSIDERING THE PRICE OBJECTION

As in handling all objections, the salesperson's job at this stage is to find out if the prospect's reference to price represents a real objection or if it is only a stall. The salesperson can probe further or decide to ignore the question. This can frequently be done by asking a question similar to this: "Aside from the price, what do you think of our offering?" A favorable answer can be followed with another question: "If the price were agreeable to you, would you buy the product?" Or, "Do you feel this is really the service you need and want?" Or, "Do you intend to buy the lowest priced offering?"

NEGOTIATING A PRICE

Price negotiations as such are a challenge to every salesperson. The prospect or customer, having a reasonable desire for a product, will frequently ask for a modified price in hopes of arriving at a figure agreeable to all parties.

Wise salespeople engaged in such a negotiation adopt the policy that they never drop a price, but may, if circumstances are suitable, reduce it to get an order.

The implications in this statement are clear to all experienced salespeople. A price should never be changed except in exchange for an order number. A wise salesperson never gets involved in a price-cutting situation. Invariably, it leads to price being used as the basis for further dickering with weak-kneed competitive salespeople who attempt to substitute low price for professional salesmanship.

If in a negotiation the customer makes a genuine offer for the business at a price, the salesperson must be guided by the company's policies. The salesperson can accept the order, at a modified price, subject to acceptance by the company within a specified time. In most cases, it's possible to assure the customer that you can respond with a firm answer within forty-eight hours. In many cases, you can reply far sooner. Customary procedure is to take all the facts pertaining to both the offering and price to management, explaining that an order can be gotten under the conditions outlined.

Even if management refuses the offer, it is frequently possible for a minimum price level to be established, which gives the salesperson a chance to go back to the prospective customer to ask for an order at a new price, somewhere between your original offering and the buyer's offer.

Unfortunately, in many cases, a prospect's feeling that a price is subject to negotiation is implanted by the salesperson, usually through lack of enthusiasm for the product, incomplete sales presentation, or apologetic submission of the price. A sales professional with a positive, enthusiastic attitude throughout the entire sales negotiation is usually the best answer to the price objection, inasmuch as it may overcome the objection before it is raised.

PLANNING YOUR NEGOTIATION

There are many areas in which to plan and prepare before you sit across the table from a prospect or customer in a negotiation session.

1. *Organization*—Before getting into the negotiation, obtain and review all possible information on the prospect's or customer's organization.
   a. Who are the decision makers?
   b. What do the prospects or customers really want from the negotiation? What is important to them?
   c. Are there any inner conflicts or political situations that may exert influence on the outcome? If the negotiation swings different ways, will there be different winners and losers within the prospect's organization?
   d. Who will negotiate for the prospect or customer? What's been your experience with him or her?
2. *Authority*—What can you bring to the negotiation to give you more or less authority or legitimacy?
   a. Historical data give you legitimacy and authority. Records or charts can show on-time deliveries, efficient operation, reliability, or other positive performances by your company.
   b. References from recognized authorities can be helpful.
   c. The more knowledge you have of your proposal or other areas of the offering, the more strength you have.

  d. Even if you have full authority you can always back away from a decision until you have had time to check with specialists. One person can't know everything.

  e. On the other hand, zero or limited authority can be a definite advantage as it will give you additional time to ask for approval of those who have the authority.

3. *Time*—Remember, deadlines can exist on both sides.

  a. Buyers have deadlines when they must have new products, equipment, and services. They are anxious to buy. If you know this deadline, you will be in a better position to negotiate.

  b. A stated firm deadline may, in reality, be very flexible.

  c. Most negotiations conclude just before the real deadline.

  d. Is there anything you can do to affect the deadline?

EMPHASIZING PRODUCT VALUE

In presenting the negotiation, you must make certain that significant emphasis is put on the overall value of the offering. Long life, performance, efficiency, reliability, service, installation, training, and goodwill must all be stressed. By doing so, you help the prospect arrive at the real value of the offering. Avoid getting into the "lowest price trap."

When prospects want the product, they should be led to think in terms of total cost or price. This includes not only the initial cost but also the cost of later service. The operating cost over the anticipated useful life of the product or service is an important factor to be considered for all products or services being evaluated.

When evaluating total cost, issues such as the following should be included:

1. The cost of replacement parts and inventory needed to assure continuity of operation.

2. The quality difference in your product and those of inferior make and lower price.

3. How the customer will save money with your quality product or service because of increased productivity and reduced down time versus that caused by inferior products or services.

SUGGESTIONS TO CONSIDER WHEN YOU NEGOTIATE

1. Negotiations are a continuous activity and not usually hurried, short-time activities. Long-term relations help toward the willingness of the prospect to want to do business with you.

2. With regard to concessions, give in slowly and get something in trade.

3. In major areas, don't make the first concession—it usually shows a weakness of your entire offering.

4. If initially the buyer says, "Let's split the difference," refuse. He or she will get more satisfaction later if you do split the difference after all other items are resolved equally.

5. Successful negotiators make large initial demands and make concessions in small increments.

6. Who is to say what is fair and reasonable? What may be fair to you may be unfair to the buyer.

7. Never attack the presenter but only the idea or offer presented. This is a good suggestion at any time.

8. If you show a real attempt to like the buyer, he or she will probably let go a little.

9. Make buyers look competent within their own organization. Always give them a way out; don't trap them.

10. Salespeople tend to overestimate their competition. Don't let the threat of the buyer to get concessions from a competitor scare you off. Competitors probably aren't willing to give away the store any faster than you are.

11. Determine how the alternatives will be decided.

12. Take notes of your discussions so you are able to review after the session is over.

13. Don't hesitate to call a break if you need time to think, check with others, or ask for help.

LOOKING FOR NONVERBAL SIGNALS DURING THE NEGOTIATION

Sales professionals do more than listen for answers to questions—they *look* for answers. The body language or nonverbal communications of a prospect or customer can be more revealing than what is said. A significant portion of what is communicated is done so without words. It's so important that it can make or break a negotiation.

This type of language is called *kinesics*. It is defined as a systematic study of the relationship between nonlinguistic body motions (shrugs, eye motions, hand movements, and so on) and communication.

Since body language usually is stimulated by the subconscious, it is often more reliable than verbal communication. In fact, many times it contradicts what is said verbally. The sales professional can get positive or negative signals from the actions of a prospect or customer. Possible positive steps you can take after noting nonverbal signals are these:

1. Determine if the prospect or customer is in a buying mood and favorably impressed with your presentation and approach to solving the problem. If the sign if favorable, go to a closer. Your negotiation is heading in the right direction.

2. See if there is doubt in what is being offered, suggesting that additional proof and supporting documentation should be given.

3. Negative buying signals suggest that you go back and ask additional questions to see if you really understand the problem.

There are hundreds of nonverbal signals that take place in a prospect's or customer's office. We'll list some of the most obvious to help set the tone for this advanced sales and negotiations technique. It is recommended that you research available books on the subject of kinesics for a more in-depth study.

Some important nonverbal signals are the the following:

1. You mention your price and the purchasing agent tilts her head back, raises her hands, and becomes rigid. This buyer is sending a "no" signal. It means you are facing a barrier. You've got to stop what you are doing, express understanding, and redirect your approach.

2. As you explain your sales features and their benefits, this buyer looks away, clasps his hands, and crosses his legs away from you. This buyer is showing you caution signs. Your own words and actions must be aimed at getting him to open up. Try to ask more questions to determine where the hesitancy lies.

3. As you review the dollar benefits of your product or service, the company president opens her arms and leans toward you. This buyer is sending warm buying signals. With no obstacles to your selling strategy, simply move on to the close.

Other nonverbal signals and their possible meanings are these:

Signal	*Meaning*
Buyer takes a deep breath and releases a big sigh.	Indecision.
Buyer sits with folded arms.	Won't buy you or what you sell.
Gentle stroking of the chin with thumb and forefinger, usually accompanied by a slight, relaxed smile.	Has made up mind favorably—now is the time to close.
The buyer looks you straight in the eye in a pleasant manner without trying to stare you down.	Is interested and will probably give you fair consideration.
The buyer is shifty-eyed, refuses to look at you directly, or drops the eyes.	Beware—probably has something to hide and will make it tough for you.

Nonverbal signals are meaningful as a guide for you to better understand your prospect's hidden thoughts and feelings. It's a sales skill that should be studied and mastered.

THE WIN/WIN ATTITUDE

The attitude you want to establish with your prospect or customer is one which, at the conclusion of the negotiation, you both feel you've won. It's commonly referred to as the win/win attitude. The outcome of this type of negotiation is that *both* parties feel that they would have preferred a more favorable arrangement, but both are satisfied. Both parties feel that they are winners.

The negotiation tempo has been one in which both parties had the time and the patience to look for the best available arrangement, one in which both the buyer and seller have increased their participation and profit.

When you and a customer have the strong desire to come up with the best arrangement, the creative juices start to flow. Fresh ideas, considerations, alternatives, plans, and aspirations start to come to the surface. False limitations or roadblocks are removed and replaced with a more up-front approach.

In win/win negotiations, both parties take the time to look for the best arrangement. You and the buyer both try to improve the other person's profit without hurting yours.

Some areas where both parties can profit from a win/win approach are

- A change in specification.
- A more closely coordinated shipment schedule.
- Revised payment terms.
- Options for more visits.
- A change in packaging.
- A tie-in of sales of one product with other products or services.
- Change in means of transportation.

In building long-term buyer and seller relationships, the sales professional strives for the win/win attitude to start a negotiation and work toward getting a win/win result.

ASPIRATION LEVELS

What you aspire to achieve during a negotiation is *goal setting*. Those with higher aspiration levels usually do better during a negotiation. Salespeople that start out higher come out better. On the other hand, buyers that start negotiations lower wind up buying lower.

Those who aspire to get more out of a negotiation usually do. Lower aspirants, regardless of their negotiation skills, prestige, or power, usually get less out of the negotiation. The aspiration level each negotiator takes into the negotiation is based on individual goals, self-esteem, risk taking, persuasion, persistence, success, and other personality traits. Each person aspires to get some personal and/or company gain out of the negotiation. The sales veteran continues to emphasize customer gain or benefit after an order is placed.

LOOKING FOR THE BEST SOLUTION

There are no limits to the number of arrangements and alternatives that a buyer and seller can consider when looking for the best.

1. *Technical specifications*—If the buyer should reduce or change some of the technical requirements of the specifications, it may be less expensive to manufacture and test. This could reduce the cost and sales price. Conversely, if the manufacturer designs a better product than required, it will last longer. This could also be a point to negotiate.
2. *Equipment, schedules, shipments, and service*—The cost of engineering, manufacturing, testing, storing, shipping, and service is all part of the selling price. If the potential buyer is willing to negotiate changes in preliminary requirements, it could affect the sales price. Some examples follow:

   a. Customer wants design drawings in eight weeks; it suits your schedule to make them in six or ten weeks. If the customer changes, can you?
   b. The prospect wants the equipment in six months; you would prefer to ship in five or eight months. This could be a negotiation point.
   c. The customer wants exclusive truck shipment; you prefer rail. Which is best?

    d. The prospect prefers special packaging—cardboard carton ship-
ment, one to a box; you prefer barrel shipment, three to a barrel.
How is price affected?

    e. You prefer to offer design sketches for engineering review; your
customer wants full-size drawings. Can this be a negotiation
point?

    f. Installation time and on-site training programs can vary; this is a
negotiable point.

    g. The dollar amount of stock, materials to be stocked, methods of
inventory, invoicing, and time to restock are all negotiable.

    h. What portion of total cost will be charged to buyer if he or she
cancels before shipment? It can range from a minimum cancellation charge to 100 percent of the order depending on engineering, design, manufacturing, and testing completed.

    i. The prospect changes specifications after the order is placed
and released for manufacture, how will these be charged back?
Is it a flat fee plus design and materials charge, or is it negotiable
on an "as occurred" basis?

    j. Will shipping costs be paid by the seller or the buyer?

    k. If the prospect or customer desires special testing, possibly
witnessed, how will it be billed? Is it free?

    l. Will there be a restocking charge for returned materials? How
much? If an item was manufactured exclusively for the customer,
maybe you can't resell it and don't want it back.

    m. For territorial protection, you may agree not to sign any addi-
tional authorized distributors or representatives in a particular
territory.

    n. The prospect may require instruction manuals in different quan-
tities than you normally supply. This is possibly a small item,
but a negotiable one nonetheless.

    o. Isn't order placement time the best time to get a replacements
parts order? It sure is—a good parts order can be very
profitable.

    p. If products are coming from many locations to one customer
location, who will handle the coordination?

3. *Terms of sale*—All the terms of sales are items that can be
negotiated.

    a. *Basic price*—This is probably the most often negotiated item.
Sales professionals continually emphasize the benefits of the
products or services they represent. If there are any "gives" in
this area, you must get something in return, such as change in
shipping schedule, change in payments schedule, parts order,
specification changes, and/or purchase order.

    b. *FOB point*—Ownership of material can pass at the shipping or receiving point. Processing claims for possible shipping damages between these points takes time and effort and must be initiated by the owner at the time of damage. On shipment overseas, ports of embarkation, ship designation, and export clearances are all topics for discussion and negotiation.

c. *Special warranties and guarantees*—The length of time a product is guaranteed can vary. It can start from the time it leaves the factory to after it's in service for a period of time. You can consider extended periods of coverage following the normal guarantee. Does your standard policy cover only the repair or replacement of the defective part? What about cost of removal, packing, and reinstallation of the defective product? What about loss of revenue while a product is out of service? Is it feasible to supply a "loaner." All these areas are negotiable.

d. *Package offer*—You may have many products you are offering for sale at one time. Will it be to the buyer's advantage to buy them all from you at a better package offer? Are there items in your total offering that you don't want taken out of the package?

e. *Payments*—When will payment be made? At shipment, upon receipt, ten or thirty days after installation, after in service, after six months? Is there a discount? On large projects or major purchases, should progress payments be made? What's the schedule? Who should decide on progress?

   On international orders, obtaining letters of credit, export clearance, type of currency, and so on are all important concerns worthy of negotiation.

   Escalation or deescalation of the base price because of materials or labor costs to the manufacturer could be a concern. What are the guidelines? Are there minimum and maximum charges?

f. *Delays*—If the project is delayed beyond the shipping date by the seller, buyer, someone else, or something, how will the cost be handled? What about storage—who will pay? How much for how long? What about extra handling or loss of revenue by the buyer?

g. *Patents*—There may be a unique feature that the buyer wants built into your products, and he or she wants patent rights. Your approval, preparation for filing a patent, and development costs are negotiable.

h. *Cancellation charges*—When capital equipment is ordered, many actions begin before the manufacturing starts. Materials must be ordered, designs started, tools set aside, financing arranged, and so on. If an order is cancelled, the seller has a right to recoup expenditures. Of course, if manufacturing has already started, additional expenditures are made. How much the seller is entitled to in the event of a cancellation is a negotiable item.

i.   *Other*—Other terms of sale that are negotiable could include cost of special options, shipping charges, returned materials, special testing, special paint, delivery date, and types of drawings. The customer's request for quotation may offer many opportunities to negotiate. You should review them closely.

In this section on looking for the best solution, we've listed some areas that can offer you room to negotiate. If the proper rapport is present, both the buyer and the seller will consider as many alternatives as possible to consummate a sale that benefits both parties. A good negotiation is one where both parties work to solve each others problems.

THE BUYER'S ROLE

The buyer's role in a negotiation is to get the best price, the best product or service, and the best terms of sale for the company. That is what he or she is getting paid to do. The buyer may not be inclined to listen to discussions of pricing that you consider reasonable or fair. Buyers have to be convinced that they are getting value. In this section, we will consider the buyer as the principal negotiator for the prospect or customer.

Buyers look at the offerings of the price the salesperson would like to get, not necessarily the price the company will accept. Just as the professional salesperson is preparing tactics for the negotiation, the buyer is also getting ready. Buyers have some apparent advantages; usually, like in sports, they have "the home-field advantage." They choose the time, place, and meeting room. This gives them the opportunity to bring in additional members of their negotiation team in an attempt to strengthen their position.

Behind the buyer there are other team members making demands, just as team members may be making demands on the seller. Buyers have to satisfy the demands of management, production, sales, engineering, union, and government. Often the buyers are caught between their organization and the salesperson.

The salesperson involved in a negotiation must recognize that rarely are buyers operating on their own. The needs of those behind the buyer must be satisfied. The other disciplines in an organization that you've been calling on all have buying influence. The professional sales negotiator recognizes that buyers must present a unified approach although they are faced with the following situations in their own organizations:

1. Conflict between departments (all behind-the-scenes parties have their own responsibilities) and demands from management.
2. Each department has different needs, wants, and priorities.
3. Some are involved heavily in the decision-making process whereas others are not.
4. Each department gains differently from the outcome.

The effective sales negotiator understands the buyer's organization as well as his or her own organization.

In addition, the salesperson must recognize that negotiations may be necessary within the sales team. Each department has a different set of priorities, needs, and wants, which it expects to be satisfied from this negotiation. The salesperson, as the representative of the whole organization, must decide, with management, the company's initial position on all key issues. As the negotiation progresses, it may be necessary to go back to consider possible changes.

WHAT THE BUYER REALLY WANTS FROM A NEGOTIATION

The products or services you offer for sale are the items that are on the negotiation table; however, the real issue that may have to surface is better understanding of what the buyer really wants—that is, one or more of the following emotional items:

- To be listened to.
- To know the truth.
- To have a clear explanation.
- To have peer and managerial recognition.
- To feel important.
- To avoid being embarrassed.
- To feel satisfied after the negotiation.
- To avoid risks.
- To be promoted.
- To work less, not more.
- To meet personal and professional goals.
- To be liked and considered fair, honest, and responsible.

These wants aren't on purchase orders, but they affect who gets them.

AVOIDING TELEPHONE NEGOTIATIONS

Sales professionals should try to avoid telephone negotiations whenever possible since they know face-to-face negotiations are more effective. The following list is a guideline for effective telephone negotiations for those times when you will have to communicate in this manner:

1. Have a complete checklist of items you want to discuss; have your files, details, paper, pencil, and other materials ready before you dial.

2. If you are called, before you say, "I'll get the file and call you back," listen. Get as much preliminary information as possible before ending the conversation and getting your files and materials together. Then call back.

3. Do not allow yourself to be forced into a negotiation over the phone if you feel it is not right. Be honest with the buyer; tell him or her you cannot discuss it now, and give a specific time when you will call back.

CONCLUSION

A sales negotiation concludes successfully when both the buyer and the seller feel they've received proper value. They are both winners. The buyer is content with paying an equitable price for the products and services ordered. The benefits to be received are clearly understood and anxiously anticipated. The buyer has placed confidence in the supplier. The seller also wins. With the order, the seller is now in the position to deliver the products or services presented. The salesperson is supporting the company's sales and marketing efforts. The salesperson is a doer.

Negotiations and advanced sales tactics require preparation and planning for proper execution. The real professionals are master negotiators.

Review Questions

1. Name ten buying and selling situations that can lend themselves to negotiation.
2. Why are sales negotiations considered a process rather than a single event?
3. Pick out three products you want to sell and name tie-breakers you would use to sell each product. Next try this material with three services.
4. What personality characteristics help the salesperson during a negotiation?
5. For each of the products and services in question 3, list at least five items that you would negotiate.

6. Why is preparation before a negotiation so important? Explain how you can prepare.
7. How does the authority of the negotiators affect the negotiations?
8. Pick out two products you are interested in selling. List typical needs, wants, and "gives" that might be considered. Next try two services.
9. Name ten buying signals you should look for and hear in a negotiation.
10. Why is it important to look for a win/win outcome in your negotiations?
11. How does the rapport you've built with your account pay dividends during a sales negotiation?
12. How can you help buyers in a negotiation? How can they help you?

module twelve
Effectively Handling Objections and Closing: the Mark of the Professional

The successful handling of a prospect's objections and ultimately closing are at the heart of the selling process. The inability to handle objections and to close are the reasons why most individuals fail in their sales career.

The fear of rejection is the prime reason why many salespeople don't even attempt to close a prospect. They fear the "no" response. They take a "no" response to their offering to mean a personal rejection of them as individuals. "No" responses or objections are usually caused because insufficient benefits were presented. A "no" response means you have to try again.

Knowledge, skills, attitude, and practice are all essential for effective salesmanship. The importance of preparation cannot be overemphasized. The professional knows why and how to stress often-asked objections as part of the sales presentation. The salesperson should take the initiative and not wait for objections to arise. If you are continually presented with a particular objection, offer a sales point to cover it in a positive manner. However, every objecting comment doesn't have to be answered, because it may be only an incidental statement. If it is a real objection, it will be raised again, and then you can handle it.

To grow as a sales professional, you must learn how to handle objections and how to close. This module will offer many helpful suggestions.

REMOVING HURDLES TO GET ORDERS

This module covers two areas of professional selling often considered the toughest. Although difficult, success and the biggest rewards go to those who can handle objections and close. The top professionals have the ability to handle objections effectively and close their sales presentation or interview by asking for a favorable decision. If any areas of salesmanship are considered part art and part science, handling objections and closing are two of them.

We've included both these important subjects in the same module because they often follow each other in the normal sequence of a sales presentation or interview, although, to be sure, there are closings that occur without any customer objections. Let's start with defining what an objection is and then proceed to show how it can help us close.

WHAT ARE OBJECTIONS?

An objection is a statement or question that a prospect or customer offers as a reason or excuse for not buying now. An objection may often be a substitute for a "yes" or "no." Some objections sound almost like a "yes" or a good "maybe." But if no order is written, or at least no favorable decision reached, it is really a "no," and we will consider it an objection. Unfortunately, we hear very few just plain, "No, I do not want to buy!" declarations. Most objections are veiled in other delaying statements.

An objection should be viewed as an implied request for more information, possibly for facts the prospect needs to justify (to him- or herself as well as to others) his or her decision to buy. Fear of making the wrong decision is a common source of objections. The sales professional should consider an objection as a challenge. Simply stated, an objection means that the salesperson did not give the prospect or customer sufficient benefits and reasons why he or she should buy. The presentation wasn't convincing and persuasive.

Welcome Objections—
They Help You Close

The salesperson should look at objections as a way of revealing what is on the prospect's or customer's mind. They should be welcome. Nothing is tougher for a salesperson to handle than a person who doesn't reply, comment, or object. Objections help to identify areas in the sales presentation that the salesperson did not cover as effectively as possible.

Through more experience, the salesperson plans a more thorough presentation that will cover all normally raised objections. The presentation should be complete and persuasive so that positive action is expected.

The ability to detect, analyze, and handle a prospect's objections are necessary sales skills. If you can determine the real reasons why a prospect decides not to buy, it is much easier to present additional customer benefits that will help convince him or her to buy now.

Directly or indirectly, the objections prospects raise can disclose the underlying cause of their reluctance and indecision. Objections are your opportunity to get at the heart of the situation. The analysis and content of your response should be such that it doesn't create further objections but rather helps to close the sale.

Prospects who do not question you usually aren't very interested prospects. Their intent may be to hear you out as quickly and politely as possible so they can do something that does interest them. However, prospects who raise objections obviously are interested prospects, actively considering the information you have presented. You have their total attention and active participation. Objections can disclose areas where more information or clearer customer benefits are needed. Maybe the prospects did not sufficiently understand, believe, or accept the sales presentation. Maybe they don't see how it applies to their particular situations and problems. Prospects' questions may also reveal areas where you need to acquire more information to present at a later date.

Successfully handling objections must become an acquired skill for the sales professional. *Objections should be expected and welcomed.* Objections help identify what is on the buyer's mind. They are a guide to the experienced salesperson and a problem to the novice.

WHY PROSPECTS RAISE OBJECTIONS

There are numerous reasons why a prospect or customer raises objections. Let's review the most important.

1. *Typical hesitancy.* It's normal for people to want to delay decisions. Buyers are no different. The status quo is a familiar and safe place to stay. You have to relate clear and undeniable reasons for making a change now. Breaking habits is hard.

2. *Fear of deciding incorrectly.* Prospects may be afraid of making the wrong decision. Right now, what they are buying has been approved by them and others in their organization. The decision has been made. Prospects want assurance that they will not make a mistake. Giving them specific customer benefit statements will give them the confidence they need to change.

3. *Insufficient evidence.* The prospect hasn't been given sufficient reasons or justification to accept the offer. Obviously, you haven't deter-minded the prospect's needs and wants effectively. Maybe it's necessary to probe a little deeper and ask more questions to get additional input. It helps to reemphasize benefits of your offer.

4. *Other priorities.* Prospects may not object to your offer per se. Their objection could mean that right now they have other priorities at a higher level than yours. Your sales offering may be in competition with other projects for the same funds. Companies have to allocate their funds, personnel, and plant resources as they feel necessary. Clients may have limited amounts of money to spend but many areas where it is needed. For example, their present objectives may be a research project or other building expansion programs rather than the service or product you offer. You should have solid reasons and specific customer benefits showing why your offer is of value.

5. *Present suppliers.* If a prospect decides to buy from you, eventually he or she has to tell present suppliers that they are losing part or all of his or her business. This is tough to do. Emphathize with your prospect. Old friendships are at stake. Remind the prospect that present suppliers received orders because of their ability to supply needs and wants; there-fore, you should receive the same consideration based on *your* ability to serve. Don't hesitate to take a small initial order if it helps get your foot in the door.

Prospects or customers may attempt to mislead you or get you confused with some initial objections. They may be delaying tactics or smoke screens to check your professionalism. They may have no real bearing on the buyers' final decision. As a sales professional you must handle these initial objections and continue to ask questions to determine if the objection is sincere.

The best way to handle objections is to try to avoid them. And the best way to avoid them is to have a thorough, well-planned presentation filled with customer benefits. Make your presentation so full of specific customer benefits that prospects will not raise minor objections because they can visualize the advantage of buying as definitely outweighing any negatives.

If the same or similar objection comes up several times, you should face that objection head on during that meeting and modify your next presentation to address it before it is asked. By taking the offensive on objections that are often brought up, you demonstrate the confidence you have in your product or service, your company, and yourself.

How you overcome final objections is the true measurement of your success in this profession.

Notice the word *final* in the last sentence. Some objections are re-lated to the product or service offered and are not final. Many objections offered early in the sales interview or presentation are requests for information, though they often sound like very strong objections. Remember, the more informative your presentation, the fewer objections or requests for information you will face.

OBJECTIONS DELAY DECISIONS

A customer's objections frequently amount to nothing more than a delaying action. Most people, buyers included, put off making a final decision. Forcing or encouraging buyers to voice all their objections is necessary to get to the real reason for any reluctance. All objections can be handled while the salesperson is with the buyer. In this way, sales effectiveness is increased, which helps the buyer and the seller by saving time and effort.

Remember, all the salsperson wants and is entitled to is a decision. "Maybe," "could be," "might be," "hope so," or "probably" don't count—only a "yes" or "no." The only thing a buyer owes salespeople for taking the time to present their products or service is a decision.

THE SALESPERSON'S FEAR OF OBJECTIONS

Salespeople often delay or do not solicit a buyer's decision because they fear the answer they may get may be "no." The fear of rejection, fear of losing the sale completely, and timidity are some of the things that make up this unwillingness to carry out the final step of a sales presentation and ask for a positive buying decision.

Another basic fear that salespeople have is that a prospect or customer may actually state an objection that they cannot answer adequately. Most salespeople have the feeling that out there, in the vast outer space of selling, there are hundreds, or thousands, yes, some say millions of objections lying dormant in prospects' minds just waiting to be used to chase them away. This is why a study of objections—the tough ones to handle—is so important.

IDENTIFYING WHY THE PROSPECT ISN'T BUYING

In probing for the reasons why prospects should buy, an effective technique is the statement and question. Simple statements such as "Apparently, I have not made it clear to you, Mr. Buyer," followed by a question, "What areas are you concerned about?" prove to be very useful in identifying specific objections.

Another probe may be, "Apparently, during my discussions, I left some doubt about the benefits to your company." or "In what area is there still some doubt?" Only when a *specific objection* is identified can a professional salesperson suggest an effective solution and close.

The professional salesperson must always be prepared to deal with general, common objections that most buyers raise. Objections such as "your prices are too high," "your delivery is too long," "we're satisfied with our present supplier," "we have no money," "we've used another company's services for many years" are all common objections. In reality, all of them can be viewed as one primary objection. Usually it means that the salesperson has not given the buyer sufficient reason and justification to buy. In reality, the buyer is saying, "You haven't sold me yet, and if you don't try harder, I have no interest in buying from you." Buyers sometimes use this stall to determine the sincerity and commitment of the salesperson.

EFFECTIVE METHODS OF HANDLING OBJECTIONS

The best way to handle any objection is to know as much as possible about your product or service, your company, your markets, your competition, your sales presentation, and yourself. You must be prepared.

To avoid being caught at a loss for words, it is important to have at least one new, *additional* sales benefit that could be shown to the customer. This additional sales point may be the final reason for a customer to buy, even after mentioning numerous objections.

Some buyers feel that they have to bring up many objections. They feel that it is part of the job. Some objections are sincere; others are insincere. Some have to be answered and some could be ignored. Objections often wear out the less experienced salesperson. The real professional has at least one more benefit that can be offered to a buyer to give the buyer one more reason to go ahead. Maybe the last benefit may be the closer.

Professional salespeople remember that after an objection is raised and answered, they must get back to selling and attempt a close. Each statement and/or question gives them an opportunity to get back to probing for any more objections or to reviewing features and additional benefits.

There are numerous objections that a prospect or customer can make. Later in this module we list sixteen of the most prevalent objections and some unusual replies. If there is ever a time for a salesperson to be effective and perhaps different, it's when a prospect or customer raises an objection.

Good buyers have heard all the "canned" replies and expect to hear them again with the same regularity that a salesperson hears "canned" objections. Handling objections differently may help to "deprogram" these buyers. Their minds may not be geared to handle these unique methods. When the pattern of doing things their way is broken, they usually get down to the serious business of making a decision.

Some typical objections which you should be prepared to answer include these:

1. *We have no need at this time.* This usually means that you didn't probe enough to identify the buyer's needs, wants, and problems.

2. *We're not ready to buy right now.* This may mean that you haven't given enough specific reasons to go ahead; you didn't emphasize the benefits to the prospect for buying now. Maybe the closing wasn't successful. You should consider another closing technique.

Besides giving reasons to buy by probing and asking questions, it's important to think of another reason for the stall. Maybe the person you are talking to doesn't have the authority to buy. Additional questioning, without embarrassment, will identify who else may be in the buying cycle. When other influences are identified, suggest that you both make an appointment to see them now. A question like, "Who else in your company should we contact to review this offer?" may be useful.

3. *Your price is too high.* This could mean you haven't been specific enough in emphasizing your benefits in terms of money and savings of time. What about comparing the initial price with the life of the product or long-term service cost, maintenance savings, stocking costs, and so on. Clarify price versus cost; find out what is "too high" and how much "too high."

Consider an analogy: "Mr. Jones, when you look for a suit of clothes, I'm sure you don't always look for the cheapest one. I'm sure you look for value and clothes that fit your needs. Don't you? Value, that's what we are offering in our products and services."

4. *We're not interested.* This usually indicates that you have not hit a responsive cord or hot button. Go back to probing. Try the following statement-and-question technique to get a specific objection.

"Mr. Buyer, we've talked about many things during the last few minutes—what particular area aren't you interested in? Is it my shipment? Is it my price? The time of year?" The key to making this probe work is to go right from the question to possible objections *without a pause.* If you stop after the question, "What particular area aren't you interested in," the prospect may say, "Everything." This reply doesn't help you identify a specific objection.

5. *We don't think it fits our industry.* An effective response to this objection is a third-party referral. This softens the blow in that you are not challenging the objection; you are only replying by using another party as a reference. A typical response could be, "I know exactly how you feel, Mr. Jones. In fact, Mr. Smith of Ajax Company felt the same way until we had an opportunity to review further with him."

It's not necessary that each objection, or apparent objection, be answered the first time it's mentioned. Prospects often raise objections just to get your reaction, maybe to get your agreement. "Your delivery is long," may not be an objection but a simple comment. Your simple reply, "Oh," may be all the buyer wants to hear. If delivery is a reason for not buying, the buyer will raise the objection again.

Patience is often the best way to handle objections. It's not necessary to answer quickly every objection raised. Sometimes a quick reply only encourages another objection, with the prospect trying to raise more objections than you can answer. You can't win that battle. Listen more than you speak and practice patience.

BEING PREPARED TO HANDLE TYPICAL OBJECTIONS

In most selling, there are no more than twenty objections. We recommend you review your presentation to make sure that you give enough specific customer benefits so that most of these are never asked. Give the prospects and customers justification on why they should buy from you to solve their problems. Be prepared to handle:

1. Your price is too high.
2. We are satisfied with our present supplier.
3. We have had trouble with your company.
4. Let me think it over.
5. We are set right now, but drop by later.
6. I need to check with someone.
7. We buy from a centralized source.
8. You cannot service us adequately.
9. Your terms are not good enough.
10. We are not expecting to make a change right now.
11. We had trouble with a previous representative of your company.

12. This isn't the season that we normally buy products or services like yours.
13. Our budget has been cut, and I have a moratorium on spending.
14. What's in it for me?
15. We have commitment of a reciprocal nature.
16. We buy on contract and it is set for this period.

If you prepare a list for your accounts you may come up with a few more.

The sales professional knows many methods to effectively handle the objections raised. Remember after an objection is satisfied, the next step is to close the sale. If prospects or customers are not ready to buy at that time, they may have other objections which are still unanswered. Probing will help identify additional objections.

Often restating the prospect's objection in a question or statement form enables you to reply with a simple answer. This usually takes the steam out of the objection. If buyers previously said they would not buy your offer but now you've convinced them to reconsider, change your offer slightly so it doesn't put them in the embarrassing position of having to change their minds after already saying no.

With a "new" revised offer, they can give you a "new" positive reply. The buyers save face.

UNUSUAL REPLIES TO OBJECTIONS

Every objection you hear has several acceptable answers, and for each one there are several methods or techniques to use. Even some of the seemingly nonsensical answers can be the basis for meaningful probing to provide opportunities to review, listen, question, and qualify.

Following are unique answers to some prospects' objections. These can be used in a professional manner. It is very difficult to give these words the inflection, sense, timing, and the full meaning they can have when said the right way at the right time. Using these can be very effective and offer a real change of pace from the too often typical sales call windup; "Bye now," "thanks," "give it your consideration," "see you next time around." Maybe these unusual replies can help you.

> *Objection:* Your price is too high!
> *Answer:* What isn't?
> *Answer:* I've had exactly 56 people tell me that already; you're number 57. Over 50 of these are now buying from me. What other reasons are there that we can't do business?
> *Answer:* You may be right! Let's review the cost comparisons again. [Note: This objection doesn't really mean anything as a rule. It is

expected that all buyers complain about price; they have to say it. It's an expected dialogue that seems to be suited to the occasion. Buyers are paid to say that your price is too high.]

Objection: We have had problems with your company or product before.

Answer: I regret anything like this has happened. [This demands a straight answer. Get the facts and the circumstances and determine what can be or has been done to correct the problem and what assurances you can give that it wouldn't happen again.]

Answer: What would it take to straighten this out to your satisfaction?

Objection: Let me think it over.

Answer: Savings of this type certainly demand your full consideration. I'm pleased that you want to think it over. Maybe we can think it over together, over a cup of coffee. How do you take your coffee? Let me get you and me a cup.

Answer: I'll be back in a few minutes after you have had a chance to think about it. [Note: This reply arouses emotion when you come back, and your chances are over 80 percent in your favor that it will be a good one. This answer is different and buyers are not programmed for it. There is not much to think about if you have done an effective job of presenting your product or service. If the buyer thinks of any substantial objections, you should be there to answer.]

Objection: We are set now; drop back later.

Answer: [Go do your homework. Check to see where the company isn't set. Come back as soon as you can, preferably within an hour; tell the buyer it is later, you are back, and here is what is required.]

Objection: I need to check with someone.

Answer: [Point to the phone, say, "Go ahead, I'll step out while you do." Note: If you really want an emotional reaction, tell the buyer that while he or she is checking to determine if a buy can be authorized, you will check with your boss to see if you can sell.]

Objection: Our budget has been cut; we can't buy now.

Answer: That's exactly why I came to see you! If you had saved 20 percent [the savings that can be realized from your products or service] of your production or service expenditures during the past year, you wouldn't have these budget problems now.

Objection: What's in it for me?

Answer: [In a stage whisper] Job security [or] The feeling of accomplishment.

Objection: We buy on annual contract.

Answer: I'm sure your contract has provisions for you to test various offerings from other suppliers. When can we get a test going so you will have an idea what you can expect from us when the bid comes up next year?

CLOSING—THE KEY TO GETTING ORDERS

Closing is bringing to a conclusion your sales presentation or interview by asking for the order. It is "pay dirt" for the sales professional. It comes from the idea of closing the discussion, closing your attaché case, and asking for your prospect's order.

Closing is the logical sequence after you have demonstrated to a prospect that the present situation is a problem; it is costing money or time and you deserve their business because you have a solution. You emphasize the specific benefits of your proposal or offering.

When to Close

The ABCs of salesmanship say that you should *always be closing*. Selecting the right time to ask for the order is a decision the sales professional has to make. We included closing in the module with objections because in a presentation a prospect or customer typically has a few objections or questions that have to be clarified. After you handle any objections, the next step should be to close by asking for the order or an opportunity to get you closer to getting an order.

The professional starts to close at the beginning of the presentation and follows through at the conclusion. Whenever enough benefits are realized, the prospect should be asked to buy. Probing identifies hot buttons. Once the hot button is touched, the professional should attempt to close.

THE FEAR OF CLOSING

Fear of closing has sent more sales novices into other fields of endeavor than any other reason. The fear of rejection looms on the salesperson's mind. Will the prospects say no? "They don't like me," "They don't like my product," "They don't like my service," "They don't like my company," and so on.

The newcomers in sales start to turn professional when they recognize that closing is a normal and natural step in the selling sequence. The fears will go away if and when they start to believe in themselves, their products or services, their companies, and the benefits the prospects will enjoy after they buy. The more knowledge and skills they have, the higher their confidence and the better prepared they are to overcome closing fears.

A LOOK AT THE CLOSING SITUATION

Trick phrasing or cute methods of slipping the pen into the prospect's or customer's hand may have a place somewhere, but not in the professional, ethical salesperson's portfolio of techniques. There are many closing techniques that must be tried, including the trial close, the alternate-choice close, presenting the order for approval, the yes technique, the balance-sheet close, and others that are nonmanipulative. Obviously, all the steps in effecting a sale must be done properly and at the right time in order to serve as a foundation to justify in the prospect's or customer's mind that the product or service is worthy of an order.

In addition to knowing the mechanics of closing, there is a great deal of pure sales psychology that must be studied and understood to help you get the order. People buy from people. Hence, the prospect or customer must feel emotionally satisfied before they decide to give you an order. They must believe you and trust you. When prospects buy from you, tell them you come with the offering. You are part of the package.

Certainly, much more is implied here than just asking for the order. The sales professional must be armed with full information of what the product or service will do for the customer and must be able to demonstrate it. Still, even with well-trained salespeople, there is a hesitancy, even a reluctance, to be aggressive in the final stages of the sales call. This is particularly true if they have not done an outstanding job of presenting what the product or service will do in terms of customer benefits. When they fear rejection, they don't ask for the order. They perpetuate the delays in making a buying decision.

The salesperson not only has fear of asking for the order; there is also fear on the part of the buyer. The salesperson knows this, and it only adds to the apprehensiveness at this critical time in the sales interview. The easy and comfortable way out is not to press too hard now, but to postpone the decision to see the buyer another day . . . and another day . . . for three or four more sales calls.

Generally, the first sale to a prospect is after the fifth or sixth sales call. The ratio of sales to calls on those considered regular customers is around one to three or four. It seems that too many salespeople have been reading those articles and books that paint persistence as a virtue to be practiced ad infinitum. It's not. There is a time following your efforts when you are entitled to an order. If you have presented your product or service professionally, confidently ask for the order.

Unfortunately, for whatever reason, salespeople will actually ask for the order, in an effective manner, on fewer than 50 percent of their calls. This is true for calls on both established accounts and for those that are still in the prospect stage. This delay in asking for a buying decision not only costs money and takes time but also keeps the door open for a more aggressive, competitive salesperson to come in and get the order.

With today's high cost of doing business and the value of selling time, anything to improve sales performance is beneficial. Actually there is very little difference in the definition of *persistence* and *insistence*. Insistence gets the job done sooner and usually better. Almost everything that can be accomplished in five or six calls can be accomplished in one, two, or the maximum, three calls, if the calls are planned and include a good probing interview and a presentation is filled with customer benefits.

Closing is the logical final step in the selling sequences. When you help your prospects analyze their problems and identify their needs and wants, the decision to go ahead should be obvious. If your presentation and discussion are effective, and you handle any objections, the close comes easily and naturally.

There should be nothing mysterious about closing. Even in sales situations where no order is actually signed, the prospect must make a definite decision that the time has come to act. Until you obtain this firm commitment to act now, you can receive no return on the time you spent or the effort you have invested.

A SHORT CHECKLIST FOR MORE CLOSES

There are many skills and techniques to increase the ratio of orders received to the number of sales calls made. Following is a short checklist:

1. Build a presentation of believability. You should present your company, yourself, and your product or service as a positive, total package. Use necessary visual aids, including charts, brochures, illustrations, testimonials, samples, and so on. End each step of your presentation by getting a positive commentment that what you're saying is understood and meets the approval of the listener. Encourage the prospect to say yes.

2. Have the proper attitude. During your discussion make positive statements emphasizing how the client will benefit from your offer when an order is placed for your goods or services. Comments such as, "When it is installed in your plant," or "Once the system is in place," puts the prospect in a positive frame of mind. It makes him or her "see" the benefits of ownership.

3. Identify the proper or prime motivators. The prime reasons people buy are pride, profit, fear, love, duty, hate, and security. By proper probing, you can determine which is the motivator that applies to this prospect.

4. Establish a good buying attitude. By asking leading questions during the probing, you can start identifying or establishing buying attitudes with questions such as, "Do you normally buy per project or on an annual contract?" or "Which do you prefer, a buy outright or lease program?" By asking questions of this type, you can determine if the prospect is in a proper buying attitude. During these closing questions, you must know when to keep quiet. After a question has been asked, it's necessary to stop talking and listen to the prospect with full attention.

In closing the sale, you get a timely decision. Your prospect must be convinced that the time has come to decide on a course of action.

Closing, like an effective sales call, requires planning. Consider how and when you are going to ask for the order? A suggestion: if you don't know how you are going to close, don't make the sales call. Plan your entire sales call before you leave your office, from your introductory comments to asking for the order.

CLOSING SIGNALS TO LOOK FOR

There are times during and at the conclusion of your presentation when your closes should enjoy a higher percentage of success. These are after the prospect gives you a verbal or nonverbal closing signal; look for it. Here are some examples:

1. The prospect relaxes—particularly if he or she assumes a pleased and relaxed expression after being cool and argumentative.
2. The prospect reexamines the model or sample of your product after you have finished discussing it.
3. The prospect picks up sales literature of your offering and reexamines some of the pages that have descriptions of features with which he or she seems pleased.
4. The prospect asks you to confirm your shipment or other terms of sale.
5. The prospect compares the details of your offering with those of a competitor.
6. The prospect has appeared pleased and nodded agreement with all the benefits you outlined in your product or service as you made your presentation.

7. You have finished your demonstration and the prospect appears pleased with it.

8. The prospect asks for your opinion—not information, but for your opinion. Take any closing signal as a sign to ask for the order.

HOW OFTEN DO YOU ASK FOR THE ORDER?

This is really an easy question to answer. There is, obviously, no limit to the number of times you can ask for an order. Upon receiving a "no," you throw a little more in the pot. Bring out an additional benefit or two that you have reserved for just this occasion. Press a little harder on the hot button and then ask again. There is no limit to the number of times prospects can say "no." And if they say "no" several times, what do you do? Ask one more question—an easy question to remember because it consists of one word—just the simple question, "Why?"

If you have enough intestinal fortitude, ask again and don't be surprised if they tell you, and in the telling, give you the clue you need to get the order.

CLOSING TECHNIQUES THAT WORK

Following are some closing techniques you may want to try with your prospects or customers. None work all the time. Some may work one time and fail the second. The sales professional considers and uses many techniques, depending on the responses and the selling situation. All these techniques have one primary objective: to get an order.

1. *Asking for it.* The best way to get an order is to ask for it. If you've delivered an effective presentation and you've convinced the buyer, ask for the order. Prospects expect you to ask for it. Don't disappoint them.

2. *Agreement on a series of minor points.* Get a series of "yes" answers throughout the presentation. Get the buyers in an agreeable mood early. If they are agreeable early, you will find it amazing how many times they will say "yes" at the end of your presentation when you ask them to buy. To use this type of close, you must plan carefully, with a benefit-filled presentation full of sales points that the buyer will agree on.

3. *Choice of positive alternatives.* This close asks a question, giving two positive alternatives the buyer can make. An answer to either alternative is an order. This is a successful close if during your presentation interview, you discover that there are two or more products or services the prospect shows interest in and is hesitant to decide which to select. Some examples follow:

- ○ "Mr. Jones, which model would you prefer, the stainless steel or the cast iron?"
- ○ "Ms. Smith, should we install the computer system on the 15th or would the 30th be better?"
- ○ "Mr. Jones, would you prefer our single payment plan or our installment program?"

4. *Similar situation, or telling a story.* This close outlines a situation that another one of your prospects faced and shows how it was handled. The key to using this close is to pick out a situation that has similar circumstances, to outline your recommendations at this time, and to state clearly the favorable results. If this situation is a story about a person or company the listener respects and can relate to, it can be very effective. For example,

> "Ms. Smith, I understand your hesitation in going ahead. It was only a few months ago when Mr. Jones of the Acme Company faced a decision similar to yours. As you know, his plant operation is similar to yours. We reviewed our offering, outlining how we could save him money on his inventory and maintenance. I outlined his savings per month. He went ahead, gave us an order, has the equipment in place, and has saved thousands of dollars in the last two months. Wouldn't you like to start saving money like Mr. Jones?"

5. *Making an assumption.* In this close, you get approval and agreement on minor decisions, making the final agreement and purchase order a logical, final step. You assume that an order is forthcoming and is in the final stage of clarification. Examples are these:

- ○ "Ms. Jones, when do you usually receive shipment?"
- ○ "Would you prefer rail or truck shipment?"
- ○ "How many people would you want to send to our free postinstallation maintenance seminar?"
- ○ "Would you want to inspect the equipment in our plant or after it's in your warehouse?"
- ○ "What accessories do you want us to ship with the original equipment?"

6. *Making a summation close.* In this close, you summarize one by one all the customer benefits mentioned and agreed to during your presentation. During this summation, the prospects are agreeing with your statements. They start to envision themselves and their companies taking advantage of the benefits your product or service offers. Now is the time to give them the opportunity to buy.

7. *Writing a balance sheet.* This close is one of the easiest and most effective. It encourages a prospect who is hesitant, cautious, or suspicious. When a buying decision is tough to get, look for help from the prospect.

Ask for a sheet of paper and make a line down the middle. Next, say, "Mr. Bostwick, on one side, let's list all the positive reasons why you should place an order now." Let him think of and write down the benefits you presented earlier. Give him gentle reminders if necessary. If you had an effective presentation and interview, you should have a long list of customer benefits and reasons why he should place an order now.

When this list of positives is complete, ask him to write down the reasons why he is delaying. *You keep quiet.* This list of negative points will be much shorter. A comparison of the two lists should be very convincing. Now say, "See, Mr. Bostwick, the go-ahead list is much longer than the delay list. Let's go ahead—what is your purchase order number?"

If he hesitates, take a look at his delay list. Handle troublesome items as you would any other objection.

8. *Reducing to the ridiculous.* This is a very effective technique that can close when the buyer is interested but apparently can't justify the financial outlay at this time. Assume she has budget approval of $50,000 for equipment; your offering is $53,000. Try this approach:

> "Ms. Jones, the difference of $3,000 over your budget approval presents a small percentage increase for a piece of equipment with all our features and customer benefits. Over the expected thirty-year life span of the equipment, that's $100 a year or less than $2 per week. In fact, it's less than $.30 per day. Now, Ms. Jones, wouldn't you want to move ahead and enjoy the many benefits of our products now for less than $.30 per day? That's about the cost of a package of gum."

9. *Inducement to buy now or timely event.* This close helps when there is a time limit to some of the conditions of your offering. If you have any special pricing, packaging, service arrangements, or other conditions that will expire within a short time, use this close. Examples are:

- "Mr. Jones, we can make this offer at this time only because we must clear our inventory before we close for our annual plant vacation shutdown."
- "Mr. Jones, this is a preadvertised special price before we announce it at the next trade show. After the 15th, the price will go up 20 percent. I strongly recommend you place your order now to take advantage of this reduced price."

10. *Specific benefit.* This close is based on the prospects' key issues or hot buttons. Stick to the benefit that interests them the most. Satisfy their minds that this is the best decision to make. When you have done your job, ask for the order and promise to see that they get the results and benefits they expect.

11. *Possibility of loss.* This can tie in with other closes. Point out to the prospect what a delay would cost because of the failure to get the benefits of the product or service at an early date. This can be effective if there are only a few models left, and you can say, "Ms. Jones, if you don't act now, I can't guarantee that this model will still be available when you decide. There are other salespeople in my company selling from the same inventory."

CONCLUSION

This module covers two crucial areas of the sales presentation—handling objections and closing. Rather than fearing objections, the sales professional learns to welcome them. They are a means of communication between you and the potential customer. They let you know where you stand. Actually, objections are a normal part of sales negotiations.

Often objections are raised as a delaying tactic. It is important to get to the heart of the delays and find out if the objections are based on real problems. Asking questions and probing will bring out any real objections.

The best way to handle any objection your prospect may have is with your thorough knowledge of your company, product, and service. Don't just give a canned reply to an objection; experiment; try something different.

Throughout the module, we pointed out many suggestions for when and how to close. We emphasized the importance of staying on the subject until you get the answer you seek. Remember, you are doing buyers a favor if you let them buy your product or service.

If they are a purchasing people, they *must* buy. That's their job. That's the reason they're being paid. You're *helping* them do their job. If they are operating people and your benefits are useful to them, you are doing them a favor if you convinced them to give you an order so they can enjoy those benefits.

As a final word on the close, when you get the order, stop selling. Thank the buyer and leave.

Review Questions

1. Why do salespeople fear customer objections?
2. If you recognize that objections are usually part of the selling cycle, why should you welcome them? Explain. How can you prepare for often-asked objections?
3. Assume you are selling small electric motors. List five objections you may hear. How would you handle them? Next, assume you are selling foreign cars, life insurance, and building maintenance service.

4. How would you handle the objections listed in the section "Being Prepared to Handle Typical Objections"?

5. Name some nonverbal signals that can indicate a customer's objections.

6. Explain why handling objections and closing should be covered in the same module.

7. Is there a "best" time to close? Explain.

8. What are some positive steps that can be taken to help close?

9. Why do some salespeople hesitate to ask for the order? How often should they ask?

10. What are positive nonverbal signals that prospects may give to indicate they are ready to buy?

11. Select five closing techniques and try them in role playing with someone playing the part of a prospective buyer.

12. Name five unusual closes that may be used. When should they be tried?

13. Why should salespeople continually strive to improve their closing ability?

module thirteen
Keeping Customers Satisfied and Staying Competitive

The effort to get a prospect to place an order and become a customer is long and arduous. It is the constant challenge of the sales professional. Although the search for prospects to turn into new customers never stops, you must never stop building rapport with your present customers. They deserve your follow-up, so that they will receive the products or services ordered. A commitment to service is required to keep your present customers buying from you.

BRINGING YOUR PRODUCTS TO MARKET

In a free-enterprise business environment, companies grow by continually bringing to the market new products and services. Professional salespeople take these marketable items to their prospects and customers and strive to get them interested enough to buy.

Because many companies and individuals are selling the same or similar products or services, a salesperson is operating in a very competitive environment.

Potential buyers have limited resources and/or limited requirements; hence they have to choose between available suppliers. Some products or services may be available from only one or a couple of suppliers (for example, large computers, aircraft, and special risk insurance), whereas others may be available from numerous suppliers (office copying equipment, electric motors, automobiles, and standard insurance policies).

The professionals in sales recognize very early in their careers that if they are to succeed they have to survive and grow in this competitive market. They recognize it; they respect it; they thrive on it. The weaker souls, those with a less competitive spirit, may linger in sales for a while and then drift into other, less competitive careers.

An emotional shock is something felt by those who get into sales because "they like people," and then find out that not all the people they meet, prospects, competitors, and some of their peers, like them. Professional selling is truly a career of survival of the fittest. It requires a strong commitment.

Recognizing that selling is a very competitive profession, we will now look at what you can do to bring your products or services to market more effectively than your competitors, suggesting ways to build goodwill and rapport to keep your customers.

HANDLING COMPETITION

Some suggested methods to handle competitors are the following:

1. Learn as much as you can about their products and services. Study how they bring their products to market, their company policies, their pricing levels or strategies, the markets they serve, and their customers.

2. Prepare your sales calls, literature, and sales aids so they bring out your strongest points. Prepare your presentation so that it will counter the best possible competitive appeal.

3. List the strong selling points of each of your competitors on a separate sheet of paper. Next to each strong point or apparent advantage, list a similar or better customer benefit from your product or service. Don't assume that every prospect or customer of yours knows your competitors' strong points. You emphasize your customer benefits during the presentation. Don't mention, and sell, your competitors.

4. Analyze why prospects or customers are buying from competitors and prepare a detailed plan to convince them that they should be buying from you.

5. Continually review and reinforce the reasons why your customers are doing business with you. Analyze your efforts to determine if you have slipped in any of the areas that convinced the prospects to buy from you initially. Continually strive to build a closer rapport with your customers so they can be more dependent on you. Earn the right to ask for more orders based on your commitment to service.

Remember: Your best customers are probably your competitors' best prospects. Keep working to keep them satisfied and buying from you.

WINNING CUSTOMERS FROM COMPETITORS

All your prospects and many of your customers are buying from and are loyal to your competitors. Through the years they have built up rapport and commitment to these suppliers. It is hard to lure these buyers to your side, but it must be done. When a company enters the marketplace or wants to increase its market share, it must get customers by luring them from other suppliers.

Some suggestions on how to get prospective customers, who are loyal to competitors, to buy from you are the following:

1. Review the original decision on why the prospect decided to buy from a competitor. You may ask, "Ms. Jones, what made you decide to buy from the Allstar Company in the first place?" The reply will give you an indication of her "hot button." In your presentation, emphasize what your company has accomplished in supplying goods and services to customers with similar needs and wants. Maybe you are better able to satisfy the reason why she decided to buy from Allstar in the first place. Tell her how you have been serving your present customers and offer the names of those who are satisfied. Mention how you can perform an important function for her company if she gave you the opportunity to bid on its requirement.

2. Discuss the necessity of a continual source of supply by receiving products and services from more than one supplier. Transportation problems, strikes, plant relocations, mergers and market changes, or other production or work stoppages can bring interruption in supply. Other sources of available goods and services could be important for your prospect's survival.

3. Continue to stress the specific benefits that your product or service can provide. Don't assume that competitors are continually emphasizing all the benefits that their products or services offer.

4. No company can afford to remain stagnant in its market. Hence, continually point out that it will be worth the prospect's time to evaluate what your products and service can do for her.

5. Emphasize the importance of continually being alert for new suppliers so the company can take advantage of the supplier's creative abilities, spurred by competition and other market of economic changes.

A competitor's customers are loyal and satisfied because the products or services they receive fit their organization and requirements now. These conditions can and do change, so customer satisfaction is relative. Strive for the opportunity to show how your products or services can give prospects more value for their buying dollar.

A suggested approach may be to ask for a trial order so prospective customers can see for themselves the quality of your product or service. A statement such as, "You can do your company a very fine service if you investigate how the new product we have to offer can help you." Encourage them to consider how their design, management, operations, or personnel department can evaluate your products so that they personally see the benefits they will receive. This approach can get an initial order for testing and evaluation. It can give you a foot in the door. Once you get this opportunity, make sure you open the door, get inside, and stay there.

BECOMING AN ACCEPTABLE SUPPLIER

In competing against established suppliers, you may first have to get on the bidder's list of acceptable suppliers. Obviously, if companies have been in business awhile, they have sources for the goods and services they need. The sources may not be the "best," but they are available. If you want to become a source you must create an awareness and then an interest and desire in your products or services. First, you have to get to the level of being considered acceptable. After this level is achieved, you must strive higher to reach the level of preferred.

Let's start by offering some ideas and statements you can use to get on a bidders list of acceptable suppliers:

1. Consider sending copies of advertisements, newspaper articles, trade journal reports, testimonial letters, and so on to buying influences. This step will alert them to your acceptance by other companies in the same or similar activities.
2. Invite members of the prospect's firm to visit your plant, your headquarters, your offices, customer installations, an open house, a trade show, or a convention.
3. You may consider a comment like this one: "I assume your present suppliers are quoting you a fair price on your requirements; however, with new products and services continually being introduced and inflation, improved efficiency, higher productivity, and energy conservation concerns to all of us, maybe you can do better."
4. Say, "What I'd like to do is have a copy of your bid specifications and requirements so we can prepare a proposal and quotation for your review and evaluation."
5. Suggest the following: "You can determine whether or not what we have proposed will give you more value for your buying dollar."

6. Or say, "What I'm asking for is a chance to prove how well we can serve you. When will you go out to buy your next requirements?"

Trial orders, sample equipment, thirty-day service evaluation period, money-back guarantees, and limited acceptances and usage are all part of what it may take for you to become an acceptable supplier. The creativity of the sales professional is really challenged by thinking of ways and means to become an acceptable supplier to prospects that are apparently satisfied by their present suppliers. In the next section, we'll give some additional methods you can use to convert satisfied buyers.

CONVERTING THE SATISFIED BUYER

Satisfied buyers of a competitor's product or services may feel content because they have determined that what they are buying is the "best" for their employers. You have to alter their buying habits if they are not buying from you. Suggestions that could help you convert buyers are the following:

1. Determine if there are people in your plant, home office, or sales force who are able to suggest ways they've tackled similarly entrenched competitors. They can help you be more effective in your presentation. Check if your presentation is emphasizing the most appealing benefits you could offer against your competitor. Review with your manager the presentation you are planning to use. Maybe together you can come up with something you may have overlooked.

Enlist the help of satisfied customers of yours who are influential in similar businesses or who belong to the same society or organization as the prospect you are trying to convince. A very effective technique is the testimonial, especially when the prospect you're trying to sway respects the person you mention.

2. Review the customers' overall operation. Study their methods of doing business, their products or services, and their competitors in the field. This will give you an enlightened approach to understanding their businesses. Can you offer recommendations on how they can improve their position in the marketplace by using some of the products and services you are able to offer? To help them break the habit of buying from the same supplier, you will automatically give them an opportunity to consider your product or services.

3. Point out that when prospective customers buy from you, they not only receive the product and service of your company but also, more importantly, your commitment to serve their accounts in the best, most professional manner. They must be convinced of your professional talents.

4. Try to identify weaknesses in competitive products or services. This is best done by probing, asking prospects why they are currently buying from their present supplier. Determine why they are presently satisfied— product specifics, delivery, terms of sale, price, or other areas of interest to them. Are they buying from competitors because of force of habit? In engineering-oriented companies, specifications identifying purchased items with model, style, or part numbers cause a hardship if they are changed. There is reluctance to change suppliers because a little extra work is involved, and buyers and engineers have to answer to their superiors concerning why the change is being suggested. You must continually look for prospects' hesitancy in making these changes, and it is necessary to offer many positive reasons why the company can benefit from them. The benefits must be clearly understood by all the people initiating these changes so they feel comfortable when they have to explain to their management. You know you have to supply the tools for these changes in specification.

5. Consider all the departments in a prospective customer's organization that would give you the receptive audience you need to emphasize your benefits. Consider all influential people at the location you are contacting, and at others, such as headquarters or other plants, where the buying decision can be influenced.

HANDLING PRICE CUTTERS

After you've gotten prospects to buy from you and become customers, you must be very diligent so you don't lose them to price-cutting competitors. Competitors can always have the attention of your established customers by quoting lower prices. Lower prices grab attention and are a very effective tool for getting a first order. If you have to compete with companies that continually cut prices, some considerations which may help you are the following:

1. Prepare a list of all the features, functions, and benefits that your products or services offer. Define what these benefits mean in dollars, time savings, increased production, lower costs, customer satisfaction, and so forth.

2. Emphasize the strong relationship you've had with that customer and how you've earned the right to maintain or increase your level of business.

3. Outline the benefits that come from long-time relations with your company, its management, manufacturing procedures, supplies, and convenience. Continually stress the value received by your offering, emphasizing that value is a combination of price and service and is the prime concern.

GETTING BACK THE CUSTOMER YOU LOST

The first action to take after you lose a customer to a competitor is to ask yourself, "What can I do to get this customer back?" Second, "What has to be done to assure myself I don't lose more customers for similar reasons?"

Prepare a list of all the things that could have gone wrong with the account. Next, set up a convenient meeting with your former customer for a frank discussion so you can clarify the position. Consider key areas such as price, delivery, proper handling of warranties or guarantees, and service calls.

Your ex-customer may try to be vague so as not to hurt your feelings. Indicate that although you've lost a particular order, it is your intention to win back the business in the future. You want to solicit support in helping you identify what went wrong by discussing your possible problems.

In retrospect, determine if you've actually made the classical salesperson's mistake of *assuming*. If you assumed you'd get the order, you probably forgot something or someone. Once you start to assume, you get complacent and forget to emphasize all the benefits that are important to maintain your customers' interest and business. Consider the following:

- Have you kept them abreast of all your new products or services?
- Have you kept them abreast of important price, personnel, or policy changes?
- Have you visited them on a frequency appropriate for their business activity?
- Have you considered all the ways of helping them improve their businesses by emphasizing products and services that would help them in the marketplace?

In order to regain lost customers, it is important to review why they stopped buying from you. Emphasize that you are interested in serving them again. Openly admit that if in some way you did not serve them properly or deserve their business when the last order was placed, you apologize for the oversight. Review anything new and beneficial about your product or service that they should be aware of. Tell them you will be calling on a regular basis to keep them abreast of new products and services, and you expect to *earn* their business in the future.

THE IMPORTANCE OF DEVELOPING ENTHUSIASTIC CUSTOMERS

Enthusiastic customers are one of your best sources of prospects because they are excited about what they buy and want to share that excitement with others.

Ask satisfied customers how they like a certain salesperson and they are apt to say something like, "Oh, he's okay. I get what I pay for." But the *enthusiastic customer* jumps at the chance to brag about the salesperson: "She's the greatest! Let me tell you what she did for me just last month." If you deliver what customers want at a fair price, without any problems, they are satisfied. Although that's better than being dissatisfied, you need more to ensure keeping the customer and increasing sales. You have to develop enthusiastic customers. Let's review how you can make your customers enthusiastic about your products and services.

First, you must deliver more than the customer expects. This breeds enthusiasm, which produces a climate that ensures loyalty and increased sales.

Here are some suggestions the professionals have for producing and maintaining enthusiastic customers. Try the ones that best fit your selling situation.

1. *Keep in touch.* Check after delivery to see that things are going well. Check again later and ask for leads on new prospects. Write a thank-you letter or make a telephone call.

2. *Handle complaints promptly.* Problems are inevitable. Don't ignore them. They grow with neglect. Do more than the customer expects in satisfying the complaint.

3. *Be a friend.* Think of the customer as a friend and do things for him or her accordingly. Send birthday cards. Send a postcard while you're on vacation. Congratulate him or her on awards or advancement.

4. *Give praise when it's due.* Look for things for which you can give legitimate praise: something the firm has done, awards, increased earnings, a big order. Congratulate the customer personally for awards, election to an office, and honors. Customers appreciate attention, too.

5. *Send prospects to your customers.* If your customers are in business, send leads or refer prospects to them. It's human nature to respond in kind to anyone who does us a favor.

6. *Ask for prospect leads.* How does this increase the customer's enthusiasm for you? We're always flattered when asked for help, suggesting that we're important. It caresses our egos.

There is a maxim in selling: "Business goes where it's invited and stays where it is well treated." Take time to treat your customers as you would like to be treated and you'll change them from so-so satisfied customers to enthusiastic sales-getters. In the next section we will give you a few more suggestions on how you can become the preferred supplier.

BECOMING THE PREFERRED SUPPLIER

The best way to become the preferred supplier is to build such a high level of good will that your customers will always think of you first. This is easier said than done. It requires a strong commitment on your part. Following are suggestions that may help you become a preferred supplier.

1. Build a reputation for customer service based on trust and dedication.
2. Stay abreast of market conditions, new products or services, industry trends, technical standards, advertisements, and personnel changes.
3. Establish yourself as a "consultant" in the eyes of your customers by using a conscientious, professional approach to their needs and wants.
4. Continually review the development of your professional sales skills to determine how well you are progressing.
5. Check your call frequency to verify that you are making enough sales calls based on actual or potential business.
6. Report back to your manufacturing plant and/or headquarters any information regarding energy saving, size, preferred performance, lower cost, convenience, better delivery, or other features or benefits your competitors announce.
7. Remember you are part of the product or service you offer your customer. If customers continue to place their faith in you and your company, don't let them down. You are the integral part of the total package you bring to your customers.

CONCLUSION

You earn your orders by pursuing potential business and professionally taking all the actions necessary to persuade a prospect to become a customer. You keep that same commitment and drive so that your present customers continue to buy from you.

Competition is a way of life. Learning how to handle the competition with customers and prospects is a big part of a salesperson's job. There are many ways to handle competition—knowledge, planning, and effective sales skills will help a great deal. Commitment to building rapport is essential.

Customers are won over from competitors daily. It can be difficult to get a customer to change a source of supply, but it can be done by a diligent, professional effort on your part.

Some of the customers that switch their source of supply may be your own. When this happens, review your past performance with these customers. Determine what went wrong. Then do everything you can to get them back.

Review Questions

1. Why is it necessary to follow your customer's orders closely?
2. Name five ways you can keep customers thinking about you in a favorable manner.
3. Explain why it's necessary to keep your present customers satisfied, while you continually look for prospects.
4. Name five methods you can use to handle competition.
5. What contribution does the field salesperson make to keep his or her company's products or services competitive?
6. Name the major selling points of each of your major competitors. Next to each point, list a similar or better customer benefit for your products or service. How do you compare?
7. Give three methods you can use to win prospects from competitors?
8. What do you do to win back a former customer you lost to competitors?

The
Final Wrap-Up

This manual covered the key topics those in sales should be aware of and continually develop. Sales professionals should always strive to improve their performance by setting higher objectives followed by action programs to meet these objectives. Selling skills and techniques, tied in with the proper attitude and work habits, were mentioned as basic requirements of the successful salesperson. Knowledge is essential. The time and effort you spend getting knowledge and studying effective sales skills and techniques, as well as developing the proper attitude and desirable work habits, is the admission fee you must pay to earn the right to take up a prospect's or customer's time.

The salesperson must be prepared and qualified to discuss the features, functions, and most importantly, the benefits of the products or services represented by his or her company.

The professional learns as much about the prospects or customers, the markets, the company, and the competition as possible. The successful application of knowledge through proven selling skills and techniques is essential to get orders. Time spent in improvement of sales skills pays dividends. The sales professional identifies prospects' needs and wants by asking questions, listening, and offering solutions to problems.

Go back and reread the modules or sections where you feel additional reinforcement will be beneficial. Check any marginal notes to see if you've taken the actions you desired. Determine if you are using the exhibits to help you prepare, plan, and be as effective as you can.

We recommend that you invest in your personal and professional growth by setting aside a portion of your annual income, possibly 2 to 5 percent, to buy sales and inspirational books and cassette tapes and to attend sales-training seminars. The time and money you spend in professional development will reap rewards.

Take advantage of modern electronic technology by getting a small cassette recorder. It is convenient to use and carry. Nonproductive time can be utilized by listening to sales-training and inspirational tapes while traveling to and from home or to and from the office. Sales interviews and presentations can be recorded and played back to help you gain confidence. The effectiveness of cassette learning is in its convenience and repetition.

Success in sales, as in any career, should be considered a continuous journey, not a destination. If we define success as "the achievement of desirable goals," we must realize that as a set of goals are achieved, they should be followed with another, more challenging set.

Selling is a dynamic field that requires personal commitment. By introducing new products and services into the marketplace, salespeople are supporting the free-enterprise system, serving their country and themselves. They realize that they are selling themselves along with their products or services and their company. Their's is truly a *people business*, of people buying from people.

In sales, the challenge is high and the rewards are great. Success can only come when goals are set and achieved, coupled with the commitment to strive for higher levels of performance.

You have the ability to make whatever you want out of your career. It is your choice, your commitment, your future. Make the commitment to be more successful—starting now.

Ambition is wanting something better . . . success is getting it.

Glossary
of Sales Terms

Note: For simplicity, we will use the letters P/C to mean prospects or customers.

Account: a P/C presently assigned or to be assigned to a salesperson.

ASK: the action a salesperson takes with a P/C to identify needs, wants, methods of doing business, and ways to get the action desired; see *probe*.

Attitude: the outlook, temperament, and reaction a salesperson has in his or her day-to-day activity toward the sales profession.

Audio-Visual: a sales aid that allows the P/C to see and hear about the product or service at the same time.

Benefit: what a P/C can or will enjoy from purchasing a product or service.

Benefit (specific): what *this* P/C will enjoy after purchasing a product or service.

Brainstorming: the consideration of all influences in the buying and selling process that can help or hinder getting an order.

Buyer: a person assigned to purchase or buy; someone who influences a purchase.

Buying cycle: the activities individuals or firms may be involved in from the time they decide a product or service may be required until it is purchased.

Buying influence: an individual or department in a company that contributes information or decides what products or services to buy.

Call frequency: how often an account is called on; can be any number of times per year, quarter, month, and so on.

Canned presentation: a tightly structured sales presentation, usually memorized by the salesperson.

Client: customer assigned to a salesperson.

Close: the end of a presentation, interview, or other discussion with a P/C.

Closing: the activities involved in bringing a meeting with a P/C to a close.

Cold call: calling on a P/C without an appointment.

Competitors: other individuals or companies selling the same or similar products or services.

Concept selling: selling of an idea (a concept), usually without the benefit of a tangible product or service.

Customer: an individual, company, or other organization that buys.

Customer benefit: what and/or how this P/C will improve from purchasing a product or service.

Deal: often used in describing the many actions and transactions between buyers and sellers; it's suggested that its use be limited because it can leave a negative impression.

Distributor: usually someone who is authorized to buy from one company and distribute to other companies.

Enthusiasm: positive excitement and drive.

Feature: something built in or inherent in a product or service; it doesn't have to be exclusive to make an important sales point.

Feedback: looking and listening for a response from a P/C to guide future questioning.

Function: how or why a feature works.

Gives: something a salesperson can give up during a negotiation if it will help get an order.

Goal: an objective or target expected to be reached within a fixed date; should be written down, measurable, and reviewed regularly.

Grabber: an initial statement or question that is intended to "grab" the attention of the P/C.

Hazardous areas: considerations in a sales strategy that may prevent a salesperson from getting an order.

Hot button: an expression referred to when a P/C is very responsive to one or more of the benefit statements.

Ice-breaker: a question, statement, or comment used in a sales call to open a discussion, to "break the ice."

Interview: a two-way, open discussion with a P/C in an attempt to identify his or her needs, wants, and methods of doing business.

Knowledge: the information necessary for a salesperson to be prepared to call on a P/C.

Major account: a P/C that is in the market frequently and buys in large dollar volume; sometimes called a A account.

Marginal account: a P/C that is in the market less frequently or buys in smaller dollar volume; sometimes called a B account.

Market(s): all the P/Cs that are potential clients or may be interested in a salesperson's products or services; can be identified by territory, type, or size of account.

Marketing: all the activities necessary to promote, transfer, distribute, and sell a product or service.

Market penetration: how well a product or service is selling in the markets served; can be expressed in percentages, dollars, units, and so on.

Maximum return per call: evaluating what dollar return in the way of orders can be expected when reviewed on the number and length of the sales call over a given period, say a year, quarter, or month.

Minor account: a P/C that is in the market occasionally and usually buys in low dollar volume; sometimes called a C account.

Needs: a product or service that is required by a P/C for personal or business well-being.

Negotiation: the activity of meeting and discussing the products and terms of sale in an attempt to reach an acceptable arrangement.

Nonverbal communications: facial gestures or other body motions that can communicate positive or negative reactions.

Objection(s): the reason(s) given by a P/C for not buying now.

Objective: what one wants to achieve; a goal, a target; must have a given date for accomplishment.

Offering: a written or verbal statement about the products or services that are for sale.

Open-ended questions: questions asked that usually cannot be answered with a simple yes or no; but encourage a more detailed reply.

Opening: the start of a sales interview, presentation, or call.

Pitch: a slang expression for a sales presentation.

Plan: the programs and actions necessary to reach a goal or objective.

Presentation manual: a binder or folder containing material that can offer supporting proof to a sales interview or presentation.

Prime selling time: the time when sales professionals should be in front of or on the telephone with a P/C; usually considered to be the normal business hours for the P/C being called.

Prioritize: set in order of importance actions that are to be taken.

Probing: the process wherein a salesperson asks questions, listens, and makes sales points to determine the buyers' needs and wants, hot buttons, how they do business, decision makers, and so on, to identify how to approach them in future sales calls.

Proof: what may be shown or explained to a P/C to verify a sales point or feature presented.

Prospect: an individual, company, or organization that has a need or want for products or services and has the ability to pay for them.

Prospecting: the activities engaged in when looking for prospects.

Prospect list: a listing of prospects showing call details, results, and action programs.

Qualifying: determining if a prospect needs or wants a product or service and has the ability to pay for it.

Referral: a recommendation given by a customer, by a testimonial letter, verbally, or other means; it can be the name of a prospect, company, or organization that can use a product or service.

Retail selling: usually a situation in which sellers wait in a store or other place of business for a P/C to come to them.

Return on time invested (ROTI): return in the way of orders received or expected compared with the amount of time required to get the orders.

Sale: when an order is received; when buyers state they want to make a purchase; a reduction in price or a special offering.

Sales aid: any person, place, or thing that will help get an order; see *sales tool.*

Sales call: the time a salesperson is with a P/C to build or maintain rapport or to get orders.

Sales interview: activities to identify the needs, wants, problems, and hot buttons of P/Cs, usually made before an effective sales presentation can be given.

Salesperson/salespeople: individuals engaged in selling products or services either by having potential buyers come to them or by going out on sales calls.

Sales plan: identifying the sales objective required, usually by product, territory, salespeople, market share, and so on.

Sales planning: the identification and carrying out of programs and actions necessary to meet a goal or objective.

Sales—planning ladder: a concept in which all the major activities required to get an order are identified in a step-by-step format.

Sales point: a benefit-filled sentence or statement that can be made about a product or service that should interest a buyer.

Sales presentation: the activities involved in bringing products or services to a buyer's attention.

Sales professional: the individual in sales who is committed to continually improving his or her performance by learning and applying sales techniques and skills.

Sales tool: an object, brochure, sample, model, document, and so on that can be used to help emphasize a point made during a sales call.

Sell: the activities involved in getting another person interested in what is offered.

Sellatechnics: the continual study and use of professional selling techniques.

Selling time: time spent in front of, or on the telephone with, a P/C.

Showmanship: using audio-visuals and sales aids in an attempt to make a sales presentation as memorable as possible.

Skills: the abilities developed from being knowledgeable about sales principles, their successful application, and the proper attitude toward the sales profession.

Statement-question technique: making a positive statement first and then asking a question; effective in probing.

Strategy: identifying a course of action required to reach a desired sales objective.

Success: the realization of a desired objective.

Tactics: identifying the specific actions, sales calls, timing, or other methods necessary to carry out a strategy.

Techniques: the actions and methods used to get a sales message across, to get the results desired.

Territorial management: the arranging of out-of-office sales calls in an efficient manner, one that will reduce backtracking and loss of time.

Third-party testimonial: a letter from or a reference to a person not present who is a customer of the salesperson's products or services and would attest to his or her satisfaction.

Tie-breakers: a customer benefit that will "swing" an order in a salesperson's favor; something that can be offered to break a tie.

Time analysis: an hour-by-hour review of where and how time is being spent so changes can be initiated for more effective utilization.

Time management: identifying what can be done to help an individual be more efficient in using time.

Visual aid: anything that can be seen during a sales presentation that would help make the presentation more memorable by emphasizing key points.

Wants: something that a P/C may desire; it may not be immediately identified without effective probing by the salesperson.

Wholesaler: someone who usually buys in larger quantities and sells in smaller quantities; a middleman.

Appendix

The following list is of well-known nationwide sales organizations:

American Management Association
135 West 50th Street
New York, N.Y. 10020

National Society of Sales Training Executives
1040 Woodcock Road
Orlando, Florida 32803

Sales Executives Club of N.Y., Inc.
122 East 42nd Street, Suite 1014
New York, N.Y. 10168

Manufacturers' Agents National Association
Box 16878
2021 Business Center Drive
Irvine, California 92713

National Association of Professional Saleswomen
2088 Morley Way
Sacramento, California 95825

Sales & Market Executives International, Inc.
330 West 42nd Street, Suite 1200
New York, N.Y. 10036

Index

Acceptable suppliers, 206–7
Account classification, 120–24
Account listing, 101
AIDA approach to sales call, 91–92
Alternative solutions, consideration of, 153
Annual reports, 84
Appointment calls, 59–62
ASK, 3, 12
Asking questions, 9–12, 32–33, 170
Aspiration levels, negotiation and, 177
Attitude, 2, 3, 7–8
Available products, services, and consultants, review of, 153

Benefits of product, 19–23, 46, 94, 133, 134
    emphasizing in presentation, 140–41, 143
Bidding change, notices of, 154
Body language, 29, 174–76
Brainstorming, 159
Brevity in written communications, 48
Business newspapers, 84
Buyer's remorse, 72
Buyer's role in negotiations, 180–81
Buying cycle, 152–55
Buying influences, 152, 155–57

Caesar, Julius, 48
Call frequency, 101, 122–24
Cancellation charges, 179–80

Cassette learning, 37, 78, 214
Churchill, Sir Winston, 77
CIMA approach to sales call, 91–92
Circular coverage, 124
Clarity of verbal communications, 34–35
Closing, 184, 194–201
    checklist for, 196–97
    fear of, 194–95
    techniques for, 198–201
    timing, 194
Cloverleaf coverage, 124–25
Cold-call selling, 80–81, 88–95
    AIDA and CIMA approaches, 91–92
    benefits of, 89–90
    objections, 89–90
    opening, 92–95
    planning, 90–91
Communication:
    reasons for, 29
    total, 28–29
    verbal (*see* Verbal communications)
    written (*see* Written communications)
    (*see also* Listening; Telephone)
Competition, 203–6
Compliments, sincere, 93–94, 133, 134
Concept selling, 151–52
Concluding sales letters, 46–47
Creativity, lack of, 75
Customer benefit opening, 133, 134
Customer contact time, 115, 116
Customer-grading worksheet, 121–22, 130

Daily activity planning, 117
Deal, elimination of word, 35
Decision to buy, 155
Delaying actions, objections as, 188
Delays, 179
Direct mail programs, 87–88
Distributors, selling to, 23–24

Emotion-packed words, 33–34
Emotions, 150
Eye contact, 136

Fear:
    of objections, 184, 188
    of rejection, 80, 90, 184, 188
Features of product, 18, 22
Flexibility, 16–17
FOB, 178–79
Free enterprise system, 2
Functions of product, 19, 22

Grabbers, 45, 142
Guarantees, 179

Habits, 151
Hazardous areas, 152, 158–59
Hopscotch coverage, 124
Hot button salesmanship, 13, 17, 22, 90
Humorous approach, 137

Ice-breakers, 92, 133–37
Inactive customers, 83–84
Industry or business-related approach, 137
Interview, 131–38

Key buying influences, 152, 155–57
Kinesics, 29, 174–76
Knowledge, 2, 3–5

Leads, sources of, 84–85
Letters, 45–50
Listening, 1, 71–79
    benefits of, 77
    cassette, 78
    checklist, 74
    importance of, 71–72
    improving skills of, 73–74
    reasons for poor, 72, 76
List of prospects, 85–86, 97
Logic, 150
Lost customers, 209–10

Mails, prospecting through, 87–88
Management planning, 100–101
Manufacturers, selling to, 24
Miscommunications, 37–39
Motivators, 20–21

Names, remembering, 35–36
National account selling, 160
Needs, identification of, 152–53
Need-satisfaction selling, 17
Negative words, 33
Negotiations, 154–55, 164–83
    aspiration levels, 177
    buyer's role, 180–81
    effective, 166–67
    nonverbal communication and, 174–76
    planning, 164–65, 169–70, 172–73
    price, 170–72
    tactics for, 167–68
    telephone, 182
    tie-breakers, 168–69
    win/win attitude, 176
Nierenberg, Gerard I., 38–39
Nonverbal communications, negotiation and,
    174–76

Objections, 4, 184–94
    in cold-call selling, 89–90
    definition of, 185
    as delaying action, 188
    effective methods of handling, 189–91
    fear of, 184, 188
    reasons for, 186–89
    on telephone, 58, 65–66
    typical, 191–92
    unusual replies to, 192–94
Objections, 17, 81–82, 100, 107
Offerings, submission and evaluation of, 154
Office time, 115, 116, 118–19
Open-ended questions, 9–12
Opening interview, 131–37
Opening sales calls, 92–95
Oral communication (*see* Verbal communi-
    cations)
Original equipment manufacturers (OEMs),
    selling to, 24

Package offer, 179
Patents, 179
Payments, 179
Periodicals, 84
Personal time, 115, 116, 119–20
Persuasion, power of, 13–14
Pitch, elimination of word, 35
Planning:
    cold-call selling, 90–91
    sales presentation, 140
    negotiation, 164–65, 169–70, 172–73
    (*see also* Sales planning)
Positive mental attitude, 7–8
Prebid meetings, 154
Preferred suppliers, 154, 211
Pre-negotiation, 164–65, 169–70, 172–73
Preparedness, 14–15

Presentation (*see* Sales presentation)
Presentation manual, 15–16
Previous prospects, 83–84
Price, negotiation of, 170–72
Price cutters, 208–9
Probing, 10, 32–33, 133, 134–35
Problem solving, 8–9
Product mix, 101
Product value, emphasis on, 173
Proof of benefits of product, 19–20, 22, 46, 94–95, 133, 135
Prospect/customer-assessment worksheet, 121, 129
Prospecting, 80–88
  identifying, qualifying, and developing prospects, 82–84
  importance of, 82–83
  list, 85–86, 97
  objectives of, 81–82
  opening, 92–95
  sources of leads, 84–85
  by telephone, 57–58, 61, 88
  through mails, 87–88
  within own territory, 87
Provocative questions, 93
Puffery, 20

Questions, 9–12, 32–33, 170
Quotation, request for, 154

Reasoning, 150
Referral, 94
Rejection, fear of, 80, 90, 184, 188
Remembering names, 35–36
Repeat calls, 75
Retail selling, 23
Return on time invested (ROTI), 125–26
Rhetorical questions, 11
Routine letters, 48–49

Sales aids, 152, 157–58
Sales-Call Planner, 107–8, 111
Sales calls:
  objectives, 107
  (*see also* Sales planning)
Sales interview, 15–17
Salesperson planning, 101–3
Sales planning, 98–111
  essentials, 98–99
  importance of, 99–100
  management planning, 100–101
  planning work, 104–7
  Sales-Call Planner, 107–8, 111
  salesperson planning, 101–3
  Sales-Planning Ladder, 98, 103–4, 110
Sales points, development of, 17–23
Sales presentation, 16–17, 139–48
  benefits, emphasizing, 140–41, 143

Sales presentation (*cont.*)
  customer participation, 144
  favorable attention, formula for, 142–43
  motivating buying, 141
  personalizing, 141
  planning, 140
  showmanship, 144–45
  techniques, 143–44
  by telephone, 64
  visual aids, 145–47
Sales strategies and tactics, 2, 3, 5–7, 149–63
  analysis of, 6–7
  buying cycle, 152–55
  buying influences, 152, 155–57
  concept selling, 151–52
  hazardous areas, 152, 158–59
  national account selling, 160
  reasoning, logic, and emotions, 150
  teamwork, 149, 159–60
  tools and aids, 152, 157–58
  written outline of, 161, 163
Satisfied customers, 210–11
  conversion of, 207–8
Secretarial and receptionist screen, 64–65
Sellatechnics, 2
Selling professional, 1–26
  asking questions, 9–12, 32–33, 170
  attitude, 2, 3, 7–8
  flexibility, 16–17
  hot button salesmanship, 13, 17, 22, 90
  knowledge, 2, 3–5
  persuasion, power of, 13–14
  preparedness, 14–15
  presentation manual, 15–16
  sales points, development of, 17–23
  sales skills and techniques, 2, 3, 5–7
  statement-question technique, 10–13
Sentence structure, 43, 47–48
Service time, 115, 116, 119
Showmanship in presentation, 144–45
Skill improvement, 101–3
Socrates, 10
Sources, analysis of, 153
Sources of leads, 84–85
Specifications, preparedness of, 153
Statement-question (SQ) technique, 10–13
Straight-line coverage, 124
Strategies and tactics (*see* Sales strategies and tactics)

Teamwork, 149, 159–60
Technical specifications, 177
Telephone, 39, 52–70
  appointment calls, 59–62
  forms, 66–67, 69–70
  habits, appraisal of, 54–57
  negotiations, 182

Telephone (*cont.*)
    objections on, 58, 65–66
    presentation, 62–64
    prospecting by, 57–58, 61, 88
    secretarial and receptionist screen, 64–65
    techniques, 55–56
    timing, 60
    voice, 39–40, 52
Terms of sales, 178–80
Territorial management (*see* Time and territorial management)
Territory, prospecting within own, 87
Thank-you letters, 49
Third-party referral, 94
Third-party testimonials, 133–34
Tie-breakers, 168–69
Time-analysis worksheet, 115–17, 128
Time and territorial management, 113–30
    account classification, 120–24
    benefits of, 114
    customer contact time, 115, 116
    daily activity planning, 117
    definition of, 112–13
    office time, 115, 116, 118–19
    personal time, 115, 116, 119–20
    return on time invested, 125–26
    service time, 115, 116, 119
    time-analysis worksheet, 115–17, 128
    travel time, 115, 116, 118
Timing of telephone calls, 60

Toastmasters International, 37
Topical subject approach, 137
Trade associations, 3
Trade journals, 84
Travel time, 115, 116, 118
Twain, Mark, 48

Vacation letters, 49
Verbal communications, 30–40
    clarity of, 34–35
    improving, 30–34, 36–37
    miscommunications, 37–39
    remembering names, 35–36
    voice, 39–40
    words to avoid, 35
Verbal masks, 38–39
Visual aids, 145–47
Voice, 39–40

Warranties, 179
WATS line, 58
Wholesalers, selling to, 23–24
Word size, 43, 47
Work, planning, 104–7
Written communications, 40–50
    clarity of, 43–44
    letters, 45–50
    organization of, 42–43
    reasons for skill in, 40–42
Written outline of strategies and tactics, 161, 153

NOW ... *Announcing these other fine books from Prentice-Hall—*

HOW TO SELL IN THE 1980s: Successfull Selling of Products, Services, and Ideas in a New Decade, by Robert L. Montgomery. Shows salespersons how to become more positive, enthusiastic, and vital. Offers tips on answering objections, remembering details of a sales pitch, speaking with confidence, and more.

$4.95 paperback, $9.95 hardcover

ON YOUR WAY TO THE TOP IN SELLING, by L. Perry Wilbur. New, from a former top insurance salesman, this book presents dynamic, professional tips and techniques for sales success. Includes 25 ways to close a sale, magic words that convince prospects to sign on the dotted line, 10 ways to overcome objections, how to avoid the 20 biggest mistakes most sales reps make, how to make the law of averages work in the salesperson's favor, and more.

$6.95 paperback, $13.95 hardcover

To order these books, just complete the convenient order form below and mail to **Prentice-Hall, Inc., General Publishing Division, Attn. Addison Tredd, Englewood Cliffs, N.J. 07632**

Title	Author	Price*
_____	_____	_____
_____	_____	_____
_____	_____	_____

Subtotal _____

Sales Tax (where applicable) _____

Postage & Handling (75¢/book) _____

Total $_____

Please send me the books listed above. Enclosed is my check ☐ Money order ☐ or, charge my VISA ☐ MasterCard ☐ Account # _____

Credit card expiration date _____

Name _____

Address _____

City _____ State _____ Zip _____

Prices subject to change without notice. Please allow 4 weeks for delivery.